European Multilingualism

MULTILINGUAL MATTERS
Series Editor: John Edwards, *St. Francis Xavier University, Canada*

Multilingual Matters series publishes books on bilingualism, bilingual education, immersion education, second language learning, language policy, multiculturalism. The editor is particularly interested in 'macro' level studies of language policies, language maintenance, language shift, language revival and language planning. Books in the series discuss the relationship between language in a broad sense and larger cultural issues, particularly identity related ones.

Full details of all the books in this series and of all our other publications can be found on http://www.multilingual-matters.com, or by writing to Multilingual Matters, St Nicholas House, 31-34 High Street, Bristol BS1 2AW, UK.

European Multilingualism
Current Perspectives and Challenges

**Rosita Rindler Schjerve and
Eva Vetter**

MULTILINGUAL MATTERS
Bristol • Buffalo • Toronto

In memoriam
Peter Nelde

Library of Congress Cataloging in Publication Data
A catalog record for this book is available from the Library of Congress.
Rindler Schjerve, Rosita
European Multilingualism: Current Perspectives and Challenges/Rosita Rindler Schjerve and Eva Vetter.
Multilingual Matters: 147
Includes bibliographical references.
1. Multilingualism—Europe. 2. Linguistic minorities—Europe. 3. Language policy—Europe. I. Vetter, Eva II. Title.
P115.5.E85R56 3012
306.44'6094–dc23 2012009131

British Library Cataloguing in Publication Data
A catalogue entry for this book is available from the British Library.

ISBN-13: 978-1-84769-735-6 (hbk)
ISBN-13: 978-1-84769-734-9 (pbk)

Multilingual Matters
UK: St Nicholas House, 31-34 High Street, Bristol BS1 2AW, UK.
USA: UTP, 2250 Military Road, Tonawanda, NY 14150, USA.
Canada: UTP, 5201 Dufferin Street, North York, Ontario M3H 5T8, Canada.

Copyright © 2012 Rosita Rindler Schjerve and Eva Vetter.

All rights reserved. No part of this work may be reproduced in any form or by any means without permission in writing from the publisher.

The policy of Multilingual Matters/Channel View Publications is to use papers that are natural, renewable and recyclable products, made from wood grown in sustainable forests. In the manufacturing process of our books, and to further support our policy, preference is given to printers that have FSC and PEFC Chain of Custody certification. The FSC and/or PEFC logos will appear on those books where full certification has been granted to the printer concerned.

Typeset by DiTech Process Solutions.
Printed and bound in Great Britain by Short Run Press Ltd

Contents

Acknowledgements	vii
List of Abbreviations	ix
Introduction	1
1 European Multilingualism: Political Scope	**10**
1.1 Multilingualism and the Diversity Debate	11
1.2 European Multilingualism: Towards a Comprehensive Policy Framework	14
1.2.1 Language education policy	20
1.2.2 Linguistic minorities policy	30
1.2.3 EU institutional language regime	38
1.2.4 Positions and challenges	43
2 European Multilingualism as a Field of Research	**52**
2.1 Multilingualism: A Multidisciplinary Field of Research	53
3 The LINEE Project	**60**
3.1 Theoretical Dimension	64
3.2 LINEE Key Concepts	67
3.2.1 Culture	67
3.2.2 Discourse	76
3.2.3 Identity	85
3.2.4 Ideology	95
3.2.5 Knowledge	105

	3.2.6 Language policy and planning	114
	3.2.7 Multi-competence	125
	3.2.8 Power and conflict	133
3.3	Methodological Issues	145
	3.3.1 Central question and methodological framework	147
	3.3.2 Basic models of qualitative social research	148
	3.3.3 Conceptual background: Levels of analysis	150
	3.3.4 Research strategy: Degree of openness	151
	3.3.5 Method(s)	153
	3.3.6 Conclusion	155
3.4	Lines of Tension Emerging from LINEE	155
4	**European Multilingualism Beyond LINEE**	**161**
4.1	Re-Conceptualising European Multilingualism	161
	4.1.1 European multilingualism: Container of national languages	161
	4.1.2 Language equality principle	164
	4.1.3 The 'legitimate' plurilingual repertoire	169
	4.1.4 European multilingualism and migration	173
4.2	Towards an Integrative View of European Multilingualism	178
Conclusion		186
References		193
Appendix		213

Acknowledgements

The manuscript at hand owes its existence to the project LINEE (Languages In a Network of European Excellence), which was funded by the European Community within the 6th Framework Programme under Priority 7 'Citizens and Governance in a Knowledge-based Society', Contract No 028388. To date, LINEE is the only Network of Excellence commissioned by the EU in order to explore European multilingualism. Against the background of several years of cooperation and knowledge exchange taking place in LINEE, both authors of this book are deeply indebted to all members of the LINEE project, and especially to the Project Coordinator in Bern, Iwar Werlen, and the Project Manager Maddalena Tognola. Only the joint efforts and the knowledge gained in LINEE could make it possible to venture an attempt at presenting the challenges and perspectives emerging in connection with European multilingualism from a comprehensive perspective.

In view of the fact that the goals set by the LINEE project have been reached, it is particularly painful that the initiator and ideational mentor of this project did not live to cast a critical eye on the results of LINEE and to share the profit of these results with us. Peter Nelde passed away during the first year of the project due to severe illness.

This book is the result of most intensive networking. Preliminary stages and partial results of this work have been continually discussed both within the framework of LINEE and within the scientific community outside LINEE. Among the many people taking the trouble to reflect on European multilingualism with us, particular thanks are due to Barbara Seidlhofer, who, as a member of the second major multilingualism project, DYLAN, which was also approved within the 6th Framework Programme, enabled us to create a link to DYLAN. Furthermore, we would like to thank Monica Heller, who brought to bear her valued expertise as a member of the Advisory Board of LINEE into the conception of the manuscript at hand. And finally, we are thankful to Henry Widdowson, who made his knowledge available to us to an exceptional degree by heightening our awareness of eminently critical interrelations of European multilingualism.

With regard to the Viennese LINEE team, special thanks are due to the colleagues who have been most closely involved in compiling this manuscript. Here, we are especially grateful to Eva Eichmair, and also to Marie-Luise Volgger and Daniela Dorner. Through their valuable content-related and critical input, these colleagues did not only make a substantial contribution to the emergence of the LINEE research platform developed in Vienna but also played a significant role in advancing the completion of this book. Finally, our particular thanks also go to Angelika Rieder-Bünemann, who was responsible for proofreading and translating the English manuscript.

Rosita Rindler Schjerve and Eva Vetter
Vienna, April 2011

List of Abbreviations

CDA	Critical discourse analysis
CoE	Council of Europe
CoP	Community of Practice
DMM	Dynamic model of multilingualism
EC	European Community
ECJ	European Court of Justice
EEC	European Economic Community
ELF	English as a lingua franca
EM	European Multilingualism
KBS	Knowledge-based society
LMT	Language management theory
LPP	Language policy and planning
RML	Regional and minority language
WP	Work package

Introduction

The book at hand addresses multilingualism in the European Union (EU), attempting a close investigation of this phenomenon in its socio-cultural and political, as well as its scientific dimensions. The particular focus on the EU can be explained by the fact that the topic of European multilingualism (EM) primarily results from the contexts of advancing Europeanisation. This is the reason why this multilingualism appears to be geared to the EU's integration process from a political perspective. Furthermore, the focus on the context of the EU is also due to the fact that this book is essentially based on the results of the major project LINEE (Languages in a Network of European Excellence, FP6 2006–2010), which was commissioned by the EU to investigate EM and which has recently been completed.

Writing this book was motivated by the following considerations: on the one hand, the desire arose within this major project to make certain components of the project results accessible to a wider scientific community. On the other hand, it had become clear in the course of working on the project that the term 'EM' appears to be vague, contradictory and inconsistent, both in its political dimension and in its scientific foundation, and that it thus seems to require a certain degree of revision. Moreover, the LINEE research gave rise to the impression that, in its profiling and policy development, EM reflects a process in the making which is essentially substantiated in the overlap between the ability to shape policy and the generation of scientific knowledge. It thus seemed promising to gauge the deficits and discrepancies shaping the conception of the term 'EM' by means of a critical synopsis of these two dimensions. And finally, the experience resulting from the authors' occupation with developing a research platform for theories and methods of multilingualism should serve to summarise and reformulate the body of knowledge created in LINEE with respect to the general theorisation of multilingualism.

When talking about EM, it cannot be ignored that from the 1990s onwards there has been a paradigmatic shift, when not only scientific scholars but also political stakeholders set out to rethink the heterogeneous linguistic landscape in Europe in the scope of the diversity framework. From a political perspective, this shift has been largely prepared by the goals and activities of two primary agents in this field, namely, the Council of Europe (CoE) and the European Economic Community (EEC), although the global initiatives launched by the UNO and UNESCO should also be mentioned in this context, albeit their being primarily geared towards human and cultural rights (e.g. the *Universal Declaration on Linguistic Rights 1996*: cf. UNESCO 1996 or the *Universal Declaration on Cultural Diversity 2001*: cf. UNESCO 2001).

Since the early 1950s (cf. European Cultural Convention 1954), it has been a major concern of the CoE to promote language learning and teaching. This was, inter alia, reflected in the development of not only basic models such as the Threshold Level and the Niveau Seuil but also of the *Common European Framework of Reference for Languages* (cf. CEFR 2001) and the *European Language Portfolio*, which have evolved into the most influential instruments in European language education policy, albeit at a later stage. The emphasis on intercultural communication and plurilingualism expressed in the language learning-related and the minority-related policy since the 1980s is entirely in line with the policy of the Council, which has mainly been directed towards the issues of human rights, democratic citizenship, and cultural integration. In fact, the *European Charter of Regional and Minority Languages* (cf. Charter RML 1992) and the European *Framework Convention for the Protection of National Minorities* (cf. Framework Convention 1995) are also to be viewed from this perspective, as well as the increased focus on the linguistic and cultural integration of the immigrant minorities. In this context, it should be stressed that the Council has repeatedly been seeking cooperation with the EEC and the subsequent EU in the pursuit of its goals.

Although the initiatives of the EEC were also concentrated on language acquisition policies and regional minorities, this policy was nevertheless underpinned by considerations resulting from the requirements of economic integration and of the search for a solution to the regionally escalating conflicts in the individual member states. The prelude to an explicit policy of EM, however, occurred only with the foundation of the EU, where the respect for cultural diversity was codified in the Maastricht Treaty. The EU's move towards multilingualism was primarily fostered by the requirements of the Europeanisation process, where multilingualism was to ensure not only economic growth and transnational communication but also sociocultural cohesion and the development of a common European identity.

Within the EU and against the background of the longstanding homogenising politics of the European nation states, the move towards multilingualism eventually occurred in an amazingly short period of time. The change was long overdue for several reasons: on the one hand, national monolingualism has been the exception rather than the rule due to the fact that from the very beginning, most European nation states have actually been multilingual. The national homogenisation of the linguistically heterogeneous communities, however, has for a long time obscured the existing multilingual reality. On the other hand, more recent immigration has brought about new and highly complex forms of bi- and multilingualism which (cf. also Vertovec 2010: 86–67), although largely neglected by the state authorities until recently, called for a solution. Another point is that in the background of ongoing European integration, the question is to be raised as to how the existing linguistic diversity might be accommodated within the scope of European unity. That is to say, it has so far remained unclear how to tackle the increased range of official languages on an equal footing within the EU institutions and, in particular, how to deal with English as an emerging supranational lingua franca in this and other transnational contexts. Another unresolved question is how to implement a reasonably balanced policy of foreign language learning that would not focus exclusively upon the large prestigious languages, as is presently the case, but would account for the diversified multilingual requirements of the various transnational and regional contexts. And the third question concerns possible modes of integrating the highly diversified linguistic resources of the old and the new minorities.

It is true that the public debate on linguistic diversity and multilingualism in Europe is of rather recent origin. However, as early as in the 1970s, public awareness about linguistic heterogeneity was raised when the European regional movement was headed towards challenging the cultural and linguistic dominance of the nation state. The struggle of regional minorities for linguistic and cultural autonomy and the conflicts it gave rise to had the effect that these minorities came to constitute a field of both scientific investigation and political commitment. At that time, the scope of these activities was, however, largely directed towards the phenomena of bilingualism and diglossia rather than towards multilingualism. Interestingly enough, this orientation also applied to those cases where more than two languages were involved.

Furthermore, bilingualism was the focus of the acquisition studies of these times, and the bilingual stance was maintained when the political stakeholders within the enlarging EEC set out to plea for increased second language learning. It was only in the 1980s that the plea for multilingualism emerged for the first time, when the European Commission and the Council started to argue in favour of two foreign languages. This plea for multilingualism continued well into the 1990s, when the famous *White Paper on Education and Training* (cf. COM(95)590) of the European Commission stated that Europeans should learn at least two community languages besides their mother tongue.

We can say, however, that the call for language learning and the preoccupation with regional minority languages largely took place at separate sites and that both were inspired by somewhat different paradigms. The same holds true for migrant minorities, who from the 1980s onwards became a focus of increasing scientific interest, which, however, developed more or less independent of the research focus regarding the regional minorities.

Rare exceptions to these separate activities can be seen in those cases where acquisition policies concerning bilingual minority schooling, for example, in Germany with a focus on immigrants, or in countries like France, Great Britain or Spain regarding regional minorities, drew upon the scientific expertise of both education and minority research.

It was only within the EU context, and especially after the millennium and the Lisbon strategy (cf. Lisbon Conclusions 2000), that the plea for multilingualism started to integrate the separate perspectives into the larger scope of the European diversity debate. In this scope, linguistic diversity is referred to as a basic quality of the EU since it is seen as reflecting the different European identities and cultures while at the same time representing a marketable resource for the New Economy. Moreover, since Barcelona 2002 (cf. Barcelona Conclusions 2002), the appeal for EM has been evolving into a political strategy in which the learning of languages is seen as a means to foster the knowledge-based society (KBS) while at the same time enhancing economic growth, social cohesion, welfare and intercultural understanding within the Union. Interestingly enough, there appears to be growing concern about how the languages of the old and the new minorities are to be integrated into the diversity scope. The reasons for this anxiety can be seen in the fact that the issue of minorities combines with the question of human rights, democracy and equality, the core principles and values on which the EU is founded.

Following the communication of the European Commission (cf. COM(2008)566 final: 4–6), 'unity in diversity' constitutes a cornerstone and a political objective of the European Union. Hence, promoting EM is seen as a comprehensive strategy which integrates languages into the wider context of the EU agenda for social cohesion and welfare. From this it can be concluded that the promotion of EM constitutes a strategy which is to ensure the political implementation of linguistic diversity in Europe.

Beyond the political dimension, which is still in the making, it cannot be ignored that EM constitutes an ever growing field of scientific investigation and research. Taking its epistemological stance from different disciplinary sites, for example, multicultural and European studies, studies in language contact concerning the old and new minorities, foreign language learning and acquisition or language policy and planning (LPP), EM has been developing into a multi-faceted cover term that embraces a wide range of theoretical and methodological perspectives. As yet, these different disciplinary strands appear, however, to be rather isolated and fragmented as they lack integration into an overall framework. Unfortunately, no such framework is available to date. Against the background of the existing fragmentation, it hence constitutes a major challenge for scholars of EM to seek for the basic common grounds on which such a framework might be developed.

When talking about EM, the question may be raised as to what distinguishes multilingualism in Europe from multilingualism in other parts of the world. The answer is to be sought in the very nature of this concept as it evolves from the specific intersection of both the political and the scientific debate. While the political concept of EM relates to strategies that evolve primarily from the European Union's integration and diversity debate, the scientific concept draws upon the interdisciplinary knowledge on which multilingualism research is generally founded. The peculiarity of 'European' multilingualism may be seen in the fact that the regionally bound political scope interacts, as it were, in a dynamic way with the multidisciplinary theorisation of multilingualism accommodating both dimensions at the same time. The intersection of policy making and research is best reflected in some large-scale studies, for instance, EUROMOSAIC (cf. Nelde et al. 1996; Euromosaic III 2004) or ELAN (cf. CILT 2006), which were commissioned by the EU in order to foster knowledge of how multilingualism interacts with the sociocultural or economic Europeanisation and how linguistic diversity can be managed for the benefit of European integration.

Since EM appears to constitute a multi-layered concept that is apparently in the making, it can be assumed that investigating the actual intersection of the political and the scientific scope in more detail might reveal its meaning more precisely. More recent influential documents on multilingualism (cf. High Level Group 2007; Maalouf 2008, 2008/2225(INI) EP 2009) indicate that there is as yet no clear-cut political strategy in place to cope with linguistic diversity in the EU. Here, it is still unclear in how far the EU possesses the power to actually interfere with the language policies of the member states. Another unresolved question concerns the languages that should be part of the promotional policies. Minority and particularly immigrant languages represent a highly contentious issue in this respect (cf. Nic Craith 2006; Extra & Gorter 2008). Moreover, it remains unclear how to combine two major and apparently contradicting objectives towards which current EM policies are generally targeted, namely, enhancing multilingualism as a marketable resource on the one hand and promoting multilingualism as an issue of equality and of fundamental rights on the other hand. As these questions have actually not been answered as yet, it is a major challenge to accommodate the divergent issues within the 'unity of diversity' framework of the EU since this framework constitutes the basic grounds from which the policies of EM are evolving.

Although in this book the focus of European multilingualism is primarily directed towards the EU as a geopolitical entity, it should not be forgotten that the political dimension of this multilingualism goes beyond the EU's sphere of influence. In this wider scope, as already mentioned, the CoE has set important benchmarks and thresholds in foreign language learning and in minority protection, and in these contexts the CoE and the EU have intensified their cooperation over the past decades. Despite this cooperation reaching beyond the EU, however, we can adhere to the fact that the EU language politics at present seeks to provide a common framework in which the many languages of the Union would be accommodated and promoted according to the basic values and principles to which the EU is committed. In this scope, it appears legitimate to talk about a concept of EM which is unequalled worldwide.

Another point which has already been mentioned is that the intersection between the political and the scientific dimension constitutes one of the major characteristics determining the dynamics of EM. In line with this dynamics, the EU has commissioned large-scale research projects such as LINEE or DYLAN (Language Dynamics and Management of Diversity, FP6 2006–2011) in the past few years. Thus, within LINEE, nine partners from different European universities collaborated in 24 sub-projects in order to find out how EM fosters European integration and the European KBS.

Clearly, EM is a very complex issue that refers to highly diversified sociocultural and linguistic phenomena which combine with the use and the learning the valorisation and the political management of the plural languages. Thus, the wide range of focuses to which EM research relates eventually makes it appear as a rather heterogeneous field of study which – as mentioned before – lacks coherent theory building. Hence, it is a major objective to elaborate on the different knowledge sets on which EM is actually founded and on how these can be brought together and further integrated. This focus is also captured and refined in this book.

In the past years, the growing interest in multilingualism has brought about a series of publications which cover a wide range of topics and aspects. In these, the diverse facets of multilingualism are approached from different scopes and perspectives. There are several handbooks which account for the state of the art of multi- and bilingualism research, in which the focus is on linguistic, that is psycho- and neurolinguistic, as well as sociolinguistic or interactional and applied phenomena (e.g. Wei 2010; Wei & Auer 2009; Wei & Moyer 2008). Moreover, apart from single monographs focusing on particular psycholinguistic and educational issues, the publications include a great many edited volumes comprising selected case studies which contribute to a specific thematic focus, for example, language and power or identity. Within the multilingual scope, minorities and multilingual classrooms are also extensively covered. Beyond this, a considerable number of more recent publications focus on the aspects of linguistic diversity and multilingualism in Europe dealing with central issues such as the 'unity in diversity' debate, the problem of the old and the new minorities, language use within the EU institutions or 'English as a lingua franca' (ELF). With rare exceptions (e.g. Nic Craith 2006; Williams 2005; Kraus 2008), most of the publications are again compilations of selected case studies which elaborate on a particular focus while, as yet, a more integrative perspective of assessing EM is still lacking.

This book cannot provide such an integrative perspective. It will, however, supply a sociolinguistic perspective in the attempt to combine the major strands on which, as it is argued, EM appears to be actually founded. At this point, it should be highlighted that attempting such an integrative perspective was possible only against the background of the large and interdisciplinary scope of LINEE, as this scope allowed for uncovering very central and as yet hidden facets of the contradicting and unstable nature of EM. The fact that this book draws upon the LINEE knowledge does not imply, though, that it will give a comprehensive overview of the LINEE research findings. Rather, it will use central issues derived from the LINEE research in developing a scope that goes beyond LINEE.

Starting from the political framework which establishes EM as a normative goal, Chapter 1 shows how multilingualism has made its way into the EU's political agenda. In doing so, a wide range of topics are covered, starting out with revealing in what way the terms 'linguistic diversity' and 'EM', which are often used synonymously, appear to be related.

As an important part of European diversity, language diversity and also multilingualism are closely linked to the diversity principle. Hence, Section 1.1 shows how the plea for EM has evolved from the diversity debate in the EU's economic and political integration process. Subsequently, Section 1.2 deals with the EM-related policy in the making, which – as argued – has developed into a cross-cutting political framework that has a direct bearing on diverse policy areas such as education and culture, economics, external relations and foreign affairs, science and research, justice or social rights. In this section, three central political fields of action of the EU are identified and discussed in relation to the overriding questions and discrepancies emerging in each case, that is language education policy (cf. Section 1.2.1), linguistic minorities policy (cf. Section 1.2.2) and EU institutional language regime (cf. Section 1.2.3).

In Section 1.2.4, the description of the historical development of EM into a field of policy making is left behind when the positions and challenges arising from the insights gained in Section 1.2 are critically identified. Here, the focus is on discrepancies and open questions, all the more as the obvious weaknesses of the EM politics could not yet be eliminated despite the continuous upgrading of the EM agenda since the beginning of the millennium.

Chapter 2 of the book is devoted to multilingualism as a field of research. It shows how multilingualism research has evolved as an independent research area only recently and in a slow process of delimitation from bilingualism research. Furthermore, this chapter reveals that the wide range of theoretical-methodological focus areas is decisive for the characteristic fragmentation of this research discipline.

Making a contribution to overcoming this fragmentation was an important mission of the LINEE project, whose results form the basis for the considerations in Chapter 3. Thus, the main focus of this discussion is on the theoretical dimension of the multilingual manifestations (cf. Section 3.1), also including methodological aspects to a certain degree (cf. Section 3.3). Since a major task of the LINEE project involved developing theoretical platforms for EM, the discussion concentrates on the results derived from these platforms. Here, a particular focus is placed upon a set of recurrent variables which, as it appeared, are to be seen in a close relationship with EM. These variables are 'culture', 'discourse', 'identity', 'ideology', 'knowledge', 'LPP', 'multi-competence' and 'power and conflict'. They are discussed with regard to their theoretical conceptualisation in multilingualism research in general and in the LINEE research in particular. Moreover, the chapter shows how the diverse and complex manifestations of EM can be grasped dynamically and flexibly through the synopsis of the different variables, and it points out, in the next step, which results this synopsis yields (cf. Sections 3.2.1–3.2.8).

Finally, Section 3.4. provides a critical evaluation of the results obtained from the analysis of the LINEE variables. This chapter contains a discussion and summary of the fault lines detected in the different manifestations of EM by analysing the variables, with regard to the present usage of the term 'EM'.

Chapter 4 of the book clearly goes beyond the scope of the LINEE project by refining the LINEE results in terms of an integrative perspective. The fault lines resulting from the synopsis in Section 3.4. form the starting point for Section 4.1, which once more employs the LINEE key variables to look into the most critical aspects of the EM concept. Here, the main focus is on the following questions: how can the many languages be tackled in a more consistent way? What are the ideological guiding principles that underlie EM? What would be the pool of languages of which EM is to be composed? How can the minorities' linguistic resources be integrated into the EU's diversity framework? By providing an analytical discussion of these questions, Section 4.1 aims at establishing a basis for reformulating the most obvious discrepancies of the EM concept. Subsequently, Section 4.2 attempts to sketch an integrative and, at the same time, multi-focal approach by drawing on the LINEE key variables. The main objective here involves pointing out scenarios in which EM is adequately conceptualised in its dynamics and complexity.

This aim is achieved by interlacing the single key variables, which are handled flexibly, subject to the respective research focus.

The conclusion finally takes up the book's central lines of argument again, thus outlining the concept of EM on the basis of the results obtained, with regard to both political and scientific points of criticism. Furthermore, the last chapter considers potential options for reassessing the discrepant aspects of conceptualising EM and for forging new paths in order to theorise and grasp EM in its complexity and dynamics.

As this book shows, EM is a multi-layered phenomenon which raises major questions both regarding its conceptual design and regarding the way it is handled. These questions are closely related to the economic and the largely underestimated cultural process of Europeanisation. Above all, problems are caused by central and ideologically inconsistent arguments and objectives which characterise the nascent concept of EM. It is hoped that, owing to its broad perspective, this book can offer answers to selected questions.

1 European Multilingualism: Political Scope

In the past 20 years and since the foundation of the European Union, the plea for EM has been a prominent feature of policy making (cf. High Level Group 2007: 22). Policy makers and stakeholders have been seeking to establish EM as a normative goal and, more recently, as a cross-cutting policy framework that relates to the major values and principles to which the European unification project adheres. Respecting the existing linguistic diversity and enhancing the multilingual competences of the European citizens have been conceived as important premises on which integration into a Union bound together by common values should be fostered. Following this politics and the normative stance it pursues, one might be inclined to argue that the EU has invented EM in order to ensure its goal of an ever-closer political and economic integration. It would appear, therefore, that EM has come to be an ideologically driven concept and that over the past two decades, its conceptualisation has undergone substantial changes. This is particularly true for the 1990s, when the issue of Europe as an information society was raised, and the new millennium, in which the scope of this politics has been widened towards integrating aspects such as migration, social cohesion, intercultural dialogue and lifelong learning. As yet, however, some crucial issues, for example, the role of minority and migrant languages (cf. Nic Craith 2006: 56; Extra et al. 2004: 395) or the question of language hierarchies within the EM project, have remained unclear (cf. Nic Craith 2006: 40–56; Phillipson 2009: 64–65). Apparently, EM has come to be an ideologically driven concept which in its functional top-down approach is not yet established well enough in the grass roots and in civil society at large.

The debate on EM relates directly to the diversity principle of the EU. The term 'linguistic diversity', often taken to be synonymous with EM in public and official debates, is used in a double sense. On the one hand, it is used descriptively to refer to the many languages that are actually spoken in Europe and particularly within the EU. On the other hand, it is used ideologically to refer to a central value to which the EU adheres in its treaties, declarations and related documents, and which constitutes a promotional objective and a political goal that the EU seeks to achieve. 'Linguistic diversity' is an integral part of 'cultural diversity' (cf. also Lo Bianco 2010: 39–54), and both are assigned crucial significance within the European unification process since the aim is to achieve political integration into the ever-closer Union without compromising the cultural distinctiveness and the linguistically defined identities of the member states.

In what follows, we will focus in more detail on how the plea for EM has evolved from the diversity debate in the EU's economic and political integration process. We will then further elaborate on how EM has come to be introduced into the EU's political agenda as a matter of policy in its own right. Finally, we will conclude by considering the main positions and challenges that arise in the pursuit of a policy which aims at respecting and promoting linguistic pluralism in Europe.

1.1 Multilingualism and the Diversity Debate

From a historical perspective, languages can be seen as intimately intertwined with the rise of national identities in Europe. The adoption of a common language has contributed crucially to the fostering of social integration and cultural centralisation within the European societies (cf. Gellner 1983). This is the reason why languages are so closely associated with cultural diversity in Europe (cf. Grimm 1995).

The EU is a multinational conglomerate which is being directed towards an ever-closer economic and political unification. The question naturally arises as to how such supranational unification can be achieved while at the same time ensuring the maintenance of cultural diversity at the national level, and finding ways of protecting pluralism without setting limits to the European unity has become an important political and legal issue (cf. Bogdandy 2007). It also needs to be noted that against the background of the enlargement and the continuing institutional and political transformation of the EU, 'cultural diversity' provides for a framework from which the overall identity and legitimacy of Europe would evolve (cf. also Weiss 2002: 62–63).

Originally, the EEC started as an economic community, which, however, soon became aware of the significance of the cultural dimension, since it provides the common basic elements and patterns of collective identification that would legitimise the promotion of the unification process. This is one of the reasons why from the 1970s onwards recurrent references were made to the common cultural heritage and to European identity based on the diversity of the national cultures and languages. The *Declaration of European Identity*, which was adopted at the Copenhagen Summit in 1973 (cf. Bull. 12-1973), is an early example for the perceived instrumental significance of culture in the process of integration. In the mid-1980s, a similar instrumental significance was attributed to language abilities within the framework of the European market and a solidarity Community. The *Report by the Committee on a People's Europe* (cf. Bull. Supp.7-1985) submitted to the European Council (which was approved by the Milan European Council 28 and 29 June 1985) underlines that 'the languages spoken in the Community form an essential part of its cultural heritage and contribute to its richness and diversity.' The subsequent Council Decision of 28 July 1989, establishing an action programme to promote foreign language competence in the European Community (cf. OJ 1989 L 239: 24–32) notes that 'greater foreign language competence will enable the Community's citizens to reap the benefits of competition of the internal market and will enhance understanding and solidarity between the peoples which go to make up the Community, while preserving the linguistic diversity and cultural wealth of Europe'.

In the 1990s, it became evident that the European unification process had to go beyond the establishment of the Common Market and that political integration into an ever-closer Union was to be consolidated on the basis of a common cultural identity project (cf. Kraus 2008: 43). However, the plea for a common European identity was by no means to imply that the national identities were to be replaced by a supranational European identity. It was believed that they would coexist complementary to the latter (cf. OJ 1997 C 340: Art. 6.3). This explains why cultural and linguistic diversity came to constitute a major value or principle, as enshrined in the founding treaties of the EU (cf. Toggenburg 2003: 19–21). It also explains why the diversity issue has been accorded a prominent place in the various declarations and documents issued by the EU. In the light of the ever-closer integration process, the EU's commitment to cultural and linguistic diversity appears to be all the more important as it does not only ensure the preservation of the national identities but also brings to the fore the common cultural heritage on which – as it is argued – the European identity is founded (cf. Cullen *et al.* 2008: 9): Diversity was represented not only as consistent with unity but also as a crucial component of it.

Thus, Art. 128 (cf. OJ 1992 C 191) of the Maastricht Treaty provides for the respect and promotion of the diverse cultures as they associate with the cultural heritage of the European peoples. The subsequent *Millennium Declaration* (cf. Helsinki Conclusions 1999: Annex I) adopted by the European Council in Helsinki (1999) refers to the EU as a community based on democracy and the rule of law, while it conceives of the EU citizens as a society bound together by common values such as freedom, tolerance, equality, solidarity and cultural diversity. This and other examples show that cultural diversity is a declared value that relates to other values and principles to which the EU is committed. Thus, the *European Charter of Fundamental Rights* (cf. OJ 2000 C 364: 1–22), which became part of the Lisbon Reform Treaty (cf. OJ 2007 C 306: 1–271), underlines the respect for cultural and linguistic diversity in its Art. 22, where a direct connection is established between diversity and the equality principle. And finally, Art. 3.3 of the actual Lisbon Treaty (cf. OJ 2008 C 115) reaffirms the promotion of cultural and linguistic pluralism and the safeguard of the European cultural heritage. From this it follows that 'cultural diversity' has come to be assigned a prominent place in the EU's architecture.

Clearly, 'cultural diversity' is an issue that directly connects with the European identity framework and, hence, associates with the values and principles this identity is built on. Moreover, 'cultural diversity' is a central issue with far-reaching consequences both for European citizenship and for constructing a European polity (cf. Kraus 2008: 47–49). The EU is not a state but a multinational political unit. Thus, the Treaty of Maastricht introduced citizenship of the Union (cf. OJ 1992 C 191: Art. 8) on the premises that a person is a national of one member state and that EU citizenship should complement and not replace national citizenship (cf. OJ 1997 C 340: Art. 6.3).

Nevertheless, the question of how to constitute a European polity that is capable of forming the primary identification basis for European citizenship has as yet remained unanswered. Here, it is argued that a common European public sphere is required since it provides an indispensable premise for such a polity. Given the multinational order of the Union, it follows that the establishment of such a public sphere calls for transnational structures that are in line with the existing multicultural and multilingual diversity (cf. Kraus 2008: 70). In other words, constructing a common public sphere that accounts for transnational will-formation presupposes communication modes that enable citizens to exchange their opinions across national borders and language boundaries.

But how are these communication modes to be conceived? Here, we return to the question of the relationship between linguistic and cultural diversity. These two phenomena tend to be equated with the promotion of the one assumed to necessarily involve the promotion of the other, so that respect for cultural diversity 'becomes in the first instance an imperative to respect [for] linguistic diversity' (Kraus 2008: 76). The assumption is that managing diversity implies, first and foremost, managing the existing linguistic pluralism within and between the member states. Within this ideology of diversity, integration into a transnational community necessitates a pluralistic language regime that would allow for democratic and civic participation while at the same time forming the common ground for plural identifications. The discourse on diversity remains, however, silent in relation to the question of how the pluralistic language regime would ensure democratic participation and plural identifications.

Diversity, and in particular linguistic diversity, thus represents the ideological basis for the project of European integration. Alternative options for achieving integration into a transnational Community via a common language are not only omitted in this ideology but, to the contrary, also vehemently rejected, criticised or perceived as a threat. A language regime based on a common language which would support European integration, as it is already emerging with English as a lingua franca (ELF) in certain areas (cf. Seidlhofer 2004, 2007), clearly runs counter to this ideology.

In summary, we may say that diversity is a multi-layered concept as the debate on European diversity appears to be closely interrelated with core factors and components associated with the EU's integration process. Linguistic diversity, it has been said, is a significant part of cultural diversity. This also explains why the debate on 'linguistic diversity' intersects so closely with the issue of EM and why both terms are often dealt with as if they were synonymous notions. A detailed reading of the legal texts, declarations and official documents reveals that in the beginning, EM was an issue primarily associated with educational matters. In the 1990s, it was mainly linked with the question of enhanced second and third language learning whereas, at a later stage, it would also include the objective of social cohesion and intercultural understanding. This is the reason why the issue of minority languages came to be included into the debate on EM. Since the central issue involves the question of how the problem of transnational communication across diverse languages can be resolved in order to make 'unity in diversity' a reality, EM has also come to cover transnational communication issues. Here, it comes as no surprise that the debate on 'English Only' and ELF, in competition with the other European languages, raises considerable concern (cf. Phillipson 2003: 6–7).

From what has been said so far, it may be concluded that 'linguistic diversity' and EM are intersecting notions, which, however, cannot be taken as fully synonymous terms (cf. also Cullen *et al.* 2008: 1). Rather, it may be argued that 'linguistic diversity' constitutes the ideological underpinning for European multilingual politics, while it also constitutes a political goal that is promoted on the assumption that linguistic diversity equates with cultural diversity, which again represents European identity as a whole. It remains, however, an open question how the desired European 'unity in diversity' can eventually be attained and how the respect for linguistic diversity can be implemented into effective communication across the diverse languages.

1.2 European Multilingualism: Towards a Comprehensive Policy Framework

Since the mid-1990s, linguistic diversity has become an issue of increasing significance on the EU's political agenda and steps have been taken to put the principle into practice by fostering and enhancing multilingualism as a common European project so as to achieve the major objectives pursued by the Union in the ongoing unification process.

From 1995 onwards, the development of multilingualism as a common European project has been closely connected with the debate on the emergent European information society. It was argued that the impact of the scientific and technological world, the development of the information society and the internationalisation of the economy would prioritise information exchange and radically change the way societies function. From this perspective, particularly in multilingual societies and in the global markets, individual and societal multilingualism has come to be seen as a valuable cultural capital and an asset that speakers should benefit from (cf. COM(95)590: 5–6). Thus, the 'Council Decision of 21 November 1996 on the Adoption of a Multiannual Programme to Promote the Linguistic Diversity of the Community in the Information Society' (cf. OJ 1996 L 306: 40–48) established a multiannual programme to promote linguistic diversity in order to overcome linguistic barriers on the EU internal and the world markets and to provide citizens with equitable access to information in their own language. Such access to information would, it was argued, be enriched by the citizens' knowledge of other languages, which, in turn, would foster initiatives to expand the teaching of other Community languages at school. In the perspective of the later Lisbon Strategy (cf. Lisbon Conclusions 2000), knowledge of languages became part of the basic skills Europeans should be provided with in transition towards a KBS. Such knowledge was seen as capital from which the evolving European knowledge-based economy would benefit.

The EEC/EU promotion of increased language learning has been strongly motivated by economic concerns since the 1970s, when language skills were assumed to contribute to professional mobility and increased employability (cf. for example, OJ 1976 C 38: 1–5). In the 1990s, the learning of second and third languages was considered a precondition for economic wealth and prosperity. In order to develop everyone's employability and contribution to economic development, the Commission, in its *White Paper* (cf. COM(95)590: 5–6), demanded that proficiency in at least two foreign languages at school be made a priority. In the scope of the Lisbon Strategy, the *Council Resolution* of Barcelona (cf. OJ 2002 C 50: 1–2) emphasises that knowledge of languages plays an important role in facilitating mobility and boosting employability, and accordingly, the Barcelona Presidency Conclusions (cf. Barcelona Conclusions 2002: 19) call for further action to improve the mastery of basic skills, in particular by teaching at least two foreign languages from a very early age. Learning languages in terms of potential economic benefit is also stressed within the *Decision No 1934/2000/EC of the European Parliament and* the *Council on the European Year of Languages 2001* (cf. OJ 2000 L 232: 1–5). In 2004, the *Action Plan* (cf. COM(2003)449 final: 43–44) suggests that EU success as a knowledge-based economy depends on how well it tackles the issue of language learning. Language skills and intercultural communication skills are seen as assuming an ever-larger role in global marketing and sales strategies. European companies, it is said, continue to lose business because they do not speak their customers' languages. In 2005, it is one of the three major aims of the Commission's multilingualism policy to promote a healthy multilingual economy (cf. COM(2005)596 final: 15) since multilingual language skills are seen to contribute to the competitiveness of the European economy and to improving the exploitation of Europe's potential for sustainable growth and more and better jobs. In 2006, it was estimated in the CILT study on *Effects on the European Economy of Shortages of Foreign Language Skills in Enterprise* (cf. CILT 2006) that 11% of exporting EU small and medium enterprises may be experiencing business losses due to language barriers. This suggests that creative ways of using the language resources are required since it is not only English as the business language of the world but also other languages that will provide EU companies with a competitive edge and allow them to conquer new markets (cf. also Phillipson 2003: 5). Beyond this, the recommendations by the Business Forum for Multilingualism, *Languages Mean Business: Companies Work Better with Languages* (Davignon Report, cf. Languages Mean Business 2008), underlines that Europe's inherent multilingualism is more essential than ever before as the industrial economy is gradually being transformed into a knowledge economy. The report thus includes recommendations for boosting competitiveness and improving employability through improved management of linguistic diversity. Moreover, the *European Job Mobility Action Plan (2007–2010)* (cf. COM(2007)773 final) concludes that linguistic and intercultural skills increase the chances of obtaining a better job and that the command of several foreign languages gives a competitive advantage. These examples show the importance ascribed to multilingualism within the framework of the European ideology of diversity: here, multilingualism is seen as an important requirement in a knowledge-based economy since knowledge of languages contributes to fostering the free movement of goods, persons, capitals and services (cf. OJ 2000 C 364: 1–64) within the European market while it helps to strengthen European competitiveness on the world markets.

Although economic integration appears to be a strong driving force for establishing multilingualism as a policy, the policy actually covers a wide range of objectives and issues that go beyond economy and connect with other areas of EU policy making. In the past few years, and particularly from the positions taken in the most recently published EU documents, it is evident that the multilingualism project has substantially widened its thematic scope. Thus, the communication from the Commission of 18 September 2008 *Multilingualism: An Asset for Europe and a Shared Commitment* (cf. COM(2008)566 final) underlines that multilingualism should be 'mainstreamed' across a series of EU policy areas, including lifelong learning, employment, social inclusion, competitiveness, culture, youth and civil society, research, translation and the media. Accordingly, this comprehensive policy framework is intended to link multilingualism to social cohesion and prosperity (cf. COM(2008)566 final: 6). The *Council Resolution of 21 November 2008 on a European Strategy for Multilingualism* (cf. OJ 2008 C 320: 1-3) points to multilingualism as encompassing the social, cultural and economic spheres. And finally, the European Parliament resolution of 24 March 2009 on *Multilingualism: An Asset for Europe and a Shared Commitment* (cf. 2008/2225(INI) EP 2009) reiterates the importance of multilingualism as a transversal issue that has a major impact on the lives of European citizens and calls on member states to incorporate it into policies concerned not only with education but also with all components of social and intellectual life such as lifelong learning, social inclusion, employment, media and research (cf. 2008/2225(INI) EP 2009: point 7).

Multilingualism policy started, as already mentioned, in the 1990s when the EU sought to come to terms with the different challenges that originated from the transition from an economic community to a supranational political unit. Under the heading of 'multilingualism', this policy was primarily directed towards accommodating the Community's policy lines of the 1970s and 1980s, which had mainly been targeted both towards foreign language learning among Europeans and towards the ethnolinguistic safeguard of the regional minorities. The Community's intervention into educational and minority language planning had come as no surprise since the national language policies of the time were not effective enough to cope with the challenges of linguistic pluralism. As a matter of fact, national language policies had traditionally been concerned with establishing monolingual homogeneity rather than fostering multilingualism in their societies. Thus, state policies could not always do justice to managing linguistic diversity within national borders and eventually proved to be largely inefficient or unwilling to meet the sociolinguistic requirements as they evolved from changes in society at the time. It has to be mentioned, though, that the Community's policy with respect to foreign language learning and minority languages had been directed at bilingual rather than multilingual achievements since it pursued the linguistic one + one strategy well into the 1980s while the minority languages policy concentrated upon a non-conflicting coexistence between the ethnic minority and the national majority languages.

In the developmental perspective, it is noteworthy that European language policies, while targeted towards bilingualism, had already been underpinned by a hidden ideological agenda a long time before the EU came into being. This agenda manifests itself in the steady and recurrent references made to European commonalities and objectives such as cultural heritage and identity, mutual understanding and peaceful coexistence among the European peoples as well as welfare and market integration. After Maastricht, the ideological underpinning of language policies was more precisely and explicitly linked to the EU's constitutional values and political principles. This is the reason why the highly contentious issue of European identity and citizenship came to be debated in connection with linguistic diversity and the political impact multilingualism has on the development of democracy, equality and the respect of human rights. This took the motivation for maintaining diversity beyond the need to ensure the mobility, employability and competitiveness required by economic globalisation and internal market integration. Beyond this, the prospective EU enlargement and increased migration constituted another unprecedented challenge in handling the increasing linguistic diversity.

From the millennium and the transition into the European knowledge society, multilingualism has evolved into a political framework in which linguistic diversity and language learning have been bound up with the highly diversified themes and objectives that relate to the emerging European KBS and its economy. In this context, multilingualism has come to be seen as a valuable resource and a capital. Thus, following the recommendations from the Business Forum for Multilingualism established by the European Commission, multilingualism constitutes an asset for successful business (cf. Languages Mean Business 2008: 14). In the *Study on the Contribution of Multilingualism to Creativity* (cf. Europublic 2009: 23), it is regarded as a potential source fuelling innovation and creativity. Due to the *Council Conclusions of 22 May 2008 on Multilingualism* (cf. OJ 2008 C 140: 14–15), multilingualism is considered to promote mobility and facilitate social integration and cohesion; it is furthermore stressed that people need to have multilingual competence in order to play an active part in the knowledge society. The *Council Resolution of 21 November 2008 on a European Strategy for Multilingualism* (cf. OJ 2008 C 320: 1–3) puts forward that the various languages are considered to be part and parcel of the European identity and its shared heritage. Moreover, knowledge of languages – it is argued – provides the means for intercultural dialogue and dialogue between citizens to strengthen respect for cultural diversity (cf. OJ 2006 L 412: 44–50). Language learning promotes mutual understanding and greater tolerance of other cultures, and it facilitates the development of skills for the knowledge society in order to support active citizenship, equal opportunities and social cohesion (cf. COM(2008)566 final Accomp.doc.: 5).

In addition, interestingly enough, minorities and in particular migrants and their inherent multilingual resources are being explicitly referred to as capital which should be exploited in terms of Europe's linguistic diversity (cf. High Level Group 2007: 20).

This short account of the latest developments shows that the issue of EM has evolved into a comprehensive political framework that has a direct bearing on diverse policy areas such as education and culture, economics, external relations and foreign affairs, science and research, justice, social rights, etc. It remains to be seen how the project of multilingualism as a transversal theme will establish itself in the respective policy areas and to what extent it will be further institutionalised as a policy area in its own right.

The first step towards institutionalising multilingualism as a political project was taken in 2005 when multilingualism as a political strategy was explicitly integrated into the portfolio of Education, Training, Culture and Multilingualism. In 2007, multilingualism received a portfolio in its own right, which, however, was re-integrated into the newly created portfolio of Education, Culture, Multilingualism and Youth in 2010.

Beyond the institutional implications, an important question relates to the possibilities of actually enacting the background of the newly established Lisbon Treaty multilingualism policy. Before the ratification of this treaty, the Union would not directly interfere into the language regimes of the member states simply due to its lack of competence to do so. The former legal framework and especially the subsidiarity principle of the Union did not allow for political intervention of this kind. Although the subsidiarity principle is still contingent, the situation has slightly changed since the provisions concerning linguistic diversity and especially the respect of linguistic minorities as laid down in the Lisbon Treaty now have a legally binding character, which was not the case before (cf. OJ 2010 C 83 Charter: Art. 21, Art. 22 and Art. 41).

The present state of affairs suggests that the emergent policy framework of EM is still of a rather programmatic nature. Many questions still remain open with regard to the implementation of statements concerning ideological principles and desirability since it remains unclear how they can be realised at the grass-roots level. In view of these difficulties, it should probably not be ignored that EU language policy is not solely to be seen as an outcome of the ideological and political constraints of the ever-closer Union since Maastricht. Rather, it appears to be embedded in certain continuity since the management of many European languages had been part of the political agenda well before the Union came into existence. Thus, over the last decades, language political actions have been contributing significantly to heightening the awareness of Europeans towards existing linguistic pluralism in society and towards the necessity to become multilingual through education. Against the background of the *de facto* linguistic pluralism in society, political action has been focusing mainly on the promotion of regional minority languages on the one hand and on foreign language learning on the other hand, whereas the major questions of multilingualism as they arise from the advancing Europeanisation and globalisation were largely ignored until Maastricht. In view of the general process of awareness raising, however, it is conceivable that the gap between EU language policy and the grass roots can be bridged provided that the programmatic announcements are now followed up by political actions. These concern very delicate questions which require clarification but have so far been avoided by the EU more or less successfully. A major question is whether the EU by encouraging the spread of individual multilingualism – which is the policy that the EU actually envisages – can really solve the communication problems. This once more begs the question concerning the development of a common and super-ordinate means of communication – ELF, for example, which, although it is common practice in many areas, is rejected by the EU for the obvious ideological reasons. A further burning question relates to how the natural multilingual resources of the minorities – and here in particular the migrant minorities – can be integrated into the EM framework. In this context, EM language policy appears to be more than half-hearted, and it thus remains to be seen how the EU will implement its EM programme in practice over the coming years.

In what follows, we will elaborate in more detail on three areas that have been particularly in focus in EM policy making over the past 50 years, namely, language education settings, the protection and promotion of minority languages, and the EU institutional language regulation. We will discuss how the political scope in these fields has been broadened and constantly upgraded over time and how the strategies adopted match the policy framework of EM. We will also draw on the difficulties the EU institutional language regime is faced with in its attempt to conform to the language equality principle and will point to the ambiguities and the practical limits that arise from a policy committed to an integral language strategy.

1.2.1 Language education policy

By EU language education policy we understand, in this context, all efforts undertaken within the scope of the EU (before Maastricht EEC) to exert influence on language learning in the member states. Its beginnings can be traced back to the 1970s, that is to say, to the *Resolution of 6 June 1974 on Cooperation in the Field of Education* (cf. OJ 1974 C 98: 2), in which the

Ministers of Education advocate 'the freedom of movement and mobility of teachers, students and research workers, in particular by [...] the improved teaching of foreign languages'. At the beginning of this resolution, reference is made to another document, that is, the final *Communiqué of the Conference of Heads of State or of Government* held at The Hague on 1 and 2 December 1969, and in particular to point 4 of this communiqué, in which the need to safeguard 'an exceptional source of development, progress and culture' in Europe (The Hague Communiqué 1969) is expressed. Educational agendas are thus related to the economic (development, progress) and the cultural (culture) spheres of activity, as well as to the social sphere, since '[c]ooperation in education shall be based on the following principles: [...] the programme of cooperation initiated in the field of education, whilst reflecting the progressive harmonisation of the economic and social policies in the Community, must be adapted to the specific objectives and requirements of this field' (The Hague Communiqué 1969). The fact that educational agendas represent an independent political field of the Community, dissociated in particular from the economy, is specifically stressed in the *Resolution of the Ministers of Education on Cooperation in the Field of Education*: '... on no account must education be regarded merely as a component of economic life' (OJ 1974 C 98).

In the subsequent decades, an abundance of documents dealing with language education was produced. It is particularly the Resolutions of the European Parliament, Council Conclusions and Resolutions, Communications issued by the European Commission, as well as reports commissioned by the Directorate General of Education and Culture which were crucial for establishing the profile of the EU language policy during this period, and which contributed to embedding language education policy not only in the previously mentioned economic, social and cultural fields but also dominantly in the diversity debate.

Over the decades, two main preoccupations of the EU language education policy can be observed, even if they are not always given equal priority. All these years, various partly contradictory answers have been proposed, but no clear conclusion has emerged. The first answer centres on internal EU relations and concerns the increasing demands on multilingualism, and the question as to how many, and which, languages European citizens should be proficient in. The second answer focuses on external relations and relates to the requirement for the EU to cooperate with organisations which are not restricted to the member states, such as UNESCO, or by extending language policy considerations to global spheres of communication, that is, spheres exceeding the member states, a decision which is mainly based on economic considerations.

The language education policy extended its scope in two ways: to cover an increasing number of languages on the one hand and to cover an increasing number of people on the other hand. While the *Resolution of 6 June 1974 on Cooperation in the Field of Education* (cf. OJ 1974 C 98: 2) concerned teachers, students and research workers, the *Resolution of the Council and of the Ministers of Education, Meeting within the Council, of 9 February 1976* (cf. OJ 1976 C 38: 1–5) extends the claims to compulsory schooling. 'All pupils should have the possibility to learn at least one other Community language'. A few years later, in the *Conclusions of the Council and the Ministers for Education, Meeting within the Council on 4 June 1984*, the Member States agreed 'to promote all appropriate measures to enable the maximum number of pupils to acquire, before the end of compulsory schooling, a working knowledge of two languages in addition to the mother tongue' (OJ 1998 C: 1) – with this step, the M+2 strategy was born, which is geared towards pupils of compulsory school age.

The requirement of proficiency in two languages in addition to the mother tongue is specified one year later in the *Conclusions of the Milan European Council* (cf. Bull. 6-1985: 13–16): The European Council approved the objective of involving the citizens of Europe more determinedly in the construction of the Community and suggested 'the acquisition by a maximum number of young people, before the end of compulsory education, of a practical knowledge of two languages in addition to their mother tongue, including at least one Community language' (Bull. 6-1985).

While the language learning policy of the 1970s and 1980s was targeted towards pupils, in the mid-1990s it addresses all citizens of the member states, as is recorded by the *White Paper on Education and Training: Teaching and Learning. Towards the Learning Society* (COM(95)590: 47): 'It is no longer possible to reserve proficiency in foreign languages for an elite or for those who acquire it on account of their geographical mobility.' Consequently, the mother tongue + 2 strategy now concerns all citizens of the European countries: 'Upon completing initial training everyone should be proficient in two Community foreign languages' (COM(95)590).

Moreover, the policy of mother tongue + 2 received further impetus through the request issued at the Lisbon European Council (cf. Lisbon Conclusions 2000) for 'new basic skills to be provided through lifelong learning' (Lisbon Conclusions: point 26). The *Detailed Work Programme on the Follow-Up of the Objectives of Education and Training Systems in Europe* (cf. OJ 2002 C 142: 1–22) highlights the importance of language skills for the linguistic diversity of Europe, since 'Europe's diversity is nowhere clearer than in its languages' (OJ 2002 C 142: 14). 'Encouraging everyone to learn two, or where appropriate, more languages in addition to their mother tongues, and increasing awareness of the importance of foreign language learning at all ages' (OJ 2002 C 142: 15) is a key issue of this work programme.

The extension to more than two languages in addition to the mother tongue implied above is also touched upon in the Barcelona European Council, since the latter called for further action to 'improve the mastery of basic skills, in particular by teaching at least two foreign languages from a very early age' (Barcelona Conclusions 2002: 19). In the Commission staff working paper, *Promoting Language Learning and Linguistic Diversity*, also published in 2002, this issue becomes explicit: 'The goal is for every European to have meaningful communicative competence in at least two other languages' (SEC(2002)1234: 3). This expansion of the requirement of language skills to more than two languages apart from the mother tongue is also found in the most recent European Parliament resolution of 24 March 2009 on multilingualism, namely, in the recommendation 'that Member States' academic curricula include optional study of a third foreign language, starting at secondary school level' (2008/2225(INI) EP 2009: 5).

Thus, language policy texts such as COM(2005)356 final, OJ 2006 C 251 E: 37–61, COM(2007)554 final, COM(2007)184 final, COM(2008)865 final, COM(2008)566 final 2008/2225(INI) EP 2009 continually remind us that from the turn of the millennium onwards mother tongue + 2 has been developing from a maximum requirement for pupils and students to a minimum requirement for all Europeans. So far, not much can be said about how far these proposals have been accepted or implemented since to date only input-data on language teaching, but no data on the teaching outcome, are available (cf. Eurydice 2008; see also Strubell *et al.* 2007: 9–33). From these, we can conclude, however, that schools are trying to put this policy into practice. Languages are learned earlier and earlier, and 'Only in a minority of countries is it not possible for everyone to be taught two foreign languages in full-time compulsory education' (Eurydice 2008: 38).

In contrast to this feature of the EU language learning policy, which shows a clear development towards an advocacy of proficiency in more languages for an ever-increasing target group, the question of the status of the languages concerned, and of deciding which should be prioritised, remains problematic and unresolved after more than four decades. While in the 1970s, 'languages of the Community' referred to the official languages of the EC (cf. OJ 1976 C 38: 1–5), the Milan European Council (Bull. 6-1985: 13–16) specifies that at least one of the two languages acquired has to be a Community language, with Community languages being defined very loosely as 'the languages spoken in the Community' (Bull. 6-1985). For a long time, this very open approach was not pursued: The Lingua programme sets a tight and precise frame (cf. OJ 1989 L 239: 24–32) since it refers only 'to the teaching as foreign languages of Danish, Dutch, English, French, German, Greek, Irish, Italian, Letzeburgesch, Portuguese and Spanish' (OJ 1989 L 239). Less precise, and also restricted to the official languages of the member states, is the selection made by the *White Paper* (cf. COM(95)590), as it refers to 'Community languages' or 'Community foreign languages' without differentiating systematically between these two categories.

In various documents, contributions dealing with the selection of the languages to be considered can be found. Within the scope of the two education and training programmes Socrates (cf. OJ 1995 L 87: 10–24; OJ 2000 L 28: 1–15) and Leonardo (cf. OJ 1999 L 146: 33–47), into which the Lingua programme was integrated, the significance of the less and least widely used and taught languages of Europe is stressed against the background of the intercultural dimension, with the following justification to lead 'to greater understanding and solidarity between the peoples of the European Union' (OJ 1995 L 87; OJ 2000 L 28: 2 – identical wording in both texts). From the introduction, we can infer to some degree which languages are referred to: 'Whereas certain languages, without being official languages of the European Union, are recognised at national level and are used to a significant extent as teaching languages in universities' (OJ 1995 L 87). While in this context, the regional languages in general could also be the subject, only the official languages of the Community are addressed subsequently in the document, except for two explicitly mentioned examples: 'All the official languages of the Community, together with Irish (one of the languages in which the Treaties establishing the European Communities are drawn up) and Lëtzeburgesch (a language spoken throughout the territory of Luxembourg)' (OJ 2000 L 28: 9). Furthermore, the less widely used and taught languages are also specifically referred to in the *Green Paper of 2 October 1996, Education – Training – Research: the Obstacles to Transnational Mobility* (cf. COM(96)462).

The question as to which languages are (to be) acquired has been critically discussed since the mid-1990s. The fact that Europeans acquire only a very limited number of languages as foreign languages meets with resistance and is interpreted as a threat to linguistic diversity. For example, the review *Foreign Languages in Primary and Pre-School Education: Context and Outcomes* (cf. CILT 1999) has been produced within a project funded through the Lingua element of the European Union's Socrates programme. In this review, the tension between 'international' and other languages is pointed out. Early foreign language learning is critically evaluated against this background: 'While it is desirable to provide parents or schools with a choice of languages at primary level, this does not guarantee diversity especially if continuity in the chosen language is to be maintained in secondary school' (CILT 1999: 2). Hence, as a possible solution for encompassing the threat to linguistic diversity, the review suggests that young children's awareness of diversity in general should be raised, rather than starting by teaching one specific foreign language at an early age. Moreover, in terms of language selection, it opts for giving preference to foreign languages widely spoken locally or in neighbouring regions.

The fact that language learning, due to the limited range of languages, does not necessarily correspond to the linguistic diversity is pointed out by the Commission staff working paper *Promoting Language Learning and Linguistic Diversity* (SEC(2002) 1234: 11), and taken as an opportunity to demand 'teaching and learning of the widest possible range of languages', by which 'the smaller European languages as well as all the larger ones, regional, minority and migrant languages as well as those with "national" status, and the languages of our major trading partners throughout the world' (SEC(2002) 1234) are to be understood.

At the moment, it remains unclear how – if at all – such a broad approach will be implemented since the language policy activities are contradictory and do not reveal any clear direction. There is continuing and massive support for extending the range of languages to be taught (cf. Strubell *et al.* 2007). At the same time, a clear reduction in the range of languages is likely to result from concrete policy activities taken recently, such as the *European Indicator of Language Competence*, as we will outline below.

As to the efforts which have been undertaken in favour of extending the range of languages, it has to be mentioned that various recommendations for the inclusion of languages other than the official EU languages are voiced, particularly in connection with cultural and linguistic diversity. These recommendations do not only concern all languages spoken in the EU, such as neighbouring, regional and immigrant minority languages and the languages of the trading partners, but also languages primarily used in writing (with a few exceptions) like the classical languages (Greek and Latin) and sign languages. The recommendations are based on the ideology of 'unity in diversity' and the equality of languages, on the social arguments in the sense of social cohesion and on the economic considerations.

The 2004 EU enlargement adds various new languages to the EU which are to be accommodated within the European framework of linguistic diversity. To give some examples from EU documents which establish the link between enlargement and linguistic diversity, the *Council Resolution of 14 February 2002 on the Promotion of Linguistic Diversity and Language Learning* (OJ 2002 C 50: 2) stresses, for example, the importance of language knowledge for European cohesion 'in the light of EU enlargement' and demands that 'the supply of languages should be as diversified as possible, including those of neighbouring countries and/or regions'. The *Council Resolution* also refers to the equality in value and dignity of all European languages. In the *European Parliament*

Resolution with Recommendations to the Commission on European Regional and Lesser-Used Languages – the Languages of Minorities in the EU – in the Context of Enlargement and Cultural Diversity (cf. 2003/2057(INI)), in the section 'Regional, Minority and Sign Languages', reference is made to the respect for linguistic and cultural diversity as a basic principle of the EU. Both the Council and the Parliament Resolution mention the enlargement, which increases the linguistic diversity that is somehow to be accounted for. The influence of the enlargement is also notable in the *Action Plan 2004–2006: Promoting Language Learning and Linguistic Diversity* (cf. COM(2003)449 final), which appeared in 2003. There, an inclusive approach is proposed, and the languages to be acquired are defined as follows: 'The range on offer should include the smaller European languages as well as all the larger ones, regional, minority and migrant languages as well as those with "national" status, and the languages of our major trading partners throughout the world' (COM(2003)449: 9; see also COM(2007)554 final). Like the *Action Plan*, the two reports ordered by the Commission, the *Report of the Group of Intellectuals* (cf. Maalouf 2008) and that of the *High Level Group of Multilingualism* (cf. High Level Group 2007), both distinctly argue for a language offer exceeding the official languages. In the *Report of the Group of Intellectuals*, the link between the language issue and the notion of the prospective Europe is particularly clear: 'To preserve all the languages of our heritage [...] is inseparable from the very idea of a Europe of peace, culture, universality and prosperity' (Maalouf 2008: 8).

For the selection of languages from such an extensive range, local considerations are increasingly called for. The Group of Intellectuals, for instance, argues for a bottom-up approach, which locates the decision at the 'grass-roots' level, 'i.e. in schools and also, increasingly, by the citizens themselves' (Maalouf 2008: 13). Taking into account local, social and cultural considerations, the Committee of the Regions on Multilingualism calls for 'a shared second language and a third language chosen on the basis of cultural affinity or the social and economic mobility requirements of the country or region of origin' (OJ 2008 C 257: 30, and – with identical wording – 32, point 18), while in its communication to the Council, the European Parliament, the European Economic and Social Committee and the Committee of the Regions, the Commission feels a similar need 'in relation to the choice of second foreign language, bearing in mind local conditions (border regions, presence of communities speaking different languages, etc)' (COM(2008)566 final: 11).

As to the policy activities which entail an apparent reduction in the language diversity, the *European Indicator of Language Competence*, constitutes a good example. The Indicator yields information on the outcome of language learning in the EU for the first time, but it is designed to provide data only on the five most frequently learned languages: '... in the first round, and for practical reasons foreign language competence should be tested in the five languages most frequently taught in the Union as a whole (i.e. English, French, German, Spanish and Italian' (COM(2005)356 final, 7; likewise, OJ 2005 C 256 E). This decision contradicts the equality principle since it is no longer the case that all languages are treated equally if a specific interest in proficiency in certain languages is voiced from a central authority. The hierarchy of languages implicated by this decision is challenged by the viewpoint of the inclusive approach. Thus, for example, the European Parliament resolution of 24 March 2009 (cf. 2008/2225(INI) EP 2009) recommends an extension of the Indicator: '[The European Parliament d]emands that the coverage of the language competence indicators should be extended as soon as possible to all the official EU languages, without prejudice to their also being extended to other languages spoken in the European Union' (2008/2225(INI) Report 2009: 9). Furthermore, the Committee on Culture and Education and the Committee on Employment and Social Affairs also recommend its extension to classical Greek and Latin (cf. 2008/2225(INI) Report 2009: 9).

Obviously, the debate is not yet completed. With the rising number of official languages, the demand for integrating the various other languages in use in the EU is also rising. Retrospectively, a substantial increase in the number of eligible languages can be observed, a development through which the question continues to gain complexity.

Another feature of this language policy which concerns external relations and economic considerations arises from the inclusion of spheres of communication extending beyond the EU. The European Economic and Social Committee on Multilingualism formulates two qualitative aims in its *Opinion on Multilingualism* of 2009 (cf. OJ 2009 C 77: 109–114): to preserve the vitality of European languages and to diversify language knowledge to include non-Community languages.

In this regard, the cooperation of the EU policy with other international institutions like the CoE and the UNESCO plays a crucial role since the political activities of these two institutions extend far beyond the EU. In the evaluation of language knowledge, particularly the cooperation between the EU language education policy and the CoE appears to be of prime importance. Thus, for example, the CoE's *Common European Framework of Reference for Languages* (cf. CEFR 2001) is used for the purposes of the *European Indicator of Language Competence* (cf. OJ 2002 C 50: 1–2; OJ 2005 C 256 E: 37–61; OJ 2008 C 320: 1–3; 2008/2225(INI) Report 2009).

The European Indicator emerged as part of the Lisbon strategic goal for the European Union, to become 'the most competitive and dynamic knowledge-based economy in the world' (Lisbon Conclusions 2000: point 5).

The Lisbon European Council called upon the member states, the Council and the Commission to establish a European framework defining 'the new basic skills' (Lisbon Conclusions 2000: point 26) to be provided through lifelong learning in order to comply with the requirements of the knowledge-based economy. Foreign languages were to be part of this framework (cf. Lisbon Conclusions 2000: point 26). Moreover, the Barcelona Council conclusions stressed the need for action to improve the mastery of basic skills. In this regard, the linguistic competence indicator was called for as early as 2002 (cf. Barcelona Conclusions 2002: 19).

As a consequence, the term 'basic skills' is replaced by 'key competences', a term which represents a broader concept since it is defined as a combination of skills, knowledge, aptitudes and attitudes. Moreover, the term 'key competences' also corresponds to international developments, such as the OECD's project Definition and Selection of Competences (cf. Education and Training 2010; DeSeCo 2005), the Asia–Europe Meeting's lifelong learning initiative (cf. Asia–Europe Meeting) and PISA 2000 (cf. Education and Training 2010: 2–3). In terms of the mastery of foreign languages, the framework again refers to the *Common European Framework of Reference for Languages* of the CoE (cf. CEFR 2001), which shows that a certain degree of cooperation is taking place.

An intensification of this cooperation both with the CoE and the UNESCO is also encouraged by the Council in the *Council Resolution of 21 November 2008 on a European Strategy for Multilingualism* (cf. OJ 2008 C 320: 1–3). Moreover, the European Economic and Social Committee on Multilingualism in its conclusions on multilingualism (cf. OJ 2009 C 77: 113–114) even suggests drawing on the UNESCO convention on diversity.

As far as the CoE is concerned, requests are in fact voiced for cooperation and 'renewed partnership' (Promotion of Multilingualism 2008: 4) in a study for the European Commission. These requests are substantiated with 'the excellent reputation of the CoE in the domain of languages; the fact that the policies pursued and promoted by both the European Commission and the CoE are "in line" (or at least do not contradict each other); the example of the European Year of Languages, which was perceived as a success and an example of good cooperation between both institutions' (Promotion of Multilingualism 2008: 4).

Moreover, the acquisition of non-European languages is also encouraged in the most recent significant reports. As the Group of Intellectuals for Intercultural Dialogue puts it with regard to the personal adoptive language: 'It is also likely that many of them would opt for languages from other continents, ideally the languages of the big Asian countries which have become major economic partners' (Maalouf 2008: 10). The *Report of the Group of Intellectuals* thus points to the economic reasons that make linguistic border crossing necessary. In contrast, the European Economic and Social Committee on Multilingualism (cf. OJ 2009 C 77: 109–114) sees the reason for acquiring non-Community languages as beneficial to cultural, social, political and economic relations with a view to promoting peace and friendship between peoples. Again, this example clearly shows that the EU language policy is actually confronted with rather heterogeneous interests and demands.

In conclusion, it can be said that the EU language education policy proves to be a highly active political field. The large number of documents devoted to this policy reflect the activities that have unfolded in this field over the past two decades and particularly from the millennium onwards. The documents reveal increasing demands on the multilingualism of European citizens. The policy of two languages in addition to the mother tongue has become the minimum requirement for all Europeans, although it is yet unclear which languages are to be pursued here. At the same time, the EU language policy is not a self-contained area of activity, but is part of a global network through its cooperation with international organisations and through its integration into spheres of communication outside the Community.

From today's perspective, however, taking stock of the EU language policy yields sobering results. The great effort and importance attributed to knowledge of languages as a key competence within the framework of the knowledge-based construction of the future Europe are faced with a multitude of unanswered questions and a contradictory policy. Thus, the question arises as to the type of language education policy – top-down or rather bottom-up – as well as the question concerning the *language* actually to be accounted for by a European language education policy. Searching for the answers to these questions leads us to the arguments and goals behind the language education policy. As our observations have clearly shown, the demands associated with language policy and ultimately with the language knowledge of European citizens are highly heterogeneous. From an EU internal perspective, there appears to be a desire for the choice of the languages learned to mirror European language diversity. With this approach, language learning would become a process reflecting the EU's 'unity in diversity' in so far as the knowledge of a great variety of languages would enable the Europeans to communicate with members of different language communities – with all languages being of equal value – as is being postulated. Ideologically, such a requirement is thus based on the equality principle. If the language education policy is evaluated against the background of this requirement, it must necessarily be regarded as a failure since the foreign languages actually selected by the Europeans constitute only a small section of the Europe's overall language spectrum. As it is also reflected in concrete policy activities, for example, the *European Indicator of Language Competence*, the practical reasons override the ideological claims.

From an EU-wide perspective, the language education policy involves the demand for tapping global communication spaces. Here, it is not so much the ideological arguments of the EU internal communication which are paramount, but rather economic arguments and the question of Europe's positioning in the world. The EU external communication points to a removal of a clear boundary between internal and external communication spaces, since migration has brought various different languages to the EU and thus – in an inclusive approach – have turned these into European languages. Global communication spaces consequently have also become potential European communication spaces to which the principle of 'unity in diversity' could probably be applied.

The language education policy presumably shows better than any other area how difficult it is to implement 'unity in diversity' if the ultimate political goal is the equality of languages. Indeed, the linguistic reality in Europe is a vivid example for the fact that languages differ in many respects. The structural equivalence of language cannot be projected onto equality in the various local, national and transnational communication spaces in Europe which are characterised by asymmetrical but at the same time widely varying functional distributions of languages. Attempts to turn equality of languages into an ideological foundation of the European construct and its communication space fail due to simple questions like what actually counts as a European language (cf. Nic Craith 2006: 171–173), that is, which languages are to be integrated into the diversity concept. Nevertheless, there is no doubt that the democratic operation of the European communication space is to be guaranteed only by means of suitable modes of communication, and that language education policy is central to planning such communication modes. The ideological basis the EU has chosen in its policy, however, is clearly reaching its limits, which, inter alia, becomes apparent in the case of concrete measures like the *European Indicator of Language Competence*. The search for possibilities of implementing the linguistic 'unity in diversity' as a coherent language policy, however, could also be an inspiration for an ideological re-orientation – but so far, such a re-orientation is not in sight.

1.2.2 Linguistic minorities policy

In the early 1980s, the European Parliament and the Commission set out to account for the conflicts as they arose from ethno-linguistic regionalism in Western Europe. Here, political attention focused upon the bi- and multilingual minorities which in various member states had started contesting the cultural and linguistic hegemony of the national state majorities while pointing to their own subaltern and discriminated status in this context. The conflict aggravated as the minorities put forward their claims for cultural autonomy and when calls for political segregation and terrorist activities eventually threatened to undermine political and social cohesion in various member states of the time. The objective of the Community's engagement in the minority issue was to identify in the first instance the reasons for the regionalist crisis and to seek for solutions that would accommodate the claims of the regional minorities within a common framework of official recognition and the respect for cultural diversity.

Thus, in the 1980s, language political action relating to regional or minority languages (RMLs) was targeted towards supporting the development and maintenance of networking and cooperation structures of the RMLs (cf. Grin & Moring 2002: 3, 30). The drafting of influential reports (cf. OJ 1981 C 287: 106; OJ 1983 C 68: 103; OJ 1987 C 318: 160) gave rise to various resolutions adopted by the European Parliament. As a consequence of these activities, the European Bureau for Lesser Used Languages (EBLUL), the MERCATOR European Network for Minority Languages and Education and the European Parliament Intergroup Committee for Minority Languages were installed. Against the background of the questions raised by ethnic regionalism, the European Parliament declared to support a *Community Charter of Regional Languages and Cultures* and a *Charter of Rights of Ethnic Minorities*. It appealed to the member states to protect and promote the RMLs particularly in the domains of education, mass media, public life, social and economic matters, legal measures and trans-frontier cooperation. In this context, the emphasis was on RMLs as a source of enrichment for European civilisation and diversity, and the Commission was called upon to review all Community and national legislation and practices which discriminated against minority languages (cf. OJ 1981 C 287: 106; OJ 1983 C 68).

In the 1990s, the CoE adopted two treaties, namely, the *European Charter for Regional or Minority Languages* (cf. Charter RML 1992) and the *European Framework Convention on the Protection of National Minorities* (cf. Framework Convention 1995), which were to set the standards for the achievement of minority promotion and protection in Europe. At this point, it has to be mentioned that by that time the CoE had established a plurilingualism policy in its own right which originated to a large extent from the human rights issue and from conceiving of European diversity in terms of a common cultural heritage and a wealthy asset that called for protection and promotion (cf. Grin & Moring 2002: 26). Minorities, as well as their languages and cultures, came to play an important part in this respect. On the one hand, they directly connected with the human rights issue since the right of minorities to use their language in public and private life has been and is still being considered an inalienable human right, all the more as minority languages and their speakers have mostly been discriminated against and subjected to forced assimilation into national monolingualism. On the other hand, including minority languages into a coherent framework of plurilingual education has been part of the CoE's plurilingualism policies since the 1990s, as actions of this kind were considered to contribute to promoting democratic citizenship, intercultural dialogue and social cohesion in Europe. Although migrant languages are not protected by the *Minority Charter*, the CoE has since the 1970s (cf. e.g. Standing Conference 9/1975; Standing Conference 10/1977) been pointing to the necessity to take these languages into account when planning and implementing language educational policies in order not to aggravate the social problems in the host countries.

The most important point is that the CoE, while developing an integrated approach to plurilingualism, has been collaborating with the EU in both the language education and the minority language policies since the 1990s. Thus, the European Parliament adopted a resolution on the basis of the *Killilea Report* (1994), in which the member states were called upon to sign and ratify the CoE's *Minority Charter* (cf. OJ 1994 C 61: 110). At the same time, adhering to the Framework Convention became part of fulfilling the Copenhagen criteria, which defined the conditionality for accession within the EU enlargement process (cf. Copenhagen Conclusions 1993). According to these criteria, the candidate countries were required to provide for measures that would guarantee democracy, the rule of law, human rights and the respect and protection of minorities. Ratifying and enacting the provisions of the Framework Convention was considered to serve as a benchmark criterion for accession to the Union.

Contrary to the *Charter*, the *Framework Convention* does not focus on linguistic issues although it does not exclude them when referring to the rights of minorities to preserve and to use their languages in privacy, in public, in family names, toponyms, and so on. Rather, the *Framework*'s focus is on human rights, non-discrimination, equality and non-assimilation whereas the *Charter* provides for minimal standards in protecting and promoting minority languages in a variety of fields such as education, legislation, administration, public institutions and the media, cultural affairs, social and economic life and cross-border activities. And most importantly, the *Charter* explicitly excludes dialects of official or national languages and the languages of migrants from these measures (for further details, see Grin & Moring 2002: 26).

Another significant step concerning the EU minority policy was set when in 1992 the project Euromosaic I was commissioned with the objective to investigate the ethnolinguistic vitality and reproduction capacities of the regional minorities in the member states of the Union. The findings were supposed to allow for conclusions concerning enhanced minority protection and promotion policies. Subsequently, Euromosaic II (unpublished) and Euromosaic III (2004) followed in connection with the EU enlargements of 1995 and 2004. Since the 1990s, the demands of the European Parliament concerning the needs of the RMLs and their speakers were also taken into account within the framework of the various EU programmes and action plans of Community policy such as Lingua, Erasmus, Tempus, and so on.

From the reading of the documents relating to RMLs, it may be concluded that until the millennium, the concern of the EEC/EU's political action was primarily directed towards protecting the RMLs and their related cultures within the framework of linguistic diversity. Here, 'linguistic diversity' is referred to as an asset. *The resolution on linguistic and cultural minorities in the European Community* (cf. OJ 1994 C 61: 110) relates to linguistic diversity as a key element in the Union's cultural wealth. 'Diversity as an asset' is also stressed in both the influential *Regional* or *Minority Charter* (cf. Charter RML 1992) and the *Framework Convention* (cf. Framework Convention 1995). Moreover, 'linguistic diversity' increasingly came to combine with the 'human rights' issue since the right to use RMLs in private and public life was considered a right to which again the *Charter* and the *Framework Convention* make explicit reference in their preambles. Following these instruments, promoting and protecting the regional minorities and their languages is regarded as an important contribution to democratic stability and non-discrimination. Here, it is quite obvious that the EU and the CoE's politics follows quite similar lines and objectives.

However, at the beginning of the millennium, the question was raised what part RMLs were actually to play within the EU's diversity framework. On the one hand, there was an obvious lack of provisions that would account for the safeguard of RMLs within the Union's legal framework. It is true that the *Charter of Fundamental Rights of the European Union* (cf. OJ 2000 C 364: 1–22) stated that any discrimination based on membership to a national minority should be prohibited (cf. Art.21) and that it acknowledged linguistic diversity as a citizen's right (cf. Art.22). However, the *Charter* came into force as part of the Lisbon Treaty only in 2009 (cf. OJ 2010 C 83 Charter: 396–403). Explicit reference to 'the rights of persons belonging to minorities' was also made in the rejected Constitutional Treaty of 2004 (cf. OJ 2004 C 310: 1–474). The reference thus had no legal weight unless it was taken up in Art.1a of the Lisbon Treaty (cf. OJ 2007 C 306: 1–271). On the other hand, uncertainties concerning the understanding of 'diversity' arose. It was not clear enough whether 'diversity' would first and foremost refer to linguistic pluralism between the member states and thus concern the national languages only – or whether it would also relate to linguistic pluralism within the member states and thus include the minority languages (cf. Toggenburg 2003).

When talking about minority languages, it has to be mentioned that besides the 23 official languages, there are more than 60 RMLs spoken in the EU, while immigrants from inside and outside the EU have brought a wide range of languages with them which are mostly used in the large urban centres of Europe. As linguistic minorities are generally considered to be bi- and multilingual 'by nature', it goes without saying that these minorities have an important share in constituting the Union's linguistic diversity within the member states.

The question of how to position the minority languages within the Union's diversity scope has as yet not been sufficiently answered although it is evident that after the millennium, the issue of minority languages became integrated into the wider scope of the EM politics. In this scope, RMLs became part of the multilingualism campaign of the European Year of Languages 2001, which the EU organised in collaboration with the CoE. According to the *Decision No 1934/2000/EC of the European Parliament and of the Council of 17 July 2000 on the European Year of Languages 2001* (cf. OJ 2000 L, 232: 1–5), all European languages were considered equal in value and dignity and in forming an integral part of European civilisation. In this scope, the promotional measures on language and language learning would include the national languages together with the other languages 'in line with those identified by the Member States' (since the arrangements of the *Minority Charter* and the *Framework Convention* stipulated that the contracting states specified the minorities and the RMLs in their territories).

In its *Resolution with Recommendations to the Commission on European Regional and Lesser-Used Languages – the Languages of Minorities in the EU – in the Context of Enlargement and Cultural Diversity* (cf. 2003/2057(INI)), the European Parliament calls for a multiannual programme for linguistic diversity in which the findings of the monitoring carried out under the CoE's *European Charter for Regional or Minority Languages* should be taken into account. Following the already mentioned European Parliament *Resolution on Linguistic and Cultural Minorities in the European Community* (cf. OJ 1994 C 61: 110), minority languages entered into the *Action Plan 2004-06* (cf. COM(2003)449 final: 9), which called on the member states to actively encourage the teaching and learning of the widest possible range of languages including regional, minority and migrant languages. In the following, promotional strategies concerning the minority languages were included in the EU's *New Framework Strategy for Multilingualism* (cf. COM(2005)596 final), where the teaching of RMLs and migrant languages was considered as appropriate as was their inclusion into the social sciences and humanities research programmes. RMLs are also taken into account in the *Amended Proposal for a Decision of the European Parliament and of the Council Establishing an Integrated Action Programme in the Field of Lifelong Learning* (cf. COM(2006)236 final).

In 2007 and 2008, three influential papers were published in which the actual scope of the EM policy is outlined in a comprehensive and programmatic manner. Thus, the *Final Report* by the High Level Group on Multilingualism (cf. High Level Group 2007: 5) puts forward that the first decade of the new century has seen the introduction of an inclusive language education policy which RMLs and migrant languages are part of. It defines the RMLs as constituent elements of Europe's linguistic and cultural diversity and wealth (cf. High Level Group 2007: 18). In their proposals, 'A Rewarding Challenge: How the Multiplicity of Languages could Strengthen Europe' (cf. Maalouf 2008: 11), the Group of Intellectuals for Intercultural Dialogue, set up at the initiative of the European Commission, argues strongly in favour of the so-called 'personal adoptive languages' which people would choose for personal interest just as they choose their profession. Minority languages, including migrant languages, would be part of this personal adoptive choice. In both the *High Level Report* and the *Proposals from the Group of Intellectuals*, there is a strong emphasis on minority languages relating to the personal and cultural identities of their speakers. Moreover, both documents recommend raising awareness of the value of the bi- and multilingual resources of the minorities instead of penalising or ignoring them. The Commission in its *Communication to the European Parliament, the Council, the European Economic and Social Committee and the Committee of the Regions Multilingualism* (cf. COM(2008)566 final) reaffirms that member states are the key decision-makers on language policy, including RMLs, and that it is the CoE's *European Charter for Regional or Minority Languages* that provides a comprehensive framework for the RML policies. Regional, minority and migrant languages are said to contribute to the common European cultural background and to be part of the multilingualism policy for intercultural dialogue and social cohesion (cf. COM(2008)566 final: 5). The Communication also points to the 'untapped linguistic resources in our society' (COM(2008)566 final: 6), referring to the multilingual competences of which particularly minorities dispose in general, and which 'should be valued more highly' (COM(2008)566 final).

The subsequent *Opinion of the European Economic and Social Committee on Multilingualism* (cf. OJ 2009 C 77: 109–114) reiterates that the European languages, comprising the regional and national languages and the languages spoken by migrants, make a major contribution to diversity, and underlines that managing cultural diversity will involve two major challenges, namely, promoting cultural diversity and fostering the respect for migrants. The European Parliament resolution of 24 March 2009 on multilingualism (cf. 2008/2225(INI) EP: 17) calls upon member states to provide immigrants with the necessary means to learn the language and culture of the host country, while allowing and encouraging them to maintain their own language. It encourages the introduction of mother-tongue minority, local and foreign, languages on a non-compulsory basis within school programmes and extracurricular activities (cf. 2008/2225(INI) EP: 24). Furthermore, it calls upon the Council to produce an annual progress report on multilingualism in formal and informal education systems, vocational training and adult education in the member states, paying attention to the relationship between the prevalence of national, regional and minority languages and immigration (cf. 2008/2225(INI) EP: 25). Moreover, it reaffirms its commitment to the promotion of language learning, multilingualism and linguistic diversity in the European Union, including regional and minority languages, as these are cultural assets that must be safeguarded and nurtured (cf. 2008/2225(INI) EP: 26). Furthermore, it urges the Commission to draw on the conclusions of the consultations regarding language learning for migrant children and the teaching in the host member state of the language and culture of the country of origin (cf. 2008/2225(INI) EP: 34). In addition, the various communications and annual reports on the EU immigration and integration policy reaffirm that immigrants should be enabled to acquire knowledge of the language of the host country in order to ensure their integration into the labour market and into society at large (cf. COM(2004)508 final: 18–19).

From all this it can be concluded that over the years, minority languages have come to form an integral part of the EM policy framework. Against the background of the problems that derive from the increasing immigration of third-country nationals, it comes as no surprise that the EU is more than ever committed to including the migrant languages into its multilingualism framework. RMLs which relate to the old or historical European minorities have been included into the promotional framework of the *Minority Charter* (1992) and the *Framework Convention* (1995), which set the standards for RML policy. However, there is a flaw in the RML policy as it still continues to reflect a double-standard strategy dividing member states into two categories in their obligations vis-a-vis the regional minorities: on the one hand, the new member states who have been constrained to fulfil the Copenhagen Criteria on the occasion of the 2004 enlargement and, on the other hand, the old member states who adhere to the promotional treaties of the CoE only of their own free will and interest. It is true that the Copenhagen Criteria have also put pressure on the old member states in signing and ratifying both instruments. Nevertheless, and against the positive move of some old member states, it can be feared that in the long run the double-standard regime will have a negative bearing on the whole RML policy.

For the time being, there seems to be a silent agreement that RMLs are being sufficiently provided with measures of safeguard and promotion, whereas immigrants, their educational and cultural difficulties give rise to major concern caused by the fear that these difficulties may aggravate the social problems particularly in the urban centres of the European host countries. Immigrants have come to be taken into account on the EM political agenda only since the new millennium although as early as in the 1970s, the Council attempted to call upon the member states to take appropriate measures concerning the mother-tongue teaching of immigrant children of member states origin (cf. OJ 1977 L 177: 32). In the scope of the Lisbon Strategy, minority languages, including the immigrant languages, were regarded as an added value since the 'natural' bi- and multilingual abilities of the speakers could be made use of on the labour market. However, the standards for an inclusive policy which, beyond the economic gain, also accounts for social cohesion and intercultural understanding have as yet not been developed clearly enough. Such a policy would provide immigrants with the necessary means to acquire the language and culture of the host country, while encouraging them to maintain their own language.

In terms of political achievement, it may be argued that the needs and difficulties concerning minorities and their languages have been mainstreamed through diverse political programmes over the past few decades, with the result that the European public has been increasingly sensitised to minority issues. It cannot be ignored, though, that political awareness has been largely concentrating on the regional minorities, whereas the problems of the immigrant minorities have remained unresolved as yet (cf. Extra *et al.* 2004: 395). Promoting and safeguarding the RMLs has been considered to contribute to the European diversity framework. Protecting and promoting this diversity connects – as we have seen – with the respect for human rights, equality and democracy, the principles and values which constitute the ideological underpinning of the official politics of building Europe.

It remains, however, an open question how immigrants can be integrated into the diversity framework of the EU. There are several reasons for this.

On the one hand, immigrants constitute a rather heterogeneous group of speakers comprising at the same time EU citizens and third-country nationals stemming from inside and outside Europe. This raises different questions about citizenship and rights to be accorded to the immigrants. On the other hand, there is a lack of clarity about what 'diversity' is taken to actually mean. The repeated references made to European civilisation and cultural heritage, of which the regional and minority languages are an integral part, seem to include only the 'old' minorities into the diversity framework. Also, the term 'European languages', which the documents continuously refer to, does not tell much about what exactly counts as a European language (cf. Nic Craith 2006: 168–186). Is it the languages which, historically speaking, belong to Europe, its culture and civilisation or is it the great many languages that are actually spoken in Europe? Would languages of communities from outside Europe be part of the European diversity? And what about the European diversity that extends beyond the EU borders? These are questions which need to be answered in order to set the political agenda for promoting immigrants' multilingualism.

1.2.3 EU institutional language regime

The EC/EU resolutions concerning the language use in its institutions are good examples for the argument that the European integration process has been a multilingual undertaking since the 1950s (cf. Kraus 2008: 11). The 'multilingual undertaking' started in 1958 when the EEC Council issued Regulation No. 1 determining the languages to be used by the European Economic Community (cf. OJ 1958 L 17: 385). Here, the official languages of the member states were declared working languages and official languages of the EEC institutional bodies. From this arrangement, it can be concluded that the first language regulation defines the EEC as a multilingual entity and that the respect of linguistic pluralism was so-to-say part of the political agenda well before the Union came into existence.

The 1958 regulation stipulates that documents submitted to the institutions of the Community may be drafted in any one of the official languages selected by the sender and that the reply is to be drafted in the same language. Documents from the institutional bodies to member states shall be drafted in the language of such state, while regulations and documents of general application shall be drafted in the official languages, as shall be the *Official Journal of the European Community*. Moreover, the language use in the proceedings of the Court of Justice is to be laid down in its rules of procedure, otherwise the institutions may stipulate in their rules of procedure which languages are to be used in specific cases.

In other words, the first regulation specifies that legislation must be published in the official languages, and it requires its institutions to deal with citizens in the official languages of their choice. In the course of the EEC/EU enlargements, the EEC directive has been steadily amended and thus the number of the languages has increased from 4 to 23.

As the institutional language regime is clearly regulated, there appear to be, in general, no difficulties concerning the questions as to what constitutes an official language and how to use it within the institutional contexts. However, concerning the effective use within these contexts, problems may arise when 'less widely used' official languages are concerned, as was the case for Maltese or Irish. For example, the lack of qualified translators in Maltese gave rise to the Council Regulation (EC) No 930/2004 of 1 May 2004 on temporary derogation measures relating to the drafting in Maltese of the acts of the institutions of the European Union (cf. OJ 2004 L 169: 1–2). In order to remedy the lack of qualified translators, it was decided that 'on an exceptional and transitional basis, the institutions of the Union are not to be bound by the obligation concerning the drafting or translation of all acts, including judgments of the Court of Justice, in the Maltese language.' The regulation also puts forward that 'such derogation be partial' (OJ 2004 L 169: 1) and therefore suggests 'to exclude from [...] [the] scope regulations adopted jointly by the European Parliament and the Council' (OJ 2004 L 169: 1), while it reaffirms that the status of Maltese as an official and a working language of the Union's institutions remains unaffected.

Yet, another regulation concerns the institutional use of the Irish language. Upon request of the Irish Government that Irish is the national and the first official language of Ireland, the Council Regulation (EC) No 920/2005 of 13 June 2005, amending Regulation No 1 of 15 April 1958 (cf. OJ 2005 L 156: 3–4), decided 'that for practical reasons and on a transitional basis, the institutions of the European Union are not to be bound by the obligation to draft and translate all acts, including judgments of the Court of Justice, in the Irish language' (OJ 2005 L: 3).

Apart from these specific regulations, the amendments concerning the range of official languages have not changed the rules of institutional language arrangement. The rules have been included in the adapted Council regulations and have eventually been reaffirmed under Article 41 of the *Charter of Fundamental Rights of the EU* (cf. OJ 2010 C 83 Charter: 389–403) and under Articles 20 and 24 of the Consolidated versions of the Treaty on European Union and the Treaty on the Functioning of the European Union (cf. OJ 2010 C 83 Treaty: 1–388).

In the interest of equity, transparency and democratic legitimacy, language use in the European Parliament is managed on the basis of 'controlled full multilingualism' (Code of Conduct 2006: 2), that is the right of members to use the official language of their choice. Interpretation services are reserved in an order of priority for plenary sittings, priority political meetings, parliamentary committees and delegations, press conferences, official bodies and administrative events.

In contrast to the Parliament language use, the European Council follows the rule under which during Council discussions, the representatives of the member states speak in their own languages, while interpreters ensure multilingual oral communication. The Council's deliberations are based on documents submitted to it in all the official and working languages. Legal acts adopted by the Council, as well as treaties and all documents published in the *Official Journal of the European Union*, are available in all the official languages. When communicating with members of the public, the Council applies the principle of multilingualism as widely as possible. However, for practical reasons and budgetary constraints, only the most widely understood languages are used. Officials are expected to know two Union languages in addition to their mother tongue, and in general these languages coincide with English, French and sometimes also with German.

The institutional language regime stands for a model of integral multilingualism in which all languages are basically considered as equal partners. The Council of Ministers and the European Parliament are those institutions which come closest to the 'ideal' situation in the sense that in formal settings such as the Parliament's plenary sessions, all official languages are used. Everyday institutional practice in informal meetings and especially in the Commission turns out, however, to be largely restricted to the use of English, French and some German. In this respect, the maintenance of the integral language regime bears rather symbolic weight since the everyday practice reflects the leading political role of the powerful states in the EU (cf. Krzyżanowski 2009: 25) rather than the democratic equality in diversity that the EU claims to promote.

Since the 1990s, and in the light of subsequent EU enlargements, there have been extensive debates on the practicability of this language regime. On the one hand, there are experts who recommend a limitation of the number of working languages (cf. de Swaan 1999; Grin 1996; Mamadouh 1999; Wright 2000). According to Schloßmacher (1997), even more than three-quarters of the EU officials and about 40% of the members of the European Parliament are in favour of a clear and limiting regulation. There is, however, no consensus on how exactly the range of languages should be narrowed down. In contrast to Phillipson (2003: 176), Van Els (2001, 2005) goes one step further when suggesting that one single working language, namely, English, should be used for internal communication within the institutions. He considers this solution fair since it would give rise to the development of 'Euro-English', which would increasingly become the property of non-natives and not orient itself towards British English as the 'golden standard'.

The fact that English appears to have long lost its status as a property of native-speakers is also stressed by the research, which has been developing towards ELF in recent years. Here, ELF is conceived as a contact language for people of different first languages who choose English as a means for communicative interactions that cannot be conducted in their own languages. The use of ELF is restricted to multilingual contexts, which is why language contact phenomena can be described as natural properties of ELF (cf. VOICE). ELF speakers are regarded as language users in their own right. From this research perspective, ELF has a special status which cannot be compared with the status of national languages and thus would not compete with the latter (cf. e.g. Seidlhofer 2004, 2007).

At the same time, however, the preponderant role of English and the digression from the commitment to linguistic pluralism and the language parity principle has also been harshly criticised. This criticism is particularly obvious in the reports published by the French Délégation Générale à la Langue Française et aux Langues de France (e.g. cf. Rapport DGLFLF 2010). Linguists such as Ammon (2006: 329) even fear that given the preponderant role of English, other big languages such as German and French might suffer from loss of their status and domains (cf. also Phillipson 2009: 87).

Moreover, the increase of language combinations in translation services and the contentious recourse to relay languages has been soliciting considerable concern. The EEC/EU has been well aware of these problems but has avoided addressing the reform of the institutional language regime, as any attempt in this direction would have caused controversies over the issue of national identities and the principal equality of the official languages. The controversy that evolved around the use of German as an official working language during the Finnish presidency in 1999 is just but one example for the fact that 'the language issue has kept its political explosiveness in spite of attempts to circumvent it over the decades' (Kraus 2008: 132). Initiatives to re-defining the existing language regime appear unlikely as long as the changing of language regimes requires the unanimous vote of the Council after consulting the European Parliament (cf. OJ 2010 C 83 Treaty: Art. 118 and 342).

In the *New Framework Strategy for Multilingualism* (cf. COM(2005)596 final: 3), which may be taken as a first comprehensive attempt at setting up an agenda of EM policies, it is stressed that the Commission's multilingualism policy aims at giving citizens access to European Union legislation, procedures and information in their own languages. It is also underlined that it is a prerequisite for the Union's democratic legitimacy and transparency to enable citizens to take part in the European project without encountering any language barriers (cf. COM(2005)596: 12–13).

Arguments of this kind are also reiterated in the latest report and the proposals drafted by official expert groups at the initiative of the European Commission. Thus, the report of the High Level Group on Multilingualism (cf. High Level Group 2007) points to the fact that 'the translation of EU legislation into all the official languages has to have absolute priority' (High Level Group 2007: 16). It acknowledges that the multilingual regime of the Commission assists in improving communication with the citizens although some concern is raised as to the actual number of languages to be included in this regime. In addition, attention is drawn to the fact that immigrant languages and major non-European languages 'were becoming increasingly relevant to the European project as well' (High Level Group 2007: 19).

In the *Proposals from the Group of Intellectuals for Intercultural Dialogue* (cf. Maalouf 2008: 21–24), it is advocated that the management of language diversity in the day-to-day running of the EU institutions could be rationalised 'by stressing the *bilateral language-to-language relations*' (Maalouf 2008: 21). In other words, the authors recommend setting up a network of bilateral and bilingual organisations which ensure that the language of each country is taught in the partner country to a number of people in order to strengthen the links between the speakers of the two languages instead of attempting to manage dozens of languages and the hundreds of language combinations they generate in translation. In the case of minority languages, the Community institutions are called upon to provide for financial assistance for teaching and training programmes.

The institutional language regime is also at the focus of attention of the *Council Resolution of 21 November 2008 on a European Strategy for Multilingualism* (cf. OJ 2008 C 320: 1–3), in which the Council invites the Commission to adopt measures which account for the linguistic needs of citizens and institutions and to 'care to provide information in all official languages' (OJ 2008 C 320: 3). And in the 'Opinion of the European Economic and Social Committee on Multilingualism' (cf. OJ 2009 C 77: 109–114), the Committee notes that more attention should be paid to the language regime of the Community institutions as it applies to non-official communications which are frequently not translated. Here, particular reference is made to the website of the European Council and the EU presidency.

And last but not least, the European Parliament resolution of 24 March 2009 titled *Multilingualism: An Assset for Europe and a Shared Commitment* (cf. 2008/2225(INI) EP), pointing to the principle of 'parity between the EU's official languages in all aspects of public activity' (2008/2225(INI) EP: point 3), underlines that Europe's linguistic diversity is a major cultural asset and that it would thus 'be wrong for the EU to restrict itself to a single main language' (2008/2225(INI) EP: point 4). It also emphasises 'the crucial role of the EU institutions in ensuring respect for the principle of linguistic parity in their relations between Member States, EU citizens and in the EU institutions themselves, as also in EU citizens' relations with national administrations and with Community and international institutions and bodies' (2008/2225(INI) EP: point 5).

Concluding, it can be said that the institutional language regime reflects a model of integral multilingualism which ensures the linguistic equality principle among the official EU languages. The equality principle has been invoked since the very beginning of the EEC and has been renewed on each occasion of the various enlargements of the Community. Despite the concerns raised against the applicability of the integral language regime, as well as its truly counter-acting every-day practices and its exploding budgetary expenditure, it can be said that this language regime is of primary importance for the EU multilingualism policy. Respecting the principle of parity between the official languages is symbolically equated with respecting the Member States and their national identities as equal partners. The agendas and positions taken in the latest policy documents on EU multilingualism reaffirm this principle.

Notwithstanding the efforts of upholding the principle of language parity symbolically despite the objections mentioned above, the examples of the special regulations concerning Maltese and Irish show that the automatic equation of official and working languages in institutional practice creates further problems in implementing the language parity (cf. Nic Craith 2006: 183). In order to ensure that the symbolic equality of all official languages in the EEC/EU is practically acknowledged, these were simultaneously recognised as official working languages. As the derogation measures concerning Maltese and Irish show, however, working and official languages are not treated equally in practice. Thus, for example, Maltese is an official language in principle but not a working language in practice. Even if it is stressed that these measures do not impact on the official status of the language, we cannot deny the fact that Maltese – or also Irish – with their symbolic significance as working languages, and thus also as official languages, are further restricted in their status as already less widely used languages. These cases show once more that the integral language regime, which should ensure the maintenance of the equality principle, is not viable in institutional practice.

1.2.4 Positions and challenges

From what has been said so far, it follows that EM is actually represented as a comprehensive policy framework which is to ensure the Union's ever closer economic, political and cultural integration. On the one hand, EM was to provide for the required mobility, employability and competitiveness of the globalised single market. On the other hand, it was seen as an appropriate means to reflect and sustain the political and cultural distinctiveness of the Member States within the ongoing unification process, thereby giving political legitimacy to the Union as an integrated democratic collectivity incorporating cultural and linguistic diversity.

The advocacy of EM dates back to the early days of the EEC, but it became particularly prominent after the Union had come into being. Recurrent references are made in the institutional language regime to the benefits of linguistic diversity as representing common European identity and cultural heritage. Before Maastricht, however, it was not accorded as much political weight as after the foundation of the Union. With the Maastricht Treaty, however, the cause of cultural and linguistic diversity gained momentum and developed into a comprehensive and normative EM policy which was seen to be integral to the nature and development of the EU as a whole. Thus, in the mid 1990s, EM was defined as 'part and parcel of both European identity/citizenship and the learning society' in the Commission's *White Paper* (COM(95)590: 47). From the perspective of the information society, EM was also to provide for the appropriate language skills in order to ensure mobility, employability and economic competitiveness. With the onset of the new millennium and the Lisbon strategy, EM developed into a key focal point of EU policy (cf. Krzyżanowski 2009). It was presented as both an economic and a cultural asset, providing for the needs of a KBS as well as promoting communal identity, social cohesion and intercultural communication. Although EM remains rather vague as a concept, the attempts to implement the Lisbon strategy can be taken as a first step towards profiling EM as a political framework in its own right (cf. Section 1.2.). It is only in the *New Framework Strategy* (cf. COM 2005/596) of 2005 that EM is defined as a political concept 'referring to both a person's ability to use several languages and the coexistence of different language communities in one geographical area' (COM 2005/596: 3). Here, for the first time, three fields of political action are listed, namely 'to encourage language learning and to promote linguistic diversity in society, to promote a healthy multilingual economy and to give citizens access to EU legislation, procedures and information in their own languages' (COM 2005/596). Another important step in the implementation of EM as a common political project was set when EM was linked to the Portfolio for Education, Training, Culture and Multilingualism (2004–2006) and when EM was established as a separate Commission portfolio in 2007.

This period was also the time when language political activities were directed towards a new comprehensive strategy for multilingualism. As a consequence, two groups of experts were set up on the initiative of the Commission to report on multilingualism policy. From their findings and recommendations and the latest Communication of the Commission in 2008, it can be inferred that EM has developed into a transversal theme with far-reaching consequences for other policy areas. Economic concerns, it is true, still appear to be a strong driving force in this framework but it is obvious that the new comprehensive approach is continuously widening its scope into social and cultural spheres. Thus, the issues of identity and shared heritage, of intercultural dialogue and mutual understanding are put forward. Equal opportunities, social cohesion and active citizenship should be strengthened through EM. Multilingual individuals are seen to contribute significantly to heightening creativity and innovation. And minorities' multilingual skills are viewed as a valuable and yet untapped capital which calls for appropriate exploitation, especially those of the migrants, to whom particular attention is accorded in the new policy framework due to their increasing importance.

Beyond the common political and ideological lines in which the multilingualism framework of the EU appears to be founded, the politics pursued by the EU in promoting multilingualism at the individual and societal level, as well as in economy and in the EU institutions, show that the mother tongue + 2 strategy has been turned into a minimum requirement for citizens to become multilingual. Second and third language competences have been termed basic skills which are to meet the requirements of the knowledge-based economy. Recent opinions and resolutions even suggest that the teaching of a third foreign language should be introduced at school.

From a critical perspective, the following questions require clarification here: What languages should be selected from the wide range of languages actually spoken in Europe? How are the smaller official languages to be integrated alongside the larger and more dominant ones such as English, French and German? Can regional minority languages be part of the selected repertoires? How are the various immigrant languages to be dealt with? Moreover, it has not been clarified whether local and individual constellations such as neighbouring languages, languages of border regions and of minorities or personal adoptive languages should and can be taken into account in the selection of the foreign language repertoire. It also remains to be seen how the non-EU languages can be accounted for and how world-wide communication spaces can be included into the multilingualism concept.

All these open questions show that so far, the EU has not succeeded in establishing clear guidelines towards which the linguistic support and protection programmes can be oriented. It still remains unclear in how far ELF can contribute to supporting multilingualism – even though research can provide answers in this respect (cf. LINEE; Seidlhofer 2004, 2007) which demonstrate that ELF does not endanger multilingualism but rather supports it. Furthermore, it is also unclear what the smaller (less widely used) national languages can contribute to EM and how the enormously high linguistic diversity resulting from the minority languages can be meaningfully and at the same time efficiently integrated into the EM framework.

Over the last decades, political support for the RMLs has helped to set up network structures and to provide for minimal standards of RML safeguard and promotion. This suggests that regional and minority speakers and their languages are sufficiently protected and promoted. At the same time, considerable concern is being raised regarding the multilingual migrant communities living in socially disadvantaged conditions in the big urban centres of Europe. Although the 'naturally' given multilingual competences of both the old and the new minorities have been repeatedly put forward as valuable resources and as added value, the new minorities have as yet not been included substantially enough into the promotional measures of the multilingualism policy.

Concerning the institutional arrangement of the EU's working languages, one can say that the integral language regime reflects the language parity principle which the EU keeps holding on to notwithstanding the criticism that has been raised against its practicability over the years. Therefore, it comes as no surprise that in the latest positions taken by the EU, the language parity principle has been reaffirmed although institutional every-day practice turns out to be largely restricted to a very small and selected range of languages.

From the various stances taken by the EU in its multilingualism policy, it may be concluded that the multilingualism agenda is still in the making since there are several issues in this framework which call for further clarification or for a redefinition of the current positions. From an overall perspective, we can say that this policy is still rather programmatic in its nature and is also indecisive in its strategic moves due to the seemingly irresolvable task.

One example to be mentioned in this context is the language equality principle, which constitutes one of the cornerstones of the EU's multilingualism policy. Here, it has as yet not been possible to politically implement this principle, i.e. neither with respect to minorities nor when it comes to providing an equally balanced language regime in the EU institutions or in foreign language learning. Minority languages are of special concern since there are more than 60 RMLs in Europe, which are spoken by more than 10% of the total EU population. Migrant languages are not even included in this number although estimates refer to a total of ca. 400 languages which are in use 'in addition to the dominant languages' (VALEUR-Report 2007: 26). It is thus more than obvious that migrants are actually excluded from the equality principle. RMLs participate in this principle to a certain degree, provided that they enjoy official recognition in the Member States. In this case, they are generally included in the local curricula in terms of mother tongue or subject teaching. In their role as foreign languages, however, minority languages only manifest themselves to a limited extent (cf. also Kenner & Hickey 2008). This role is, if at all, reserved for the languages of the regional minorities which are state languages in the neighbouring country like for example German in South Tyrol (Italy) or Slovenian in Austria. The autochthonous minority languages which lack such a support, like for instance Breton in France or Sardinian in Italy, remain largely excluded from the foreign language curricula.

The EU institutions and learning settings are contexts in which it is still the national languages that determine the debate on language equality. There are, however, clear power asymmetries between the smaller and the big national languages which are reflected in their selective use in educational and institutional settings. Therefore, it can be argued that contrary to the strong plea for language equality, hegemonic multilingualism continues to be furthered and sustained in the institutional and educational contexts. Hegemonic multilingualism stands for the hierarchical dominance of the great and prestigious languages, i.e. primarily English, followed by French and to a lesser degree German (cf. Krzyżanowski & Wodak 2010; Phillipson 2003). Here, the debate is still open on whether and how the smaller official languages of the EU might be accorded an equal share in the EM framework.

Moreover, the equality principle is also called into question because it is far from clear whether it would also apply to languages other than the official EU languages. This raises the question of what languages will be part of the EM framework on equal terms. As already mentioned, the minority languages can be seen as largely excluded from the EM project. And yet another point is whether and to what extent non-EU languages, for example, neighbouring languages, migrant languages, or languages of big trading partners, should be included.

The equality principle connects directly with the persistence of cultural and linguistic diversity within the unity framework of the EU. Not only do the many languages stand for the diverse European identities but they also form a constitutive element of the common cultural heritage, which serves as a basis of reference for the patterns of diversified European identifications. Hence, the respect of the diverse European identities – and preferably of the national identities – is also one of the reasons why the EU has, as yet, rather avoided than seriously resolving the contentious issue of the language equality principle in the EM framework.

Clearly, diversity and the common cultural heritage are major issues on which the multilingualism policy appears to be founded. Restricting language learning and language skills to a selected number of languages would not meet the conditions on which to sustain European diversity and the shared cultural heritage.

The same applies to multilingualism and economy since it cannot be ignored that restrictive language learning and hegemonic multilingualism have a negative bearing on meeting the requirements of a knowledge-based economy. Although recent studies on multilingualism and economy call for a better management of linguistic diversity in order to overcome linguistic barriers on the EU internal and the world markets, language learning policies largely remain restricted to the prestigious European languages and in particular to English as the business language of the world.

It is true that linguistic diversity is a major political issue of the multilingualism framework, but it remains as yet an open question whether the EU can enact this policy in the various fields of action at all. Here, it should not be overlooked that in principle the EU lacks the competence to interfere into the language affairs of the member states. Following Art. 126 and 127EC of the Maastricht Treaty (cf. OJ 1992 C 191: 1–115), it may support the member states only in their actions within the educational area. After the legal amendments in the Lisbon Treaty (cf. OJ 2007 C 306: 1–271), it remains to be seen how the Union will enact linguistic diversity to which it adheres as a general principle. Moreover, it is still unclear how the Union will act when it comes to minority languages, which in the Lisbon Treaty are explicitly referred to in connection with diversity, non-discrimination and human rights.

Respecting and promoting linguistic diversity connects intimately with the issue of human rights. The human rights issue is particularly relevant for regional minorities and migrants and their possibilities to use the minority language in private and public spheres (cf. Skutnabb-Kangas 1995: 7). As to the EU's regional minority policy, it has already been mentioned that there is a flaw in the double-standard strategy which divides the member states in their obligations vis-a-vis the regional minorities. Unfortunately, there are good reasons to assume that in the long run, the double-standard regime will have a negative bearing on the whole RML policy. As long as member states are still the key players in RML policies, it remains to be seen how, against the background of the newly enforced Lisbon Treaty, policy making in this field will develop.

It has been mentioned that migrants who are third-country nationals have come to be included in the EM political agenda only since the new millennium. Despite repeated appeals to exploit the untapped multilingual resources of these communities, their integration into the EM project has not been attended to seriously enough. So far, it still remains unclear how to appropriately integrate the language skills of the migrants and, in particular, how to include second-generation migrant children into the national education systems. A particularly contentious issue in this context is whether the migrants' languages of origin should figure at all in the national language curricula and on what grounds the standards for a well-balanced inclusive EM approach are to be formulated.

Democracy and democratic citizenship are also linked to human rights and form yet another crucial issue that directly connects with diversity and the multilingualism policy. Linguistic pluralism, in fact, appears to be an obstacle to constituting an overarching political space and a common public sphere which should allow for democratic will-formation among the Union's citisens. It is not only an obstacle but also one of the main challenges for implementing democratic European citizenship. However, the multilingualism policies appear to be unfortunate and discrepant in this respect. The best example for discrimination is the institutional language regime itself, where the principle of citizens' access to political and legal information remains impaired as long as this information is not covered in all official languages on the Union's websites. Another example would be minorities whose participation in the democratisation process is often seriously hampered because they are not allowed to use their mother tongue in the public spheres. A third point concerns language learning and hegemonic multilingualism since holding on to this practice while excluding minor languages gives rise to the fear that enhancing multilingualism of this kind might sharpen the divide between those who are in possession of highly valued language skills and others who are not or who are being discriminated against because of their language skills (cf. Phillipson 2003: 176).

Language learning and knowledge of languages, it was argued, would promote mutual understanding and greater tolerance of other cultures, and would support active citizenship, equal opportunities and social cohesion (cf. OJ 2006 L 412: 44–50). However, most recently, attention has been drawn to the fact that insufficient language skills might aggravate the communication gap between individuals with different cultural backgrounds and might also deepen the social divide between multilingual and monolingual people (cf. 2008/2225(INI) EP 2009). In other words, the EM policy is well advised to avoid excluding people from equal opportunities in the Union because of their lack of language skills.

Here, it becomes evident once more that multilingualism is seen as a key competence for access to equal opportunities, but that it remains unclear what kind of language knowledge actually facilitates this access. The kind of multilingualism which accrues, for example, from the linguistic diversity of minorities is not suited to guaranteeing equal opportunities for its speakers on the globalised language market. In this respect, also smaller and less widely used languages remain subordinate to the big languages in general and to English, in particular. In this context, the question of how to account for the local and individual requirements of being or becoming multilingual is an unresolved and contentious issue. Analysts have been repeatedly pointing to the problem of reconciling both a bottom-up and a top-down policy approach, all the more as the EU lacks the power to enforce its policy on the member states and as the EU policy has as yet not clearly enough made its way through to the people.

As a matter of fact, and provided that ensuring equal opportunities and social cohesion is not an empty wording, it will be necessary to reassess some of the major criteria and strategies on which the actual multilingualism project is founded. Otherwise, EM as the Union's major integration project will be at risk of running counter to its own agenda.

In conclusion, we may say that the agenda of the EU's multilingualism policy is still in the making. It is a policy that appears to a high degree streamlined by the EU's architecture, its values and principles. At the same time, it has to be stressed that this policy is still far from constituting a coherent agenda of political strategies. Ensuring linguistic diversity has been a major driving force for establishing the EM policy. Thus, EM as a common project has come to be assigned crucial importance in the European integration process although it is not clearly identified how EM should be tackled in order to match the declared political objectives. This is also the reason why the actual EM framework reveals a large number of tensions and ambiguities. These arise from the continuous upgrading of the EM agenda since the millennium, and they connect with the changes the EU has undergone due to its enlargements and to globalisation. And at the same time, they point to covert ideological influences like linguistic nationalism and hegemonic multilingualism which the EU has as yet not been able to successfully override. It is true that the EM project is to ensure linguistic diversity within the unity framework of the EU. However, as long as it is the primary goal of this project to warrant that the national languages and identities are not impaired, it appears legitimate to question whether the EM policy is merely a continuation of the nation state policies at a multinational level. The point here is that changing from a monolingual to a multilingual regime presupposes first and foremost a critical reassessment of the ideological stances which have been governing national monolingualism in order to not incur a form of multilingualism in terms of an additive or multiple monolingualism. Multilingualism of this kind is very likely to generate a hierarchical order of language preferences as shown in institutional language practice and in foreign language learning. And language hierarchies, it is largely known, generate inequalities and social exclusion. It cannot be ignored that EM was conceptualised to ensure a democratic and equitable multiple society and to avoid sociocultural discrepancies of this kind. It thus appears that EM is, in its current state of affairs, still a policy in the making which reflects the changes the Union has undergone in over the years. This explains that some of the tensions and ambiguities result from ideological stances where various facts and circumstances have been presupposed and driven by political concerns stemming from the Europe of the nation states. Therefore, if EM is to successfully attain its normative goal, it will have to take a perspective on the Union beyond the nation state, that is, a Union in terms of a multiple inclusive society.

2 European Multilingualism as a Field of Research

Beyond the political dimension, EM has also been developing into a scientific field of research in its own right since the 1990s. EM research is a field of study of rather recent date and is highly indebted to previous research on bilingualism and languages in contact. At the same time, it is to some extent also related to the development of the EU language policies which have been setting the agenda of EM within which EM as a field of study would evolve. EM is, therefore, both a large cross-cutting research enterprise and also a transversal political issue, with these two dimensions being in a complex dialectical relationship. On the one hand, multilingualism research in general may in some cases constitute the grounds for informed EM political planning being engaged in investigating hitherto neglected or contentious issues, or in questioning specific constellations concerning EM. On the other hand, EM policy making is setting the frame within which multilingualism research is called upon to either address specific issues or to seek answers to problematic phenomena and practices of EM. This relationship is not to suggest, though, that the initiatives to assess and to tackle EM undertaken on both sides would always map onto each other since the positions and perspectives of research and those in policy making do not always correspond. The relationship may at times turn out to be problematic in cases when scientific investigation touches upon contentious issues that policy making would rather silence or when policy making expects scientific research to provide ready-made political solutions which research cannot deliver.

Until the 1990s, Europe was first and foremost a conglomerate of separate nation states and the issue of multilingualism did not figure as a major concern. Although the European nation states were themselves far from being monolingual, scientific interest in bi- and multilingual matters was not mainstreamed but remained restricted to specific research niches for a rather long time. It is true that from the late 1970s, individuals and small research networks in Europe set out to investigate the various phenomena of languages in contact with respect to linguistic minorities, language acquisition, second language learning, code mixing and contact-induced language change. As a consequence of the rather isolated European initiatives towards investigating individual and societal bi- and multilingualism, a first stock-taking of the various studies in this field in the 1990s showed that theory-building and methodologies were still rather fragmented (cf. Goebl *et al.* 1996). The foundation of the EU, however, with its emphasis on collaborative unity, has motivated the emergence of EM as a field of research in its own right, albeit one still lacking in disciplinary coherence. It goes without saying that the EU has had, and still continues to have, a great bearing on EM research as has the CoE, when it comes to EM concerns (cf. Section 1.2). In recent years, the Union has repeatedly called for intensified research on EM and has financially sustained and promoted large scientific projects on this issue over the past two decades. Therefore, it can be argued again that EM is characterised by a dialectical intersection between scientific and political interests.

In what follows, we will briefly outline how multilingualism research can be defined in general and we will point out the specific aspects distinguishing European multilingualism in particular.

2.1 Multilingualism: A Multidisciplinary Field of Research

Multilingualism research is a heterogeneous field of study concerned with the diverse contexts in which the various manifestations of multilingualism originate, for example, minority languages, diglossia, language maintenance and shift, language acquisition and learning, code switching, borrowing and mixing, pidgins and creoles, LPP, language attitudes and ideology, or intercultural communication. This implies that multilingualism research covers a wide variety of phenomena which are studied from diverse theoretical and methodological perspectives within a range of different disciplinary contexts. This highly interdisciplinary diversity makes it difficult to give a coherent and comprehensive overview of this field of study.

The major publications on this topic over the past decade show various attempts at structuring the scientific space and its research agendas. Thus, for example, Li Wei (2010), in accounting for the different research foci in the field of multilingualism, identifies four major perspectives. One is the linguistic and developmental perspective, which includes multiple grammars, interaction of grammatical systems in code-switching and other forms of multilingual speech, multiple language acquisition, multilingualism and linguistic change. The second viewpoint emerges in the psycho- and neurolinguistic perspective, which focuses on the issues of the multilingual brain, as well as on the acquisition, storing and processing of different languages. The third perspective relates to the sociolinguistic and interactional issues of identity and culture, to language and a nation's social, economic and political development and to social motivations for code-switching. Finally, the fourth and applied perspective comprises the issues of language loss, sign bilingualism, language planning and language policies, speech and language disorders, attitudes, immigration and citizenship, and the media. Clearly, the listing of the phenomena and contexts assigned to the various perspectives may raise the question concerning the relative arbitrariness of such categorisations, but nevertheless it reflects, at the same time, the difficulty of defining the study of multilingualism in terms of a multidisciplinary field of research. There are several factors which might explain this difficulty.

First, research on multilingualism is relatively young, with its origins only dating back to the 1980s. This was the time when the debate on multiculturalism and intercultural communication came to impact upon traditional bilingualism research, in particular with respect to old and new minority speakers. Globalisation, internationalisation and growing multiculturalism in society led to a reconceptualisation of the notions of language, culture and identity. Moreover, critical theory and poststructuralist thinking made bilingualism research expand its scope through integrating a more critical and dynamic stance into the existing binary paradigm of bilingualism, thus situating 'the study of bilingualism in the domain of studies of ideology, social practice and social organisation' (Heller 2007a: 2).

The bilingual paradigm, in turn, had evolved since the 1950s from various North-American studies on languages in contact, diglossia, language attitudes, language acquisition and learning. Although bilingualism research also included the study of more than two languages, the focus remained restricted to the relationship between two languages. In other words, multilingualism was seen through a bilingual lens. In the 1980s due to rapid societal changes induced by globalisation and migration, the concerns about the limitations of this bilingual perspective led to the conceptualisation of bi- and multilingualism in more fluid and dynamic terms (cf. also Heller 2011). The traditional understanding of languages as distinctly identifiable entities came to be seriously questioned and critics argued that conceiving of bi- and multilingualism simply as a collective container of separate parallel monolingualisms could no longer be maintained (cf. Martin-Jones 2007).

Multilingualism research, in the relatively brief period of its existence over the past 20 years, has been undertaken in highly diversified disciplinary contexts and consequently with reference to a range of different perspectives which, in terms of theoretical concepts and notions, are not always sufficiently enough elaborated. As a result, there has been a degree of theoretical discrepancy and inconsistency in conceptions of multilingualism, which has had a negative effect not only on the interpretation of empirical data but also on the categorisation of specific subfields of research.

The problem is compounded by the fact that as yet there is no clear-cut distinction between multilingualism and bilingualism research. The reason for this vagueness is due, in part at least, to the intertwined theorisation of bi- and multilingualism research mentioned earlier. In recent publications, bilingualism is often taken to include multilingualism (cf. Wei 2010) or multilingualism is in turn used to include bilingualism (cf. Pavlenko 2005: 5). Alternatively, both terms are used in conjunction to indicate the distinctiveness and yet similarity of bi- and multilingualism, with both phenomena placed within a common theoretical and methodological framework of reference (cf. Mackey 1987).

It should also be noted that within linguistics in general, bi- and multilingualism research has been of rather marginal importance until recently. As Pavlenko (2005: 4) points out, in spite of the fact that most of the world's population is bi- and multilingual, the traditional bias in linguistics has been to study language as a monolingual phenomenon and to dismiss bi- and multilingualism as being of only marginal interest. It appears, however, that globalisation and migration, and to some extent also the contribution of poststructuralist thinking, have had the effect of raising awareness of the multilingual reality in society. It may be assumed that mainstreaming of bi- and multilingualism in society at large will have a positive effect on the development of multilingualism as a field of research, and that this development will provide multilingualism research with increased prestige and financial support, and will move it from the margins into the centre of linguistic enquiry.

EM research exemplifies this trend, since it has gathered momentum as multilingualism itself has come to be assigned increasing importance in the European Union over the past two decades. When the EU defined multilingualism as a strategy to ensure cultural and linguistic diversity, the scientific community started to adjust the research agenda of multilingualism to correspond to the specific European premises and prospects, taking EU multilingualism policy as a major framework of reference for its enquiries. The increase in academic interest in multilingualism as an object of scientific endeavour has been further stimulated by the regular funding by the EU of multilingualism research projects. Some of these, like Euromosaic, Eurydice Key Data on language teaching and language Eurobarometers, have aimed to take stock of the various manifestations of linguistic diversity. Others, like DYLAN or LINEE, have sought to develop new insights, to bring together already existing knowledge concerning multilingualism or to re-discover parts of the historically submerged EM in studies of the periods of the Habsburgs and Hanseatic League (cf. Braunmüller 1995; Nelde 1989; Rindler Schjerve 2003). A survey of the publications on EM over the last five years shows that the focus is on major themes such as language use within the EU institutions, old and new minorities, multilingual classrooms, code-mixing/-switching, translation, ELF, European identity, and globalisation (cf. e.g. Barni & Extra 2008; Blackledge & Creese 2010; Castiglione & Longman 2007; Cenoz 2009; Extra & Gorter 2008; Hellinger & Pauwels 2007; House & Rehbein 2005; Warren & Benbow 2008; Williams 2005). All this indicates that EM research has to a considerable extent come to accommodate its focus and scope of enquiry to the questions and challenges that figure most prominently in EU political thinking.

It is, one might suggest, this partially intersecting scope of EM policy making and academic research that lends EM research its distinctive features. This is not to say that research embraces the cause of the Union's policy. It is rather that neither the EM research agenda can be conducted in disregard of the political agenda nor can the political agenda ignore research. On the one hand, the EU political framework serves as a point of orientation for the research agenda and on the other hand, the EU needs to draw upon the expertise of academic research to formulate or revise its political strategies.

It would be wrong, however, to conclude that the dynamics between policy making and research evolved only when the EU came into being. Rather, it should be stressed that their interaction started off in the 1970s well before the Union was founded. Although, as already pointed out, earlier research was primarily bilingual in orientation, it reflected a growing recognition in the 1970s that there was a need to confront multilingual issues as post-War prosperity in Western Europe came to an end and the situation called for ever closer economic and political integration. This early research reacted to a situation in which the nation states' monolingual bias had run into difficulties in that it could not deal with the existing bi- and multilingualism of the regional minorities in Great Britain, France, Italy and elsewhere. Moreover, it could not adequately meet the requirements of increased foreign language learning among European citizens in different nation states.

It should be stressed that under the impact of the dominant North-American paradigm of languages in contact, the focus of early European bilingualism research was on regional minority languages. Regional societies living within the boundaries of the nation states and using a language other than the national language had been forced into adapting to the dominant culture and language, and in cases where they did not assimilate, they constituted a deviation from national homogenisation and were eventually turned into regional minorities. From the nation states' perspective, regional minorities were seen as an impediment endangering the national integration process since they stood for linguistic and cultural heterogeneity. The increasing tensions that arose from the hegemonic relationship between national majorities and regional minorities constituted a conflict problem which research was called upon to help to resolve. Thus, the regional minorities came to be the preferred subject of early EM research although academic mainstream research continued to turn a blind eye to these phenomena.

Although early research on bi- and multilingualism relied heavily on a North-American paradigm, it has been developing its own theoretical and methodological perspectives to cope with the specificities of EM, which differed in several respects from what defined multilingualism in other regions of the world. Thus, for example, the North-American notion of 'diglossia' was critically revised against the background of the societal conflicts raised through minority language shift and substitution (cf. e.g. Martin-Jones 1989; Rindler Schjerve 1998), particularly in the national majority contexts of Great Britain, Spain and France (cf. Kremnitz 1979, 1982; Williams 1987). Generally speaking, it can be said that research on bi- and multilingualism in Europe came to be strongly focused upon conflict issues which have constituted a major interest within European contact linguistics (cf. Goebl *et al.* 1996; Nelde 1980 and 1987; Weber 1999) and other related areas since the 1980s.

In the late 1970s, and as a consequence of increasing immigration into Europe, migrants became a centre of interest for early bi- and multilingualism research. This focused first on questions of acquisition and subsequently also on contact linguistics phenomenon, and on migrant children's educational integration (cf. e.g. Apeltauer 1987; Auer 1984; Extra & Vallen 1997; Gogolin 1994; Klein 1975; Krumm 1994; Meisle *et al.* 1983).

Furthermore, we can say that language learning in general has also developed into a major subfield of bi- and multilingualism research since the 1970s. At the beginning, research concentrated on the furthering of foreign language competences and on methods of language teaching which were heavily inspired by the behaviouristic framework of the contrastive analysis hypothesis (cf. Jessner 2008: 17), whereas at a later stage and especially under the impact of migration, attention was also directed to second language learning, that is, learning the language of the host society. It was only in the 1990s that language learning processes came eventually to be seen as an integrative part of multilingualism.

Another point worth mentioning is that EM research has already been connected with the language policies of the EEC and to a certain extent the CoE, as these institutions, despite their diversified political interests and objectives, have been collaborating to safeguard minority rights and values (cf. Framework Convention 1995 or Charter RML 1992) and language learning (cf. CEFR 2001).

To identify EM research as a field in its own right is to imply that it has distinctive thematic, theoretical and methodological features. As far as themes are concerned, the minorities issue and the increased requirement for foreign language learning in the 1970s, for example, prompted EM research to challenge the unquestioned paradigm of the nation states' homogeneity. And since the 1990s, it has had to take account of the 'unity in diversity' concept, which came to establish the idea of the Union as essentially and uniquely diverse, both culturally and linguistically.

With respect to theoretical and methodological development, there is, however, the problem that EM research is in many respects rather fragmented. A number of reasons can be suggested for this fragmentation: for one, different issues were addressed at different levels depending on the interests and concerns of the national or supranational institutions that provided funding. For another, the research was often informed by different and at times incompatible theoretical perspectives. Much of this research appears to be strongly rooted in the different scholarly traditions of the European study of 'language in society', which from the beginning of the 1990s were determined by the political and ideological orientations of the old and the new member or candidate states. Thus, in Eastern Europe and under the impact of Soviet research on bilingualism, the former Socialist countries had developed a multilingual paradigm of their own, which, however, due to language- and ideology-driven discrepancies between Eastern and Western research has not been integrated into a larger-scale European scope of enquiry. These discrepancies became particularly evident at the time when the EU was headed towards its 2004 enlargement (cf. Euromosaic III 2004) and immediately after the new member states had joined the Union. At present, therefore, serious attempts are being made towards decreasing fragmentation in the field of EM research. The LINEE project is an example of such an attempt since it has been targeted towards bringing together and seeking to reconcile discrepancies between theories and methods of EM within its research platform.

Concluding, we may say that EM as a field of research has been operating as a discipline in its own right within the evolving international paradigm of multilingualism research. The major reasons for its distinctive development are to be seen in the specific cross-cutting issues of the scientific and the political agendas which derive from the peculiarities of multilingualism in Europe. Here, nation-state ideologies and the monolingual bias have been impacting upon the research of EM over the decades. It is only since Maastricht and the foundation of the EU that the principle of linguistic diversity has come to weaken the still dominant monolingual bias. The principle of linguistic diversity and the shift of scope from bi- to multilingualism have ensured the development of EM research into a highly dynamic field of studies within the international inter-discourse on multilingualism.

At this point, it has to be mentioned, though, that the intersection between policy and academic research is not as unproblematic as it might appear at first sight. It is true that EU policy has influenced EM research positively and has rendered it distinctive in that it has provided a focus for its enquiry. At the same time, however, the question must be raised how the requirements of policy and the integrity of academic research can be reconciled without reducing the independence of academic enquiry. This poses a serious problem, especially in relation to the kinds of projects that are funded by the EU. Larger-scale projects, for example, LINEE or DYLAN, constitute ample proof that the EU decides what research should be carried out in order to direct its policies. The intersection between the political and the scientific agendas might turn out to be particularly problematic at times when the findings of academic enquiry are not favourable to the policies. As a consequence, policies may then simply choose to ignore the research results or may even direct research to the findings which are favourable to them.

With regard to EM research, it appears, however, that the research contract has hitherto been awarded in the sense of policy advice based on academic expertise. The reasons for this can primarily be found in the fact that EU language policy cannot interfere with the linguistic concerns of the member states and thus has to restrict itself largely to recommendations. The decision as to the promotion and implementation of EM in the individual member states lies with the respective states, which are generally still strongly bound to the tradition of national monolingualism. This results in a certain clash between the goals of EU language policy and the policies at the national level. At the moment, it thus seems unlikely that the EU policy should aim at employing research in order to palliate its goals. Rather, research appears to provide the planners of EM policy with the empirical foundations by means of which they put pressure on the member states, in the sense of the integration required, to promote and establish multilingualism in their particular sphere.

3 The LINEE Project

As already mentioned, the LINEE project (Languages in a Network of European Excellence) constitutes a good example for the intersecting nature of policy and research. LINEE was conducted within the 6th EU Framework Programme under Priority 7 'Citizens and Governance in a Knowledge Based Society' between 2006 and 2010. It was commissioned by the EU in order to 'focus on the role and implications of linguistic diversity in European populations, and in particular on the efforts to create a European KBS which respects cultural diversities and cross-cultural understanding' (LINEE Annex I 2006: 11, 21). The general aim was 'to investigate linguistic diversity in Europe in a coherent and interdisciplinary way, by developing an innovative, visible and durable scientific network that can overcome fragmentation and serve as a world-wide quality and knowledge-based reference framework' (LINEE Annex I 2006: 4, 11). Although LINEE was commissioned by the EU, it should be noted that the project came into being when a research network consisting of nine universities followed the call of FP6 under 'Priority 7'. In following the call, it was, however, not the EU but the LINEE partners who formulated the tasks and aims they wanted to commit themselves to.

The research network consisted of nine partners (Adam Mickiewicz University Poznan, Charles University Prague, Free University of Bolzano, Institute for Anthropological Research Zagreb, University of Applied Languages Munich, University of Bern, University of Southampton, University of Szeged, and University of Vienna) and was focused upon four thematic areas which constituted the analytical backbone of the whole LINEE research, namely, 'Language, Identity and Culture', 'Language Policy and Planning (LPP)', 'Multilingualism and Education' and 'Language and Economy'. While the first thematic area dealt with the sociolinguistic features of the nature of multilingualism, the other three areas concentrated on the types of intervention undertaken both to promote and to exploit it. It cannot be overlooked that the diversified contexts of meaning to which the actual debate on European linguistic diversity and multilingualism relates are reflected in the thematic design of LINEE. Thus, the four LINEE research areas were seen as starting points from which the major driving forces interacting with the various phenomena of linguistic pluralism were to be elaborated upon. At the same time, it was also hypothesised that the four thematic areas would provide information on how the EU and its member states identify with linguistic diversity, how they plan and implement linguistic diversity, how they provide the educational prerequisites for linguistic diversity, and how they attempt to meet the multilingual requirements of a single market.

Following the assumption that different polity levels within the European architecture, that is, the supranational, national and regional level, would provide for different political solutions and outcomes, each of the four thematic areas was subdivided into these three levels. It was also expected that research accounting for these dimensions should not only yield level-specific policy results but would also have implications on methodological and theoretical choices.

The four thematic areas and their level-specific differentiation made up for 12 Work Packages (WPs), which were projected for two years (cf. Chapter 8: Appendix). Within the 'language, identity and culture' area, which was to yield information on how the EU and its member states identify with linguistic diversity, the thematic focus was on carriers and symbols of European culture and identity (WP1), language and concepts of national identity (WP2) and on local and regional varieties as markers of identity (WP3). The 'Language Policy and Planning' area concentrated upon the aspects of European discourse(s) on multilingualism and multiculturalism (WP4), language policies, citizenship and migration (WP5), as well as on regional and minority languages in the process of EU enlargement (WP6). Research in this thematic area was expected to inform about how linguistic diversity is planned and implemented at the supranational, the national and the regional level. Research in the 'Education' area, in turn, which was to provide information on the educational prerequisites for multilingualism, was directed towards English and multilingualism (WP7), traditional pedagogic cultures in foreign language education and the need for multi-competence (WP8), and Inter-regional case studies of multilingual education (WP9). And finally, the 'Economy' area with its focus on labour markets, the Knowledge Economy, language and mobility in Europe (WP10), multilingualism amongst minority populations (WP11) and on linguistic diversity in large multinational companies and their regional allocation (WP12) was carried out to gain information about the ways in which multilingualism is handled and exploited by the New or Knowledge Economy. During the first two years of the LINEE project, multilingualism was thus explored with respect to Europeanisation and nationalisation processes, aspects of immigrant and regional minorities, ELF, diversified pedagogic cultures, multilingual classrooms, multinational companies, and migrants in the labour market.

After this two-year period, the WPs were replaced (with the exception of WP 4) by newly conceptualised WPs scheduled for another two years (cf. Chapter 8: Appendix). Since LINEE was commissioned as a Network of Excellence, the second phase of research was targeted towards further enforcing the network integration. Integration was generally implemented through changing cooperation among partners within the WPs. Thus, integration enhancement was primarily a question of who would be able to cooperate with whom in a common theme within the WPs of the second phase. As a result, the major themes of the first phase (with the exception of regional minorities' language loss) were further elaborated and cultural tourism and multilingual cities were integrated into the range of the LINEE themes. This is particularly evident in the 'language, identity and culture' area, where the focus of the second LINEE phase was on Europeanisation and the reshaping of cultural tourism and cultural industry (WP1a), promoting national identity internationally (WP2a) and on politics and strategies of identity in multicultural European cities (WP3a). In the 'Language Policy and Planning' area, attention was directed towards European discourses on multilingualism: language policy-planning at the supranational level (WP4a), the impact of 'new' migration on contested linguistic spaces: implications for national language policies (WP5a), and language management in the linguistic landscapes of multilingual cities (WP6a). The 'Education' area continued to elaborate on aspects of ELF, multi-competence and minority schools with the WPs 'Learning, use and perceptions of English as a Lingua Franca communication in European contexts' (WP7a), 'In search of multi-competence: exploring language use and language values among multilingual immigrant students in England, Italy and Austria' (WP8a) and 'Language use and language values in minority school settings' (WP9a). Similarly, the thematic area 'Economy' maintained its former focus on large multinational companies: linguistic diversity and communication in parent and daughter companies (WP10a) and on multilingualism, transcultural capital and social exclusion amongst migrant minority populations (WP11a), while it integrated the city theme in its thematic repertoire 'Economic participation, language practices and collective identities in the multilingual city' (WP12a).

Beyond the thematically focused WPs, a special WP (WP0) was designed with the task of integrating the work conducted within the WPs and of developing area-specific research platforms which should be merged into a single platform for theories and methods of multilingualism in Europe. Apart from the WPs, LINEE research was sustained by additional Task Forces, which were in charge of management and coordination, media and infrastructure, gender issues and training and mobility. At the end of 2008, yet another Task Force was implemented, which was to provide for the future sustainability of the research network after the project's completion in October 2010.

Within the general scope of the LINEE project, a major objective involved restructuring the scientific space through new methodological and theoretical platforms. In this way, integration and defragmentation of the scientific space were to be enhanced, and the knowledge derived from this research should be passed on to the scientific community as well as to policy makers, practitioners and stakeholders. Given the broad scope of the LINEE research, an integrated and multifunctional perspective was required in order to assess the implications of linguistic diversity among European populations, and in order to answer the question of how linguistic diversity relates to the promotion of the KBS. The research platforms were to provide for the theoretical and methodological framing of these phenomena. The rationale behind these research platforms was threefold: on the one hand, they were aimed at providing the comparative perspectives from which, it was hypothesised, diversified insights into both the power and the conflict potentials of EM should be attained; on the other hand, they should ensure scientific pluralism; and finally they should allow for combining fundamental and applied research in order to test the existing scientific paradigms against the empirical background of the ongoing integration process and the transition of the European nation states into a Europe beyond the nation state (cf. LINEE Annex I 2006: 11, 21).

As the research platforms were expected to cater for the redefinition and reassessment of existing disciplinary knowledge and paradigms, three specific tasks concerning the working procedure were defined, involving first the discussion of theoretical and methodological issues relevant to the thematic areas, second the identification and assessment of parallel and cross-cutting issues and third the proposal of new strategic lines of research.

It was evident that the multidisciplinary LINEE scope would draw upon quite different theoretical and methodological concepts and that assessing these concepts was to be developed through different stages of integrative research. In the first step, the area-specific theories and methods which comprised all levels of analysis (supranational, national and regional) were elaborated upon. At a more advanced stage, these thematically focused inventories should allow for a comparative view of the area-specific similarities and discrepancies, which, again, should yield the basis for the third stage, when the area-specific platforms were to merge into a single research platform.

An important first finding of the area-specific assessment was that a significant overlap existed concerning theoretical and methodological issues. Originally, the four research platforms had set out from thematically quite different theoretical and methodological inventories as they focused on identity and culture, policy, education and economy. The findings proved, however, that on the one hand, the different theoretical approaches commonly related to a set of recurrent variables which interacted with multilingualism, such as the variables ideology or 'power', while on the other hand, methodology appeared to be based on similar methods of data analysis and interpretation.

In the following, we will focus on the results of the research platforms as they are reflected in the work of the area-specific studies, and as they emerged after having undergone extensive re-elaboration by WP0. The re-elaboration consisted of several steps: starting out from a general stock-taking of theories and methods applied within the four thematic areas, the task was to compare the area-specific commonalities and discrepancies. These commonalities and discrepancies should then form the common grounds from which, on the one hand, the major categories associating with multilingualism were to be identified, and from which, on the other hand, the methodological profile of studies in multilingualism would emerge. From a theoretical point of view, it was expected that this procedure would eventually allow for identifying the key variables which impact upon and interact with multilingualism.

For practical reasons of presenting these results in a readable way, we will first take a look at the theoretical findings and then outline the main characteristics as they emerge from the methodological investigation.

3.1 Theoretical Dimension

The starting point for investigating the theoretical dimension was to take stock of the major inventories as they emerged from the area research, to compare them and to identify salient commonalities and discrepancies. As mentioned above, taking stock of the area-specific research revealed that the different approaches commonly related to a set of recurrent features which, as it appeared, interacted in variable degrees and measures with the diverse phenomena of EM. These features were mentioned in all WP reports of the first and second phase – they were identified as 'terms' or 'variables' for which there was reason to assume that they are in an implicational relationship with each other, as well as with EM, due to the frequent references in the WP reports. Their appearance as 'terms' does not necessarily imply that these features rely on a common conceptual basis. As the discussion of the features will show, the underlying concepts can in some cases differ considerably.

The following features were identified: 'culture', 'discourse', 'identity', 'ideology', 'knowledge', 'LPP', 'multi-competence', and 'power and conflict'. Due to their interactive saliency with multilingualism phenomena in the various thematic areas, they were to be taken into further account in order to assess the highly complex and diverse manifestations of EM within the LINEE framework.

One feature that might have been expected to stand out in discussions of multilingualism is gender, as it could be assumed that gender was likely to impact upon multilingualism. From the WP reports of the two LINEE phases, it turned out, however, that gender was not an issue at the WPs' central focus of investigation. It remained rather implicit in most WPs, being used as a methodological device to decide on the selection of the subjects investigated, and being studied explicitly in one exceptional case in terms of gendered discourse and ideologies. Therefore, gender did not figure strongly enough in the research findings to include it as a substantial key variable within the LINEE project.

The next step involved investigating how the variables mentioned were conceptualised and how they interacted with the shaping of multilingualism within and across the thematic areas. This undertaking turned out to be difficult in various respects. The first point was that the WPs were far from adopting generalised and common theoretical concepts concerning the individual variables. Thus, identity would be conceptualised in more fluid and variable terms of identifications in some instances, while it would also refer to a presupposed stable state of mind in others. Another difficulty pertained to the fact that the variables under investigation derived from quite different ontological and epistemological settings, which, again, raised the question of how to relate them to one another. Assessing, for example, the intersection of knowledge and LPP in precise analytical terms might be problematic since knowledge refers to levels of abstraction which are quite different from those on which LPP as a highly pragmatic category is founded.

Another point was that the variables associated with the various thematic areas in different ways. Some categories figured most prominently in specific areas, for example, identity in the identity area or LPP in the policy area, whereas they would remain rather vague and implicit in other areas. Other variables, such as power and discourse, impacted on the shaping of multilingualism in all areas although their salience was less evident.

Moreover, some variables appeared to combine very closely with others, that is, identity and ideology, so that it was difficult to draw the line or to assess the dynamics which define their specific interrelationship. On the other hand, there were variables the interaction of which remained blurred or vague, for example, identity and multi-competence, or even identity and knowledge since they appeared to interact with one another in some way, but how they precisely related to each other still remained unclear.

Against the background of these difficulties, WP0 initiated an extensive debate in the second phase of the project, in which the WPs were asked to clarify their theoretical position with respect to the single variables. From this debate, it followed that first of all, the elaborated set of key variables came to be largely confirmed. It could not be ignored, however, that some variables (e.g. knowledge) would have to undergo further elaboration as to their interaction types, and that some (such as discourse or multi-competence) would be reassessed with regard to their conceptual framing. Yet another point concerned the integration of newly salient categories, for example, 'attitudes'. It was evident that 'attitudes' connected very intimately with other key concepts such as knowledge or ideology. Concerning the interrelationship between 'attitudes', knowledge, and ideology, it seemed quite obvious that 'attitudes' could be subsumed under knowledge, whereas it was not as clear whether 'attitudes' were to be subsumed under ideology or rather vice versa ideology under 'attitudes'.

A major challenge for further investigating the variables in terms of key components of multilingualism was involved in determining how to put them together in an emergent theoretical framework of multilingualism. The LINEE research had indeed identified most crucial and constitutive features of EM, but these findings were tantamount to an itemisation which does not reveal anything about the variability and interactive dynamics of the single items with respect to multilingualism in the various contexts. In this connection, it has to be stressed, however, that the identification of these features was only the first move and not in itself an adequate account of the relations accross the research in different WPs. Hence, the crucial question was how to cope with the dynamic relationship between the diverse features while integrating them into an overall coherent framework. It is true that such a framework would have presupposed identifying commonalities and this, in turn, would have implied the risk of oversimplifying at the expense of existing diversity. However, EM typically points to highly diversified phenomena and manifestations which – it is argued – do not seriously allow for generalised or compromised definitions and explanations. Thus, the question was how to arrange these components in order to provide for coherence while at the same time accounting for diversity. This is all the more relevant given that the conclusions drawn from the LINEE research suggested that the different multilingual contexts called for specific alignments of the single variables in the form of flexible relational clusters. Against this background, it was self-evident that multilingualism was to be conceptualised in terms of complex and unstable relationships instead of a fixed and compounded range of variables. Approaching multilingualism in this dynamic perspective would also have allowed for accounting more precisely for the specific 'local' variability of EM in contrast to multilingual manifestations elsewhere in the world.

In what follows, we will first focus on the single key variables which will be discussed against both the background of the LINEE conceptualisations and the current theoretical debate on these issues. In the second step, we will then give an account of how these variables impact upon the various thematic areas and how they correlate with one another within and across these areas. This should allow for a first and tentative assessment of the relational clusters and their variability with respect to the major topics of the LINEE project.

Since the findings of the single WPs (cf. Chapter 8: Appendix) are not publicly accessible as yet, we will draw upon the outlines in the Position Papers on Theoretical and Methodological Issues 2006–2008 and 2008–2009 available online (cf. LINEE online), in which the primary focus was on the theoretical conceptualisation of the key variables and on their interaction within and across the thematic areas in order to define their salience and interaction force with respect to the central themes and topics of LINEE. Beyond this, we will also draw upon the Research Reports per Thematic Area 2006–2008 and 2008–2009 and the Research Reports per Level of Analysis 2006–2008 and 2008–2009 (cf. LINEE online), in which the findings of the 24 WPs are outlined according to the thematic and level-specific focalisations of the whole LINEE project.

At this point, it should also be mentioned that seeking to identify the variability of the single key variables and their relational context-dependent clusters implies focusing upon one and the same phenomenon from different perspectives. The repetition that this necessarily involves can be helpful in providing a deeper insight into the thematically differentiated interaction patterns of the key variables under investigation.

As to the actual presentation of the single key variables, it should be stressed that at the present stage of research, it is not possible to establish an order that would adequately reflect the interdependence between the single variables since, as yet, it is not at all evident how the correlational patterns are to be defined. This is the reason why, in the following, we will keep to a simple alphabetical order in the listing of the variables, as this neither predetermines nor obscures the view on the variable dynamics of these concepts.

3.2 LINEE Key Concepts

3.2.1 Culture

Theoretical concepts of culture

Within the humanities and the social sciences, culture is a key, albeit heterogeneous, concept. In post-modern thinking, particularly in the humanities, the ways of defining and studying culture have come to constitute an influential paradigm, although conceptualising culture is historically rooted in the early modern times (cf. Eagleton 2001: 39). In the traditional view, culture was generally seen in terms of a normative concept defining the peculiarities of 'high' vs. 'low' lifestyles and social routines. At the same time, it was also conceived as a holistic entity referring to homogeneous communities which are characterised by specific collective lifestyles. The holistic view also includes the Herderian version of nationally diversified cultures. Later, influential approaches which were inspired by System Theory conceived of culture in terms of functionally differentiated social sub-systems (cf. Parsons 1976). And finally, culture was also conceptualised in terms of commonly shared and acquired knowledge sets or learned skills since until the 1980s and within the behaviourist paradigm, cultural theory primarily theorised culture as derived from social learning and adaptive socialisation processes (cf. Hejl 2008a, 2008b).

In the 1980s, the theoretical stance changed when modern cultural theory came to view culture in terms of active negotiation processes and as symbolic systems generating meaning. In this view, it is argued that cultural codes and social practices are contingent (cf. Reckwitz 2006). Symbolic orders and value hierarchies are reflected in specific cultural practices which produce meaning and imply knowledge about how to act. Thus, culture can also be seen in terms of ideational or cognitive constructs which are collectively shared within a social group.

Another important point is that post-modern thinking argues for culture as comprising heterogeneous and hybrid processes. In pointing to the pluralistic nature of culture, Said (1994: 30) maintains that cultures are neither unique nor pure nor monolithic. In this perspective, the notion of fixed and homogeneous cultural or speech communities posited by the 'one language–one culture' assumption is seriously put into question.

Theorising culture has to involve the recognition of language as a central interacting force. Language can be seen as forming an integral part of culture since negotiating cultural meaning largely depends on linguistic communication. Communicative practices, norms and ideals are at the same time culturally bound and can be subject to change and transformation as the cultural meaning changes.

Within the nationalist paradigm, language and culture have often been equated, since constructing the nation state presupposed that the common use of standard national languages within the state territories would act as a unifying force generating political and cultural homogenisation and integrating the state's population into a common citizenry. Conceiving of language and culture in this way suggested that language is taken to stand for culture and culture is viewed as being shaped through a specific language (cf. also Ehlich 2006: 55).

Moreover, language came to mark the borders of cultural inclusion or exclusion in that it confirmed the identity of subjects as members or non-members of an ethnic community. Identifying with specific cultural representations implies sharing the knowledge of cultural space and participating in cultural practices.

Culture within LINEE

Within the LINEE project, culture is given a wide range of meanings which may be related to Appadurai's distinction between primordialist and constructionist concepts of culture (cf. Appadurai 1996). When investigating culture as a scientific concept, the LINEE research generally tended to be constructionist whereas in those cases where culture is treated in an implicit manner, it happened to be associated with rather primordialist views. According to the primordialist approach, culture and its impact, that is, in terms of underlying values and preferences or in terms of knowledge, are taken for given. From a constructionist perspective, however, people mutually construct culture through interaction, when, for example, they agree upon a given element of cultural knowledge in a specific situation.

Inspired by post-structuralist approaches, those WPs within the LINEE research which focused explicitly upon culture view it as a heterogeneous, dynamic and conflicting issue which is defined as a set of processes and practices through which individuals and groups make and exchange meanings (cf. Hall 2003). Culture is seen as signifying a practice which is intimately intertwined with language since language actively constructs social and cultural reality in interaction. The dynamic view of culture taken in LINEE also implies that the notion of fixed and homogeneous communities bound in one language and culture is seriously called into question. Another point is that beyond language, aspects of ideology and power relations are central to culture since it is assumed to be constructed through social, economic and political relations.

Culture in the thematic areas

As to the role of culture in the four thematic areas, it can be observed that this variable is most salient in the identity area whereas it remains rather implicit in the other areas. Culture and language are conceived, however, as intrinsically related and interwoven categories in all thematic areas.

From an overall LINEE perspective, culture is developed in a more systematic manner as a key concept only within the identity area. Following cultural and postcolonial scholars (cf. e.g. Bhabha 1994; Brah 1996, 2000; Hall 1996), as well as anthropologists (cf. e.g. Appadurai 1996; Clifford 1997; Hage 1998, 2003; Shore 2000), it was argued that culture, 'language' and identity signify a historically variable nexus of social meanings as they are primarily discursive articulations. However, speaking a language does not necessarily position one's membership in a given culture and vice versa. Therefore, language diversity and cultural diversity are not coextensive concepts (cf. RePa WP3a 2009). The conflation of linguistic and cultural identity as reflected by the dominant EU discourse on cultural diversity appears to rest on the assumption that the adoption of languages automatically entails the adoption of other aspects of cultural practices.

The findings also point to a close linkage of culture and ideology. Thus, the analyses of public language debates in Croatia and Cyprus and secondary analyses of surveys in Latvia revealed that in spite of historical and social differences the dominant linguistic ideologies in all three contexts are tied to the Herderian view that language, identity and nation are inextricably linked in a naturalised primordial unity. In all three cases, the dominant language ideologies conceive of the national language in terms of an abstracted homogeneous entity and a mode of identification with a unique and distinct unity. The analyses show that the standard-language ideologies ultimately contribute to valorising the national culture and its language and to devaluing non-standard cultural forms, such as regional varieties and minority languages which tend to be appropriated by the national language as its 'dialects' (cf. Area Report A 2008: 6–7). However, the Croatian example also shows that resistance against the dominant language ideology may strengthen the regional culture and languages. This particularly applies to the multilingual region Istria, where the hegemony of the Croatian standard language is met with reserve and where the regional culture is viewed as a fluid and transformable concept with no uniform and stable connection to the national language (cf. Area Report A 2008: 8; RePa WP3 2008).

The LINEE findings also point to the tensions that are displayed in European cultural policies and in the practices of cultural tourism to adopt and reshape the concept of 'European culture' in the 'unity of diversity' scope. On the one hand, the term 'European culture' is used to indicate sameness based upon the common European cultural heritage while the different national cultures are subsumed under the same concept. On the other hand, European culture is presented as a sum of different cultures, a total which enriches each individual regional or national culture creating a European added value. In the first case, culture is seen as taken for given, static and fixed, and as something that is rooted in the European past but can be displayed in the present. In the second case, culture is used in terms of heterogeneous and dynamic processes which are in the making. This duality has the effect that the tourism industry, in accommodating the notions that make for supranational 'European culture', adopts strategies such as re-reading European history in excluding traumatic elements from the past or displacing cultural memory in focusing on selective and purified narratives, with the result of changing traditional heritage into new heritage as it emerges through the intersection of the past and the present of the different national and regional cultures (cf. Area Report A 2009: 9). The perception of this new 'European culture' is revealed in the study of Polish migrants in Szeged (Hungary) and in Jersey (UK), who expressed concern about their 'feeling at home' in the world. From their statements, it can be inferred that European mobility may be problematic in terms of its implied alienation from the EU rather than alienation from the culture of the host country in which the migrants have their 'home' (cf. PoPa RLL 2009: 6).

In the LPP area, culture impacts on the different policy and planning activities in various measures and degrees. This comes as no surprise since language policies are strongly informed by ideologies, that is, cultural systems of ideas about social and linguistic relationships or cultural conceptualisations of language that are politically and morally loaded (cf. Irvine 1989: 255; Mannheim quoted in Woolard 1998: 8). From the investigation of European discourses on multilingualism, it follows that culture in these discourses is referred to as a fixed and static entity that points to the national peculiarities which are seen to be primarily reflected in the diverse European languages. European policy makers and stakeholders conceptualise multilingualism as the sum of all official languages. They strongly object against the 'English Only' option or the selected regime of privileged languages, which, however reflects a widely used practice, particularly within the EU institutions, since they fear that it would not duly reflect the national cultures of the European citizens (cf. RePa WP4 2008).

Culture also impacts on the maintenance and loss of regional minority languages in terms of a resource or capital. Thus, speakers of these languages, for example, the 'Germans' in Lorraine, Prague and Transylvania are confronted with a clash between language as a cultural, social and economic capital. This is articulated in a corresponding tension involved in balancing a generally weak desire to maintain local cultural singularity with a stronger need for social belonging and economic prosperity associated with the respective 'national' or 'standard' languages (cf. Area Report B 2008: 4).

Another point is that in the policy contexts in which migrants and old minorities happen to live together, the cultural component of multilingualism policies appears to be problematic. As the findings in these contexts show, the old or regional minorities, such as the Catalan society, are not sufficiently sensitised towards the new social reality as it emerges from immigration and the mixture of cultures (cf. RePa WP5 2008). Moreover, the relationship between language and culture is particularly evident when it comes to citizenship in the acculturation of immigrants. Investigation of immigration into European regional minority contexts in the UK, Spain and Switzerland shows how language policies directed towards social cohesion give rise to contrasts concerning citizenship and cultural inclusion between the two categories of linguistic minority communities (cf. RePa WP5a 2009: 33): Whereas formal citizenship testing concerning immigrants increasingly requires evidence of cultural savoir-faire, of the language of the host country and of residence qualifications, non-dominant regional minorities can only lay claim to cultural forms of belonging in which ('the right to speak') the heritage language is all-important. Cultural representation and inclusion appears more difficult to achieve for the immigrant communities since the 'right to speak' their heritage languages is far less evident and would require linguistic rights that do not exist.

In the thematic area 'Multilingualism and Education', various dimensions of culture emerge. In the foreign language classroom, culture constitutes a content of teaching and learning and, what is even more important, it figures prominently in the shift towards the multi-competence paradigm. Multi-competence is not just the addition of several language codes but has to do with the expansion of managing the variability potentially offered by the linguistic codes (cf. Hall et al. 2006). Conceiving of multi-competence in this way implies that multi-competence cannot do without cultural knowledge since it entails knowledge of an extended linguistic repertoire which can be used dynamically and appropriately to express a range of diverse cultural values (cf. CEFR 2001; RePa WP8 2008; Sercu 2004; Sercu et al. 2005).

Culture also figures in students' multilingual Communities of Practice (CoP), where ELF turns out to be a successful means of intercultural communication. CoPs are sites in which members negotiate their shared linguistic repertoires (cf. Hall et al. 2006). In this context, ELF speakers coming from various linguacultural backgrounds act as multicultural speakers who cannot rely on shared knowledge, either of the code or cultural schemata, and thus have to carefully negotiate mutual understanding (cf. RePa WP7 2008; RePa WP7a 2009). The focus on the cultural dimension reveals that the wide-spread idea that English constitutes a serious impediment to EM cannot simply be taken for granted and is not tenable if the traditional notion of languages and cultures as distinct and compound entities is rejected. This corresponds to the results of recent ELF research, where all the evidence suggests that ELF interactions exemplify the kind of natural dynamic use of linguistic resources as appropriate to context that is consistent with a performative or constructionist view of culture (cf. Seidlhofer 2003, 2004, 2007).

The findings concerning Albanians in South Tyrol show that in the context of immigrant networks, culture appears to be strongly linked to language since maintaining the heritage language is supposed to express solidarity towards the community's cultural values (cf. Area Report C 2009: 21). The strong relationship between language maintenance and culture is eventually confirmed by the findings within regional minority settings in which students belonging to the German minority and attending German schools in Transylvania (Romania) regard German as an important item for their own culture and life (cf. RePa WP9a 2009: 23).

The strong link between culture and language is also mostly sustained by the teachers' beliefs within multilingual schools in Italy, Austria and the UK. Accordingly, teachers in these schools mostly disagree with the statement that immigrant students would maintain their home culture without maintaining the home language (cf. RePa WP8a 2009).

As regards pedagogic practices, the findings from the comparative study of pedagogic cultures concerning the teaching of German as a foreign language in Italy, the UK and Hungary indicates that contrary to the European perspective, which is referred to in many policy papers, these practices remain grounded in the nationally framed images of specific pedagogic value hierarchies which may vary from one country to another (cf. RePa WP8 2008).

When talking about culture in the educational context, yet another meaning of culture emerges, namely, 'multilingual culture'. 'Multilingual culture' does not relate to specific languages but rather to values concerning intercultural tolerance and acceptance (cf. RePa WP8a 2009). And still within the education area, culture figures as one of the four main dimensions that define language acquisition and language education (cf. Hornberger & Corson 1997). Here, the focus is on culturally determined predispositions that guide (linguistic) behaviour. Examples from Bolzano, Transylvania, Vojvodina and 'Felvidék' indicate that these predispositions have a strong bearing on regional minorities' efforts to preserve their ethnic languages while acquiring a profound knowledge of the respective state languages (cf. RePa WP9 2008).

Within the economy area of LINEE, culture also constituted an implicit but nevertheless influential category since the New Economy, in creating globalised markets, meets with the boundaries as they emerge from the varying linguistic and cultural competences of the participants in this economy. Thus, it comes as no surprise that in the economy area, culture appears in close conjunction with language, and more precisely with knowledge of languages which constitute a more or less valuable capital in the realisation of economic processes (cf. Phillipson 2003: 149). In this light, the use of English within the context of Polish migrants in Southampton and Jersey relates to the potential of English as a cultural capital which impacts on the access to power and mobility of this migrant group (cf. RePa WP12a 2009: 26). However, the findings from the research settings of Vietnamese immigrants in the Czech Republic and of sub-Saharan Africans in Germany show that these speakers do not strive for improving their competences in the host language since their social and cultural integration into the local labour markets do not require or motivate them to do so. Contrary to their parents, young children entering a country as first-generation immigrants benefit from attending elementary and secondary schools, which makes their host language acquisition highly successful since these settings have become the ideal CoPs where these children are simultaneously exposed to formal education and informal cultural knowledge acquisition through their local class mates (cf. Area Report D 2008: 13).

In the light of the Knowledge Economy, which encourages the use of knowledge for greater economic gain, the concept of culture also appears in terms of specified know-how concerning the symbolic orders, values and peculiarities of far-off contexts in which business is to be carried out. An investigation of the practices of multinational companies in negotiating language issues showed that large multinationals contain special departments which are oriented towards training future delegates for their assignments abroad, both in language and in cultural issues, thus encouraging them to use explicit knowledge of this kind for greater economic development (cf. Area Report D 2009: 8).

Conclusion

Concluding, we can say that within the LINEE project, culture is given a wide range of meanings which may be related to the distinction between primordialist and constructionist concepts of culture (cf. Appadurai 1996). When investigating culture as an explicit scientific concept, the LINEE research generally tends to be constructionist whereas in those cases where culture is treated in an implicit manner, it happens to be associated with rather primordialist views. Despite these differences within LINEE, there is, however, common agreement that not only culture and language but also culture, identity and ideology are to be seen in a very close relationship. This appears to be particularly relevant when it comes to multilingualism in connection with old and new minorities, when the teaching and learning of languages is concerned, or when the questions of multilingual speakers' access to power and mobility are addressed.

It is true that multilingual research in the past was well aware of the fact that it accounted for culture as being intimately connected with language. Unfortunately, the intersection between these two concepts has not been clearly enough elaborated as yet. The findings from the four thematic areas within LINEE indicate, however, that culture impacts on the shaping of multilingualism in different forms and guises, that is, in terms of the use of linguistic resources as value or capital, as predisposition or as competence, and even as a prerequisite for citizenship. Therefore, research on multilingualism has to take into due account the intersection between culture and language, although it is commonplace that notwithstanding their very close relationship, culture and language cannot be equated.

Since negotiating culture is largely dependent on linguistic communication, it is not surprising that discourse is a salient interacting variable through which cultural meaning is produced. From this, it follows that investigating culture is mostly inspired by discourse-theoretical approaches which allow for assessing culture through the discursively negotiated practices and the symbolic orders, codes and meanings which they produce or from which they evolve. Culture also implies collectively shared knowledge about how to act. Therefore, knowledge is a variable that interacts with culture in various guises, like, for instance, in the provision of the ideological stances for nationalist and European language policies, or in terms of knowledge of languages, for example, in the realisation of economic processes, or alternatively in the form of communicative competences as developed in the various CoPs. It goes without saying that according to the specificities of the contexts which combine with multilingualism, LPP, multi-competence and ideology also pertain to the concepts figuring as intersecting forces in the production or reception of cultural practices. Still another point is that a discussion of culture as a constitutive component in assessing multilingualism cannot ignore the power and the conflict potential generated by specific cultural practices. Thus, it cannot be dismissed that advocating a European culture of 'unity in diversity' goes along with conflicts concerning identity formation and the management of language political strategies.

Following the hypothesis that language and identity form a historically variable nexus of social meaning in the context of EM, a major topic of LINEE involved the question of how European cultural policies and cultural tourism contribute to shaping European and national identities against the background of regionally diversified cultures and languages. Multilingual cities formed yet another central topic on the basis of which the everyday encounters of locals, migrants and tourists were investigated in order to find out how languages contribute to the formation of local identities and how migration and tourism shape the cultural diversity of urban spaces. Migration, in general, turned out to be a major topic co-involving culture in different ways and meanings. From a language political point of view, citizenship and sociocultural inclusion figured as major themes. In the education area, it was the question of what kind of cultural capital is implied in the learning of regional minority languages in Hungary, Romania and South Tyrol (Italy). And from an economic perspective, the focus was on how migrants use their multi-cultural resources in order to benefit from these in terms of economic capital.

Clearly, the LINEE research reaffirms that culture is a major component when it comes to defining EM. Conceiving of culture as a variable in its own right that cannot be equated with language appears all the more important within the study of EM since the primordialist stances which are often taken in European and national policy making and also in scientific research take culture for given and as naturally reflected in diverse languages. Concerning culture, the LINEE findings might also be read as underlining that interpreting culture in primordialist terms might run the risk of undervaluing the dynamics inherent to multilingualism and of sustaining the idea that European 'unity in diversity' is merely to be equated with the simple addition of the different cultures and languages.

3.2.2 Discourse
Theoretical concepts of discourse

In the past decades, the notion of discourse has been given a wide range of meanings. Different theoretical concepts have been developed in order to assess the working of discourse(s). The diversity of meanings and concepts is mainly due to the very complex and multi-faceted nature of research on discourse. On the one hand, in the process of defining discourse in different languages, research has developed different scopes which may diverge significantly, for example, when comparing German 'Diskurs' with French 'discours' and English discourse (cf. De Cillia & Wodak 2004: 1639). On the other hand, discourse has been assigned different meanings within various disciplines which have used and developed discourse as a concept, such as linguistics, anthropology, sociology of knowledge, literary analysis, or philosophy, to name but a few (cf. Blommaert 2005: 2–3; Mills & Kriest 2007: 1; Van Dijk 2006: 25–27). In Blommaert's terms, there are two influential developments which have substantially impacted upon the current understanding of discourse, namely, intensified interdisciplinary research on the one hand and developments within linguistic theory on the other hand. Within linguistic research itself, Blommaert points to three factors which primarily account for the theorisation of discourse: the new focus on more activity-centred approaches to analysis, the language-in-use perspective and the widened scope in conceiving of the structural working of language beyond the sentence boundaries.

Thus, within international research on discourse, current definitions of discourse may differ widely, which results in a kind of polarisation. These definitions may range from classifying discourse as language use beyond the boundaries of the sentence to conceptualising it as ways of thinking and interacting beyond language itself (cf. Gee 1999: 17; Schiffrin 2004: 597). Moreover, researchers also differentiate between discourse as 'language in use' on the one hand and discourse in a critical perspective on the other hand. Whereas discourse as 'language in use' points to the study of how meaning is produced when language is used in particular contexts for particular purposes, the critical perspective concentrates on discourse as a 'set of presuppositions in circulation about a particular phenomenon' (Cameron & Kulick 2003: 16). In the face of the substantial differences between these various strands of discourse, the individual conceptualisations are generally not seen in terms of exclusive but rather as complementary perspectives. In line with these different classifications of discourse, there are quite a range of research scenarios that have been developed in the past decades depending on the various research purposes (cf. Keller 2004), like the analysis of political discourse (cf. e.g. Wodak et al. 1999; Wodak 2001 2009), discourse in a concrete setting, for example, the classroom (cf. e.g. Cazden 2001; Smit 2011) or the discourse of knowledge in historical times (cf. Kempf 1991).

Despite the obvious heterogeneity in approaching discourse, the current concepts show some commonalities: most of them refer to influential social theories, they conceive of discourse as dialectically related to social practice, and they establish a theoretical relationship between discourse, power, ideology and knowledge.

From a social theories perspective, the influential work of Michel Foucault continues to inspire discourse studies, as it still constitutes a major reference point in theory building on discourse. In *The Archaeology of Knowledge*, Foucault (1972) refers to discourse as a system of statements which are produced in an ongoing discursive stream. Preceding statements build the context of ongoing statements. The ongoing statements, however, have to respect the set of rules which rendered the previous statements possible and which are inherent in the context of these statements. In this scope, discourse analysis refers to identifying the systems of statements as bearers of their own rules of formation. These rules of formation result from the socio-historic process in which the discourse evolves in terms of a field of knowledge and a system of rules (cf. Diaz-Bone et al. 2007: 6). Post-Marxist discourse theory, particularly the work of Ernesto Laclau and Chantal Mouffe, represents another theoretical starting point for current discourse studies. According to Laclau, any institutional practice and any technique 'in and through which social production of meaning takes place' may be considered part of discourse (Laclau 1980: 87).

As to the dialectics between discourse and social practice, Blommaert (2005: 3) points out that discourse entails 'all forms of meaningful semiotic human activity seen in connection with social, cultural, and historical patterns and developments of use'. In his view, '[t]here is no such thing as a "non-social" use of discourse [...] [D]iscourse is what transforms our environment into a socially and culturally meaningful one.' In a similar way, and from the perspective of critical discourse analysis (CDA), Fairclough and Wodak (1997: 258) argue that discourse 'is socially constitutive as well as socially conditioned. It is constitutive in the sense that it helps to sustain and reproduce the status quo, and in the sense that it may contribute to transforming it.' Concerning the close relationship between discourse, power, ideology, identity and knowledge, the perspective of CDA is particularly explicit about the intersection between language and power. One of its major aims is to critically investigate social inequality as it is expressed, constituted and legitimised in discourse (cf. De Cillia & Wodak 2004; Van Dijk 2003). In this scope, ideologies figure primarily as a link between collective group interests and individual social practices. They are discursively communicated and help to reproduce power in society (cf. Van Dijk 2003: 26–27; see also Blackledge 2009: 14–15). Discourse, it is argued, also impacts identity formation since identities are produced and legitimised through discursive interaction (cf. e.g. Blackledge 2009: 36).

Notwithstanding the multitude of meanings and concepts related to discourse today, a clear 'common understanding' emerges with respect to discourse as social practice which is tightly interwoven with power, ideology, identity and knowledge. As regards the social theory that conceptions of discourse can be related to, there are several options, with Foucault continuing to represent a frequently chosen reference point.

Discourse within LINEE

Against the background of the multidisciplinary nature and the diversified range of studies in LINEE, it comes as no surprise that the term discourse is not used in a unified way within the project. In fact, various theoretical options are pursued in LINEE. Most frequently, LINEE research on discourse associates with the work of Foucault and with CDA, although it also includes other options, for example, the discourse-theoretical approach following Laclau and Mouffe (1985). Here, it is argued that identities and societies are incomplete processes which are constructed within specific discursive formations. Thus, discourse theory, following Laclau and Mouffe, is particularly interested in the discursive attempts which fix the meaning of societies and identities.

Another example for a theoretical option diverging from Foucault and CDA is provided by social representations theory following Davies and Harré (1990). This framework focuses on the transformation process from scientific knowledge to common-sense knowledge, where both types of knowledge are assumed to be rational. The analysis of this kind of process emphasises the tension between reflection and unreflected or 'automatic' cognitive behaviour and thus addresses issues of reflexivity concerning the individual's constructive efforts towards arriving at a consensual agreement (cf. Area Report B 2009: 5).

The discourse-theoretical embedding opens up a wide range of options for investigating discursive manifestations, in so far as the focus can be more or less markedly on texts or texts in combination with other non-linguistic discourses. Thus, conceiving of discourse within LINEE may include all kinds of manifestations, such as artistic, scientific and cultural work, as in the study of discourse in the multilingual city of Pula, in which, for example, public signs, entertainment facilities, nightlife were also investigated as discursive properties of the tourist resort (cf. Area Report A 2009: 32). At the same time, discourse may be confined to precisely defined sets of texts, for example, in the official EU discourse on LPP, for which a clearly delimited corpus of texts was defined (cf. Area Report B 2009).

Despite the varying conceptualisations of discourse, two central characteristics are common to all approaches within the LINEE project, namely, the multi-level and the ideological nature of discourse. The first feature relates to the fact that discourse is considered as a multi-level concept in which texts, the contexts of their production and reception, as well as the wider socioeconomic and political contexts are linked together. To give an example, the investigation in the discursive construction of multilingualism in speeches given by the former European Commissioner for Multilingualism indicates that multilingualism policy is embedded in a wider European discourse on social coherence and economic prosperity. Here, contextualising discourse helps to understand why only a limited number of languages is included in the multilingualism variant proposed by the EU: On the one hand, economic interests call for regulating linguistic diversity on terms that suit the economic goals of the EU, whereas, on the other hand, this discourse appears to be strongly inspired by the principle of language equality. It is obvious that the discursive strand focusing upon economic efficiency is in conflict with the language equality principle. This is clearly reflected in the fact that being multilingual in, for example, German, Kurdish and Turkish, will be of less value on the European job market than being multilingual in German, French and English (cf. Area Report B 2009: 17).

Another example is provided by the conceptualisation of the discourse on European tourism as a specific type of social discourse with specific topics, configurations, means of space-, time- and actor-use as well as power relations. Concerning its contextualisation, this tourism discourse has to be put in the wider context of consumption since the cultural industry leads to a situation where the 'authentic European' sites become part of a 'game of producing, packaging and consuming a range of different themes' (Area Report A 2009: 10), while at the same time encouraging tourists to consume and experience the forms of cultural tradition and heritage offered by the visited countries.

As to the ideological working of discourse, we can say that it emerges in various manners and degrees in the LINEE research. Thus, the analysis of the focus group discussions on multilingualism in Switzerland, Austria and the Czech Republic shows, for example, that the participants take and pursue distinctive ideological stances in their discourses on multilingualism, which may be quite ambivalent. The debates on language refer to broader ethical themes, such as social competition for advancement, or superiority of particular languages and language skills. At the same time, however, they also reveal underlying broader ethical tensions as the participants appear to be attracted by their admiration for those who dispose of certain language skills on the one hand but are well aware of the discriminatory power of such admiration on the other hand (cf. PoPa EL 2009: 11).

Another example for the close intersection between discourse and ideology is the dominant discourse on languages in officially bilingual regions with high immigration rates. In the case of Morella (Valencia/Spain), the official discourse is clearly in line with the language ideology that underlies the official recognition of regional languages in Spain. In the interviews with official actors, the presence of both, Castilian and Valencian, was never construed as problematic, whereas the interviews with Romanian immigrants in Morella revealed that they preferred Castilian rather than Valencian and that they evaluated the kind of bilingualism politically institutionalised in this region far less positively. By this group, learning Valencian is perceived as an effort which is to be undertaken in addition to learning the more widely spoken Castilian, and which they also profit less from, since Valencian appears to be geographically and functionally restricted (cf. Area Report B 2009: 21–22).

These examples illustrate that there are quite varied conceptualisations of discourse in the LINEE research. It becomes very clear, however, that this research shares a common understanding of discourse as a carrier and producer of meaning. In this view, discourse is closely related to social practice and cannot be separated from ideology (cf. Section 3.2.4).

Discourse within the thematic areas

As regards discourse, the identity area adopts a broad and explicit approach which integrates Foucault's view and which draws upon discourse in terms of 'a network of meaning articulating both linguistic and non-linguistic elements' (Stavrakakis 2004: 255). Here, discourse is not only seen as words 'but also as practices directly connected to the discursive logic that formulates them. A central aim is to locate and analyse the mechanisms by which meaning is produced within particular texts, speeches, images and sites. In that context cultural and language policy, as well as cultural tourism are understood as elements of a wider field of discourse incorporating both organisational and linguistic elements' (Area Report A 2009: 6). The investigation reveals the multifaceted nature of tourism discourse and the power it wields when constructing worlds of meaning and experience and when creating specific, idealised representations of the place of destination. Moreover, the power of this discourse is characterised by the fact that dissonant voices are muted if they do not match the desired European image of the touristic place (cf. Area Report A 2009: 38).

Within the policy area, the conceptualisation of discourse is mainly inspired by CDA, although the integration of discourse largely depends on the research design of the single projects. Thus, discourse relates to concepts such as 'transnationalism' (cf. Basch et al. 1994: 6) or 'cultural citizenship' (cf. Rosaldo 1994) when in regions with two or more co-official languages and high immigration rates, national language policies are under investigation and if the question at stake is whether the two multilingual language communities, that is, regional and migrant minorities, are supporting or impeding each other. And yet, in a somewhat different way, discourse is also used within the framework of language management theory (LMT) in order to analyse the judgement of the European Court of Justice (ECJ) concerning language use and free movement of European citizens in the labour market. From the perspective of LMT, the initial stage of the language management process involves perceiving a problem. Subsequently, the discourse participants evaluate this deviation and design an adjustment which they finally implement. This can be illustrated by referring to Christina Kik's action against the Office for Harmonisation in the Internal Market (Trademarks and Designs). Here, Kik argued that Art. 115 of Council Regulation 40/94 (cf. OJ 1994 L 11), distinguishing between the languages of the Office and the other languages, was unlawful since it infringed upon the fundamental principle of non-discrimination and language equality. With this act, she questioned the rules governing the use of languages at this Office (cf. ECJ C-361/01P). The ECJ agreed that the regulation of the language use was adopted for the legitimate purposes of reaching a solution to language problems in cases of opposition, revocation or invalidity proceedings between parties who do not have the same language preference and cannot reach an agreement by themselves on the language of proceedings. Moreover, the ECJ argued that no principle specifying that all official languages of the Community must be treated equally in all circumstances may be inferred from the EC Treaty. Focusing upon discourse from an LMT perspective, it can be derived that the European institutions which participate in the discourse at the macro-level note the danger emanating from language inequality and formulate corresponding adjustment strategies (cf. Art. 115 of Council Regulation 40/94).

However, when implemented, these strategies are obviously not successful, as is demonstrated by Kik's lawsuit. Not reaching the micro-level with its interactions among the language users, the language management process thus ends at the second to last phase (cf. Area Report B 2009: 10–13).

Shifting now to the education area, the conceptualisation of discourse in this area is inspired by Fairclough (2007: 124; also in Area Report C 2009: 5), who conceives of discourse in terms of 'representations of the mental world, including feelings and beliefs, and of the material social world with processes, relations and structures as component elements'. Consequently, the investigation of discourse also relies on CDA, which attempts to reveal the hidden and opaque relationships of dominance, discrimination, power and control as they are manifested and reproduced in discourse (cf. Blommaert 2005; Wodak 2007). The research results in this thematic area indicate that according to the specific topics, different discourses are at stake, such as the discourse on the state language, discourse on the minority languages, the school's public discourse and so on. Analysing these discourses reveals underlying symbolic power asymmetries which impact upon language learning in specific contexts, such as regional minority schools. Thus, the investigation of the students' discourse on the Romanian state language confirms that this language is less positively evaluated as it is seen as something imposed by the state power (cf. Area Report C 2009: 9). Negative attitudes towards the state language may also be seen as a reason why the Romanian competence of Hungarian minority students in Szekler Land has decreased in the past 10 years.

In the economy area, in turn, discourse figures within the framework of LMT, which attempts to incorporate 'a wide range of additional problems comprising discourse, politeness and communication in intercultural or multilingual contact situations' (Jernudd & Neustupny 1987; Area Report D 2009: 5–6). In this scope, discourse constitutes a necessary condition within the language management cycle, particularly when language management is organised at the institutional level since institutionally organised management is, *inter alia*, defined by its trans-situational nature, by the involvement of a social network or an institutionalised entity, and by communication about management (cf. Nekvapil & Sherman 2009). At this point, it has to be mentioned, though, that the use of discourse within the economy area, where language was primarily analysed from the LMT perspective, differs from its definition in the other areas, as in the LMT perspective, discourse has not been assigned a central discourse analytical role.

As a comparison of the approaches to discourse in the four thematic areas shows, the ideological working of discourse is most prominent in the policy area and in the education area, which in their theoretical design follows the tradition of CDA. In contrast, the anthropological approach of the identity area most clearly exceeds the boundaries of language, in so far as non-linguistic elements, such as entertainment programme or nightlife, form constitutive components of the understanding of discourse as a 'network of meaning' and of the analysis. In the economy area, whose view of discourse is embedded in LMT, discourse figures less prominently than in the other three areas. Apart from these differences in the meaning and conceptualisation of discourse, it can be concluded that the LINEE research provides for evidence that discourse is a salient category which pertains to all four thematic areas.

Conclusion

Against the background of the theoretical approaches to discourse, ranging from language use beyond the boundaries of the sentence to ways of thinking and interacting beyond language itself (cf. Gee 1999: 17; Schiffrin 2004: 597), LINEE is generally positioned towards the 'language in use' perspective. A salient feature of the LINEE approaches in this respect concerns the emphasis on the social nature of discourse since in all the various contexts and on different levels, discourse is always closely linked to social practice. In doing so, the LINEE studies clearly show the connection between discourse and power in most diverse contexts, such as when dissonant voices are concealed or when the language learning process and the linguistic competence of speaker groups develops into a certain direction due to social power relations.

If we reflect upon the term discourse with regard to its relation to the other key variables and themes investigated in the LINEE project, specific patterns emerge. Although discourse is linked to all other key variables and themes, these relationships exhibit different degrees of strength and explicitness.

As to discourse and the various key variables, the closest intersection appears to exist between the variables discourse and LPP. It cannot be ignored that there is a very intimate relationship between discourse and LPP since, in each case, discourse is conceptualised as a substantial part of the LPP process (cf. Section 3.2.6). Moreover, the LINEE results suggest that language policy making is an essentially inter-discursive process which implies different agents, that is, European policy makers, member state representatives, independent stakeholders and experts, and citizens themselves. Their inter-discursive interaction, which may associate with different and changing ideological stances, eventually brings about LPP. As research findings indicate, the construction of discourses on EM is substantially shaped by ideologies as they evolve both from the formal contexts of official text documents and political positions or statements and even from the informal contexts such as everyday talk and interactions at the grass-roots level (cf. Area Report B 2009: 40).

Depending on the specific focus of the research in the thematic areas, the LINEE results also point to a link between the discourse and the other key variables. Thus, the relation between discourse, knowledge and culture is particularly evident in the discourse of cultural tourism, which provides for new forms of knowledge to be consumed and experienced, such as the connection of particular tourist sites to other European sites (cf. Area Report A 2009: 11). Furthermore, in the contemporary EU official discourses on the 'European identity culture', culture also constitutes a major issue which is discursively constructed and which suggests that cultural and linguistic differences can coexist both peacefully and free of contradictions within a European identity (cf. Section 3.2.1). The intersection of discourse with identity and culture is also illustrated in the public and informal discourses on minority language promotion in Wales, which appear to be strongly motivated by an attitude on part of the Welsh minority to protect a Welsh-speaking heartland, whereas in Valencia similar discourses do not appear to be primarily motivated by the fear that Valencian might be an endangered minority language in need for protection (cf. Section 3.2.3). From the different attitudes towards language promotion in both regions, it can be derived that the self-awareness and the relationship between the self and the others of Welsh and Valencian speakers differs considerably since the discursively constructed cultural reality in terms of underlying preferences, values and knowledge varies in these two regions (cf. Area Report B 2009: 42).

Finally, discourse is also associated with multi-competence in that multi-competence is an implied key issue in the diverse discourses on multilingualism (cf. Section 3.2.7). At the EU level, the concept of multi-competence relates to the questions of how many languages and what languages to learn and of how to teach and to use them. Economically invested discourses, for example, presuppose and create a specific kind of desired multi-competence which is advantageous for the economy, whereas politically invested discourses targeted towards broader societal objectives suggest their own forms of multi-competence which may include migrant and regional minority languages. At the same time, this also points to the ideological and power-specific implications of discourse. The difference between the economic and the political discourse reflects the fact that both are ideologically loaded and powerful discourses and that in terms of their consequences and outcomes they have a different bearing upon the planning of multilingualism.

As to the themes that combine with discourse, it goes without saying that generally research projects like LINEE cannot but rely on discourse when investigating multilingualism. It is true that there are some themes which relate to multilingualism in a more explicit way than others, for example, in the case of the diverse debates in which multilingualism is discussed as a political objective or where it is investigated in terms of a constitutive component in constructing identity. At the same time, the working of discourse may remain rather vague and blurred within the manifold opinions and attitudes that combine, for instance, with language learning and teaching or with the economic management of linguistic diversity. Here, we can clearly see that discourse constitutes a category which is difficult to separate from other categories and which is in a particularly close interaction with knowledge and ideology (cf. Sections 3.2.4 and 3.2.5).

It can be concluded that the LINEE sub-projects offer quite a variety of options for conceptualising discourse which are elaborated in accordance with the specific research questions and designs. Due to the intersecting nature and the variable explicitness of discourse within LINEE, different discursive dimensions come to the fore to varying degrees, depending on the research questions. An example is provided by the connection between discourse, culture and identity, which is particularly paramount if questions are raised concerning the implications of cultural tourism. This varying emphasis on the different dimensions of discourse is intensified by the specific theoretical modelling process. The LINEE research clearly shows that discourse requires an explicit theoretical embedding. That is to say, if the theoretical framework remains rather implicit, the risk of 'discourse' mutating into a 'passe-partout' for all kinds of linguistic and social manifestations is particularly high. With this development, the usefulness of discourse as an analytical category would be fundamentally questioned.

Despite this theoretical and analytical pluralism within LINEE, the single projects share the understanding that discourse is a producer and carrier of meaning and a multi-level concept connected with social practice. As such, discourse pertains to all areas, levels and themes related to multilingualism. At the same time, it is connected to all other LINEE key variables, which, in turn, are mostly discourse-based variables. It appears to be, however, most visibly connected with LPP, which is itself conceived in terms of an inter-discursive process (cf. Section 3.2.6). And yet, a most important point is that the LINEE results strongly confirm the ideological working of discourse since this forms the basis on which the underlying tensions and contradictions concerning EM emerge. From what has been said, it can thus be concluded that discourse is an important key variable when theorising multilingualism and linguistic diversity and that, also due to the fact that it is open for a variety of theoretical options, it is an apt device for assessing the multifaceted nature of EM more precisely .

3.2.3 Identity

Theoretical concepts of identity

In recent decades, identity has come to constitute a central issue in the social sciences and the humanities. However, it is extremely difficult to assess identity empirically and to conceptualise it as a process that duly accounts for the variability of individual interactions and of societal changes which constitute the basic grounds for the formation of identities. Identity is a complex and multi-layered phenomenon; therefore, it comes as no surprise that there is a wide range of conceptualisations which focus upon the various personal, social, collective, cultural and ethnic components of identity from quite different disciplinary perspectives.

Since the 1980s, post-structuralist thinking and the rapid changes caused through globalisation and intensified intercultural encounters have led, however, to a notable shift from conceiving of identity in terms of a stable and unitary category towards viewing it as a more dynamic and flexible process that is very often discursively negotiated and constructed (cf. Blommaert 2005: 203–232; Straub 2004: 279–280). In this dynamic perspective, the focus is on identification rather than on identity. Identifications emerge through the relation to the 'other', in which individuals negotiate a dynamic image in confronting their view on themselves with external views of others. Contrary to traditional essentialist views in which identity was seen as a fixed internal quality or as a stable form of inherent self- or other-awareness, post-structuralist identity refers to a fluid formation that is constantly destabilised and in a process of change and transformation (cf. e.g. Brah 2000; Butler 1993; Hall 1996; Holt & Gubbins 2002; Laclau 1990). In this scope, identities are negotiated through discursive and cultural interaction. Identity formation is thus seen as a dynamic process that aims at individual uniqueness within a group having a shared sense of belonging, and that involves multiple social dimensions constrained by social power relations (cf. Area Report A 2008: 3). Collective identities are shaped through collective experiences of shared cultural spaces of belonging; they are also socially constructed and subjected to the power relations as they emerge from the social negotiation in these cultural spaces.

Identity within LINEE

The conception of identity within the LINEE research was strongly inspired by post-structuralist approaches and linguistic anthropology, particularly within the thematic area that explicitly focused on identity, culture and language. Here, identity was seen as intimately connected with the interplay of discourses as they emerge within the exercise of power. In line with the anti-essentialist stance, it was maintained that the idea of the stable core of the 'self' or the homogenous notion of identity actually masks the plurality of positions that exist behind each identity (cf. Area Report A 2009: 8). The articulations of collective identities were seen as mainly social constructs disguised as naturalised givens (cf. Area Report A 2008: 10). Hence, constructs such as European or national identities were to be put 'under erasure' (Hall 1996: 2). As there appeared to be common agreement that European identity includes the possibility for multiple identities, where local, national and supranational identifications can exist alongside each other, the aim was to investigate the reasons for such identifications and their implications.

A major question to be answered within the LINEE research was how language, culture and identity relate to each other in terms of dominance and subordination or of hegemony and resistance within the European, national and regional or local dimension, and how the multiple forms of cultural European, national and regional differences are reflected in the various identification processes.

The LINEE research started out from the assumption that identity, language and culture imply each other in a dynamic and heterogeneous way. Identities were conceived in terms of formations negotiated through cultural and linguistic interaction, and thus they implied questions concerning the use of the resources of language and culture. For example, identifying with a nation involves participating in the idea of a nation not only as a political entity but also as a system of cultural representations. A nation is thus a symbolic community represented in the national culture and it is this status which accounts for the power to generate a sense of identity (cf. Area Report A 2009: 8).

Viewing language, culture and identity as mutually inseparable and discursive articulations also implied that they could not be separated from social, political and economic issues and that they were actually constructed through these relations and the power the latter conveyed. In this perspective, it was argued that cultural identities such as national or European identities are not stable but are subject to change according to the social forces from which they evolve.

Identity within the thematic areas

As to the variability of identity within the LINEE research, it can be said that apart from the thematic area of 'language, identity and culture', where identity was in focus, it turned out to be a salient interactive force in the context of policy planning, education and economy as well.

Within the identity area, research showed how language and culture are used to forge a sense of European identity founded in the concept of 'unity in diversity'. In this process, it became apparent that the construction of a European identity which largely omits the inconvenient facts of the power relations and the histories of antagonism and struggle among the different European nation states and which suppresses the traumas of the past results in ambivalent attitudes towards European identity. As the study in Istria showed, only few interviewees stressed their attachment to Europe as being important, although they mostly reacted positively to Europe and the EU and to belonging to the same civilisation and culture (cf. Area Report 2008: 5). From this, it follows that the political objective aiming at a widely neutralised European identity does not always match the people's views and awareness of self and others.

The tendency in constructing a well-balanced European identity is particularly reflected in the activities of cultural tourism. Here, the LINEE results show how cultural tourism contributes to rewriting the cultural memory of the European peoples in a way that fits the prescribed picture of 'unity in diversity' developed by EU policy makers and stakeholders. Thus, cultural tourism in Pula, Poznan and Gdansk, for example, is based upon selective histories in which the multicultural past of these cities is mostly experienced through issues which are conducive to commodification such as archaeological sites, buildings etc., while less saleable issues which are also part of the multicultural past of these cities, for example, ethnic minorities, are removed from the carefully painted picture. At the same time, however, the findings also indicate that through rewriting history and cultural memories, new perceptions and opportunities for new identifications are constructed in which something like a European commonality emerges (cf. Area Report A 2009: 14–15). At the same time, one cannot fail to notice, however, that the political demand for intensified European identification on the part of the citizens within the area of cultural tourism appears to be targeted towards economic rather than towards truly intercultural Europeanisation.

From investigations focusing on various aspects of national identity, it could be derived that national identities do not always correspond to homogeneous or unitary images but can be constructed from the different regional images through which the diversified national nature comes to the fore. Thus, for example, in Croatian tourism promotion, the national identity is being presented as the sum of different regional identities since the promotion focuses on the various regions and thus constructs the image of the country primarily on the basis of its diversity (cf. RePa WP2a 2009: 35).

Concerning the role of language in the creation of national identities, it has already been pointed out (cf. Section 3.2.1) that in Croatia, Latvia and Cyprus, language, identity and nation constitute an inextricable linkage in which the national language constitutes the central reference point for identifying with a distinct and unique cultural community. At the same time, the homogenising power of the national language entails the subordination of identities associated with the coexisting non-standard and minority languages.

Studies at the regional and local level furthermore reveal that belonging can be expressed through multiple identifications. Individuals may construct their multi-layered identities by positioning the local, ethnic, national or state layers in relation to one another. In Pula, many interviewees, particularly those born in the city, accommodate their multiple identifications as a kind of hierarchy where the local layer comes first. In turn, members of other ethnicities, for example, the first generation of immigrants, often associate their sense of belonging with citizenship of their country of origin. The two identities, immigrant identity and indigenous identity, construct two forms of belonging: a dialectical sense of belonging of an immigrant who is also a member of the cultural minority and, in contrast, a pronounced sense of belonging of an indigenous person who expresses a strong bonding to his/her home and city (cf. RePa WP3a 2009: 21). Another point is the role which languages play in the tension of identity building between the global and the local. The case study in Istria shows that in this tension, the local or minority language has become a powerful means of cultural resistance reinforcing local/regional otherness and providing its speakers with cultural gain (cf. Area Report A 2009: 22–25).

Unlike the identity area, the policy area did not primarily focus upon identity. Within the policy area, it could not be ignored, however, that identity played an important role in relation to regional and migrant minorities since a considerable part of the policy and planning manoeuvres in this respect appear to be involved in the management of multiple identities and belonging. The findings indicate that identity is implied in all strategies targeted towards reconfiguring the notion of citizenship and belonging against the background of traditional territorial and language-based forms of identity. Citizenship implies that citizens share common cultural values and identify with one nation or state. This conception of citizenship, however, generally disregards the recognition of difference and is accompanied by an assimilation of difference. It is true that the recognition of regional minorities commonly takes place on the basis of their territorial and descent-based forms of identity which derive from language-based belonging. At the same time, however, they are required to identify with the national language and culture as well by becoming bilingual. The situation is completely different in the case of immigrant minorities, which, in suppressing their heritage language, have to gain recognition by providing evidence of adequate knowledge of their host country's language and culture.

Investigation of language policies in Spain, the UK and Switzerland, where regional minorities live together with immigrant minorities, show that there is a range of parallel, competing discourses of belonging, multilingualism and the right to difference. This raises the question whether multiple belongings are possible at all. As citizenship is traditionally associated with language-based belonging and the requirement of proficiency in the national language rather than plurilingual competence, a major question of LINEE related to the mode of incorporating in particular new migration through the notion of 'cultural' citizenship (cf. Miller 2006; Rosaldo 1994). Cultural citizenship is a notion which derives from non-language-based belonging. It rejects assimilation and insists on the recognition of difference and the right to cultural representation of this difference. The findings show that there appears to be a shift in emphasis away from the preoccupation with equality – that is, the equal treatment of majority and minority, which controlled the traditional politics of recognition of regional minorities – to a recognition of difference (cf. Delanty 2003) which applies to the old and the new minorities alike. As the results in the three countries mentioned above indicate, new forms of inclusion must be identified to address the problem concerning the difference of culture and identity, in view of the fact that minorities are increasingly demanding recognition and the maintenance of their identities (cf. Area Report B 2009: 8).

Identity is also an important issue when talking about policy making at the EU level. Here, an important body of LPP work not only neglects the internal processes of policy formulation and the underlying hegemonic relationships within the EU institutions but also fails to mention the diversified ideologies and identities involved in this policy making. Critical investigation of the discourses on EM, and particularly on relationships between the formalisation of language policy and reflections on the policy-making process on part of key political actors within the EU institutions, showed that 'the concept of multilingualism is still beset by unresolved tensions within the discourses on LPP that circulate at the highest levels' (cf. Area Report B 2008: 5–6).

At the same time, EU policy making often ignores the impact of policies on the target groups since it remains unclear how the policies comply with the endeavours and identification potentials of the affected groups and how these groups or individuals position themselves in relation to the social orders shaped by these policies (cf. Area Report B 2008: 3). Research on the reception of EU language policies in Switzerland and Austria equally shows that the multilingualism policy of the EU seems to reflect an attempt at utilising EM as a platform to foster a sense of Europeanness and European identity rather than to respond to the needs and controversies of linguistic communities at the national and regional level (cf. Area Report B 2009: 39).

Furthermore, identity also figures in the education area (cf. RePa WP8 2008; RePa WP9 2008), where it is likely to combine with the competence model, since linguistically, multi-competent persons are hypothesised to have a particular type of identity that also comes to bear on their intercultural awareness, which forms a part of their identity. Unfortunately, no comprehensive theory of identity in relation to foreign language learning has been provided to date (cf. Ricento 2005), and in this respect the results attained within the LINEE research do not substantially contribute to a further elaboration of these phenomena.

The findings concerning attitudes within the education research of the second LINEE phase do, however, suggest that attitudes reflect a dimension which impacts upon the dialectics between multi-competence and identity. Thus, for example, immigrant students in Austrian multilingual school settings do not feel motivated to learn the languages they speak at home in addition to German. They do not think that their home languages are appreciated or even permitted in the classroom. These findings suggest that migrant students' identification with the home language is seriously hampered within the specific school setting (cf. Area Report C 2009: 29). Another example is provided by young Europeans in different school and university contexts in Hungary, the UK and the Czech Republic identifying positively with ELF although their judgements still underpin an orientation towards the native-speaker norm (cf. Area Report C 2009: 15; PoPa RLL 2009: 16). In this context, the research results suggest that there appears to be an ambivalent attitude towards developing the ELF component within the multilingual repertoires of these students since, on the one hand, they are strongly oriented towards efficient communication through ELF while, on the other hand, they implicitly refer to English native-speaker norms (cf. Area Report C 2009: 15).

Although identity is not a focal issue within educational research, the LINEE results do show that identity interacts with multi-competence in various ways and degrees (cf. Section 3.2.7). Again, ELF communication is a notable example in this respect. ELF speakers prove to be multi-competent communicators who, in adjusting their language use to the needs of the multilingual context, use communication strategies such as code-switching, which reflects the creative potential of multilingual repertoires and can be seen as evidence for multi-competence. Here, identity comes into play when code-switching is used as a device to signal membership to or accommodation with the identity that is negotiated within the group or CoP. The findings suggest that in ELF contexts, the multi-competent speakers signal their multicultural identity by integrating elements of their different codes while switching (cf. Area Report C 2009: 11).

The intimate relationship between language and identity is also reflected in migrant students' multi-competence since identity has a strong bearing on the migrant students' use of their heritage language in the school context and outside school. The comparative study of multilingual school settings in Austria, Great Britain and Italy showed that the plurilingual repertoires of migrant students develop positively as long as the heritage language is a salient part of the students' identity, whereas it appears to be severely hampered if this is not the case. Thus, identity proves to be decisive for the maintenance or restriction of the plurilingual repertoire of the multi-competent migrant students (cf. Area Report C 2009: 44).

As far as the role of identity in the Economy area is concerned, the LINEE investigation indicates that identity plays a role in the negotiation of communicative practices in multilingual workplaces and thus impacts on the realisation of economic processes in the knowledge-based economy. As to the communication within multilingual companies and its subsidiaries, the LINEE findings assert that English is generally perceived as a language not ridden with national identity symbolism, whereas languages such as Czech, German and Hungarian continue to symbolise national identities. This explains the use of English in multinational companies which are interested in finding the most effective medium of communication suitable for most participants involved in the economic process. The other languages are used for social purposes, that is, in communicative settings of the enterprise in which the signalling of specific identities forms part of the negotiation process (cf. Area Report D 2008: 14; RePa WP12 2008).

Clearly, in the KBS, knowledge of languages is a marketable skill which is used for greater economic and social development. Multilingualism is one of the major prerequisites for moving and being flexible within the markets of the New Economy. A major problem concerning multilingualism in its relationship to the Knowledge Economy, however, relates to the fact that for reasons of efficiency, languages are mainly seen as simple devices that facilitate intercultural communication and encounters. The symbolic power of these languages as carriers of social meaning and as markers of identity is not given serious consideration in this context (cf. Area Report D 2009: 8).

As regards the context of working migrants, the negotiation of communicative practices in multilingual cities in Great Britain, Croatia, Austria and the Czech Republic reveal that migrant workers employ specific identification strategies, which means that they often maintain transnational relationships sustaining their original 'home' identities, while adapting in different measures and degrees to the language and culture of the host country (cf. RePa WP12a 2009: 20).

Conclusion

As to the role of identity within multilingualism research, the LINEE findings underline that identity is a dynamic, fluid and multilayered phenomenon that is subject to change. Moreover, it is a category which intimately connects with the various variables cooperating in the manifestations of multilingualism. Thus, identity strongly connects with culture since identity is seen as a contextually embedded and discursively formed phenomenon that is articulated through collective experiences of shared cultural spaces of belonging (cf. Section 3.2.1). It goes without saying that as a discursively constituted phenomenon, identity also intersects with discourse (cf. Section 3.2.2). From the LINEE findings, we may further conclude that identity is highly important when it comes to multilingualism policies since policy manoeuvres of this kind appear to be heavily involved in the management of multiple identities, even though political strategies do not always take due account of identity issues. Beyond policy, identity also intersects with multi-competence with respect to the selection of second and third language learning and when the heritage languages are at stake in the maintenance of migrant and regional minority speakers' multi-competence (cf. Section 3.2.7). Yet another point is that the power relations which exist among the various languages in Europe impact upon the self- and other-awareness of their speakers, thus creating tensions and conflicts particularly when the identity and belonging of minorities are concerned. The intersection of identity with power and conflict is also reflected in the case of the politics of European cultural tourism, where power issues and traumas of the past are repressed and important histories of antagonism and struggle are neutralised, as there is no longer a place for them in the construction of the European identity (cf. Section 3.2.8). However, the interlacing of power and conflict with identity also emerges distincly in those cases where the use of local varieties may be associated with identifications that express resistance to the symbolic domination of national or European identities. Knowledge is yet another variable that closely relates to identity, particularly in those cases when tacit knowledge and attitudes intersect with identification processes, especially in the context of the various CoPs investigated in LINEE (cf. Section 3.2.5). And finally, a cross-cutting reading though the thematic areas brings to the fore that identity is an issue that very intimately combines with ideology. Here, it cannot be overlooked that ideological stances which imply language in terms of a valuable resource, or of social status or function, co-decide upon identification routines. Thus, European identity is framed by various kinds of ideologies about how Europeanisation should work, or national identities are constructed with the help of standard language ideologies, to mention only a few examples (cf. Section 3.2.4).

It has been pointed out that identity intimately associates with language and culture. Therefore, linguistic and cultural nationalisation as well as Europeanisation processes constituted major themes within the identity area, although the various manifestations of the interaction between identity, language and culture were also pursued under the thematic perspectives which are central to LPP issues, to educational matters and to the dynamics of the New Economy. An important thematic focus was on how European administrators and policy makers use culture to forge a common European identity and how the role of language contributes to the deeper investment in the 'unity in diversity' concept. Another focus was targeted towards investigating the politics of national identity by examining the role of language in the creation of national identities in selected countries.

Moreover, investigation of cultural tourism and industry in different countries allowed for assessing how the European 'unity in diversity' concept is promoted by tourism and how tourism contributes to constructing a common European identity and sense of belonging. The thematic focus on tourism also provided information on the national strategies applied in various countries in order to promote the national identity abroad, while at the same time the images constructed to reflect this identity contributed to reinforcing national identity in the countries under investigation themselves.

Beyond this, multilingual cities constituted so-to-say a bottom-up approach to map urban spaces in terms of the perception of the various identities and languages in negotiation with one another. Multilingual cities, it was assumed, would provide insights into the multiplicity of identification processes and spheres of interaction in which locals, migrants and tourists engage under particular historical and socioeconomic contexts in everyday encounters with each other.

Another major issue that closely related to identity concerned regional and migrant minorities and their strategies to develop multiple ways of belonging and to maintain or abandon their heritage languages in different sociocultural settings and conditions. Thus, identity-related issues arose in quite diverse contexts such as the mentioned multilingual cities or multilingual schools and minority children's language education. Identity was also an issue in the context of multilingual labour in the knowledge-based economy, and particularly in migration including the competing discourses of belonging and the contested political issues of citizenship.

Identity and identification strategies were also under debate when the multilingual context was defined through the negotiation in CoPs. CoPs are characterised by negotiating a shared common interest. This presupposes identification strategies which motivate specific strategies of negotiation. In this scope, the communicative negotiation in multinational companies, multilingual schools or student settings sharing ELF could basically be seen as CoPs where the multi-competent speakers signalled their multiple identities through specific strategies of language selection, for example, code-switching.

Against the background of what has been said so far, we may conclude that identity is a variable that impacts on all major themes which actually relate to multilingualism. Against the background of the complex and multiple forms of cultural differences at the European, national and local levels, it appears to be all the more important to conceive of identity in terms of dynamic and flexible processes which are discursively negotiated and socially constrained, in order to deconstruct national identities commonly disguised as naturalised givens or to investigate how these identities are destabilised in the process of change and European transformation. Conceiving of identity in terms of fluid and discursively constructed formations evolving from the experience of shared cultural spaces of belonging, further allows for gaining insights into the power relations which contribute to constituting these cultural spaces. This, in turn, enables us to gain insights into the way language, culture and identity are related to each other within the European, national and local dimension and how the European, national and regional differences of culture and language are reflected in the various identification processes. It is commonly maintained that European identity includes multiple identities where local, national and supranational identifications can exist alongside each other. Approaching European identity as a dynamic formation makes it possible to grasp this identity as a multi-layered process without, however, mistakenly assuming that this identity is a simple succession or addition of differently acquired identities.

3.2.4 Ideology

Theoretical concepts of ideology

Ideology is another most prominent concept that has been developed within the social sciences over the past decades. A particularly salient feature of ideology seems to be its conceptual vagueness. Consequently, Van Dijk (1998) argues that ideology is another significant term which as a concept, however, remains rather vague. Van Dijk (1998: 1) compares ideology with 'catch-all terms' such as 'society', 'group', 'action', 'power', 'discourse', 'mind' and 'knowledge' in that it points to very 'complex sets of phenomena'. Yet, he assumes that ideology differs from the other catch-all terms in that its common-sense usage is generally pejorative (cf. Van Dijk 1998: 1). Generally, it can be observed that both conceptual vagueness and a pejorative component are two properties which are frequently referred to in the rich scientific literature on ideology. A common starting point for grasping this term would be conceiving of ideology as a text 'woven of a tissue of conceptual strands which recur with particular salience' (cf. Eagleton 1991: 1). Like Eagleton, most researchers distinguish several strands of ideology which have come to be differently reflected in the wide range of conceptualisations available to date.

Following Woolard (1998: 6–7), there is a great divide between conceptualising ideology in a neutral way as dependent on the material and practical aspects related to a particular social position, and in a way that assigns ideology a negative value by linking it with the practice of dominant social groups. Similarly, Blommaert (2005: 158) suggests a distinction between ideology conceptualised either as 'a specific set of symbolic representations [...] serving a specific purpose, and operated by specific groups or actors, recognisable precisely by their usage of such ideologies', and 'as a general phenomenon characterising the totality of a particular social or political system, and operated by every member or actor in that system' (Blommaert 2005). He classifies Gramsci as a theorist pertaining to the first group, whereas in his view, Bourdieu, Foucault and Althusser are scholars who rather correspond to the second group. Blommaert further differentiates between ideology as a cluster of cognitive and ideational phenomena on the one hand, that is, in terms of particular sets of ideas and perceptions, and ideology as a collection of material phenomena, that is, as ideas produced by particular material conditions, on the other hand (cf. Blommaert 2005: 161; see also Gal 1998: 319). Blommaert also recommends combining the ideational and the material strand in conceptualising ideology. Ideology researchers commonly share Blommaert's assumption that ideas themselves do not define ideologies but that 'they need to be inserted in material practices of modulation and reproduction' (Blommaert 2005: 164) which eventually lift specific sets of ideas to the level of ideology.

Furthermore, it can be derived from research that there are different dimensions of ideology, which are, however, diversely conceptualised in the various approaches to ideology. First, ideology is a discursive phenomenon that is dialectically related to linguistic practice (cf. Eagleton 1991; Silverstein 1998; Van Dijk 1998). Although discourse is not the only social practice that associates with ideology, it is considered a highly important dimension for expressing, implementing and reproducing ideologies (cf. Van Dijk 1998: 316–317). Another point is that ideology goes along with power and hegemony. According to Thompson (1990), ideology is intrinsically linked with power-regulating institutions which pick up ideas and insert them into the ideological reproduction system. In his more general approach to ideology, Blommaert (2005: 169) suggests bringing ideology into a 'complex and layered space in which ideational, behavioral, and institutional aspects interact along lines of consent and coercion'. This also explains why in strongly coercive systems people behave as if they shared the hegemonic beliefs and ideas 'just because there are no other options' (Blommaert 2005: 169).

From the perspective of multilingualism and linguistic diversity, there are three more aspects to be mentioned, namely, the link with knowledge and with identity, and eventually the salience of language ideologies as a specific ideological subset. Van Dijk argues that theorising identity implies taking into account the role of sociocultural knowledge and shared beliefs of specific groups on the one hand and of whole societies and cultures on the other hand (cf. Van Dijk 1998: 10). In his conceptualisation, ideologies 'are not simply a "world view" of a group but rather the principles that form the basis of such beliefs. [...] In most, but not in all cases, ideologies are self-serving and a function of the material and symbolic interests of the group' (Van Dijk 1998: 8). Moreover, ideology appears to closely interact with the formation of identities. Following Van Dijk, the intricate relationship between ideology and identity can be seen in that ideologies reflect group identity and interests since they define group cohesion and solidarity and coordinate goal-oriented social interaction (cf. Van Dijk 1998: 316).

The interrelationship between ideology, identity and power is particularly evident in the case of language ideologies. Language ideologies have been very broadly defined as explicit or implicit representations constituting the link between language and humans in a social environment (cf. Woolard 1998: 3). Gal (1998: 323–324) has described them as a link between language and other arenas of social life, such as political, religious or scientific conflicts. In this perspective, Irvine and Gal (2000) have identified iconisation, fractal recursivity and erasure as three important semiotic processes which are responsible for the way ideologies recognise or misrecognise linguistic differences.

Concerning identity, Blommaert and Verschueren (1998: 208) point to the serious discrepancy between the popular ideology to conceive of language as a natural aspect of a specific group identity on the one hand and the way language is actually used in multilingual societies on the other hand. Still another point is that different language ideologies are likely to arise and to compete with each other. This may create tensions, particularly when multilingual language policies are invested by different ideologies (cf. Hawkins 2001: 21).

Concluding, we may say that despite the considerable variability in conceptualising ideology, it cannot be overlooked that the different approaches always point to connecting ideology with a complex set of phenomena such as identity, knowledge, power, and discourse. As we will see, these issues are also at the very centre of interest within the LINEE research.

Ideology within LINEE

The LINEE scope in terms of ideology remains rather implicit since explicit or extensive conceptualisations of ideology are rare. Ideology is, however, a substantial component of the projects' theoretical framework, and, in line with research of ideology in general, the LINEE sub-projects draw upon ideology in close connection with identity, power, knowledge, and discourse. Although it is quite obvious that the LINEE focus is not explicitly directed towards theorising ideology, the strength of this focus can nevertheless be seen in that it provides for detailed insights into the working of ideology in close intersection with the other components of multilingualism.

In general, the theoretical profile of ideology within LINEE highlights the ideational component of ideology. Despite a very high degree of implicitness, ideology turns out to be viewed as a specific set of representations which serve a specific purpose and pertain to specific groups. By stressing the ideational component, the ideologies which conflict with the conception of EM are eventually elaborated and emphasised.

As to the use of the term ideology, the theoretical stance taken within LINEE appears to be pejorative in those cases where ideology is associated with certain conditions of power. An example for such a use is provided by the dominant linguistic ideologies investigated in Croatia, Cyprus and Latvia. Assuming that language and identity constitute a naturalised primordial unity, these ideologies proved to be strongly inspired by the national language ideology and the power it displays when powerful groups or institutions are sustaining the national languages. In this context, the national language ideology also coincides with the ideology of the standard language, which favours an idealised, homogenous state language (cf. Section 3.2.1). Due to this overlap, these ideologies initiate the 'language subordination process', which valorises the standard language and culture, while at the same time devaluing historical and social differences concerning language and culture (cf. Area Report A 2008: 6).

In general, however, the LINEE approach to ideology remains rather neutral, for instance, when analysing the role of language ideology in the LPP processes as they evolve from the grassroots or from specific phenomena at the institutional level (Area Report B 2009: 7). Thus, in Woolard's (1998) terms, the LINEE sub-projects tend to conceptualise ideology as dependent on the material and practical aspects related to a particular social position and do not always and in all cases link it with the practice of dominant social groups.

Although the LINEE research attempted to identify the kinds of ideologies that are at stake when linguistic diversity is planned and managed, its focus was mainly on language-centred ideologies. The LINEE approaches are based on the assumption that language ideologies are related to larger ideologies which go far beyond language and linguistic behaviour and pertain to the wider economic and political spheres in society, such as market-driven freedom, modernisation in the globalised world, or nation building. Even though language ideologies are paramount within LINEE, larger ideologies are always present as well. The ideological aspects of EM itself are an example for this since they address social cohesion and democratisation as well as socioeconomic realities. Placed between major EU discourses, that is, 'the discourse on democratisation, and the discourse on the knowledge-based economy', as Wodak (2011: 8) puts it, multilingualism is embedded in ideological contexts transcending language ideologies. A particular strength of manner in which identity is developed in the LINEE research can be seen in that the interweaving of language ideologies and large-scale ideologies is addressed.

Ideology in the thematic areas

Ideology is a component which figures implicitly or explicitly in the theoretical designs of all four thematic areas. Although it remains rather implicit in terms of a theoretical concept within the identity area, the research results derived from investigation of this area point to the ideological working of cultural and linguistic policy in the formation of identities. As already mentioned in Section 3.2.3, the linguistic ideologies appear to be strongly inspired by the Herderian view that language, identity and nation are inextricably linked in the form of a naturalised primordial unity. In this perspective, the standard norms defining the national language are maintained and imposed by dominant power institutions such as academies and schools. These institutions form the common grounds on which the national identity is produced and reinforced while linguistic aspects other than the national language are devalued and subject to a sociolinguistic subordination (cf. Area Report A 2008: 6).

In the second phase of the LINEE research, the concept of governance as developed by Rose (1999) and Bennett (2005) was integrated into the theoretical designs of the identity research. This allowed for investigating ideology in more explicit terms since the concept of governance is directed towards understanding the processes and strategies which guide and shape the actions of others and the self. In this perspective, the orders of governance are closely linked to ideology, which is seen as a discursive reconfiguration of the social space (cf. Lefebvre 1974). The research findings concerning the impact of cultural policies on identity formation suggest that European tourism is a field of political and ideological struggle from which new power relations emerge. The prospect of economic benefit and the desire to match the supranational objectives of European identity construction impact significantly upon the construction of local identities and cultures, with the consequence that aspects of the local past which do not match the image of European identity are omitted in the promotional material. However, counter-memories relating to highly contentious or painful parts of history continue to circulate in everyday practices and may thus represent a source of further repulsion and conflict (cf. Area Report A 2009: 37–38).

LPP is intimately linked with ideology, and ideology thus constitutes a salient dimension within the theoretical framework of the policy area. Following Ricento (2000), language policy is concerned with various historical and cultural processes that impact upon the attitudes and practices regarding language use, acquisition and status. (cf. also PoPa NL 2009: 13). In this sense, policy is ideologically positioned.

Yet another point would be 'contested linguistic spaces', that is, areas in which communities are constituted, contested, and often reconfigured; here, the focus is on 'highly-charged linguistic environments' (Pavlenko 2009) and the ideologies and attitudes that are productive in the relative process of contestation. The element of contestation includes the struggle over real geographic spaces, that is, neighbourhoods, public spaces and public institutions. Conflicts can arise if these geographic spaces are occupied by a specific language and groups which do not use this language are excluded. Examples include the Spanish town Morella investigated in LINEE, which presents itself almost exclusively as monolingually Valencian with regard to the municipal linguistic landscape, shops, bars and restaurants. The large group of Romanian immigrants working and living in this town, however, do not use this language (cf. Section 3.2.2). Furthermore, they opt for Spanish rather than Valencian if they have to decide which language their children should learn since Spanish is perceived as the more advantageous language due to its greater regional coverage (cf. Area Report B 2009: 7).

Within this scope, the LINEE sub-projects approach linguistic ideology as 'a set of beliefs about language articulated by users as a rationalisation of justification of perceived language structure and use' (Silverstein 1979: 193). Generally, language ideologies may be seen as naturally integrated into larger relationships since they are conceived of as 'a cultural system of ideas about social and linguistic relationships, together with their loading of moral and political interests' (Irvine 1989: 255) and as 'representations, whether explicit or implicit, that construe the intersection of language and human beings in a social world' (Woolard 1998: 3).

With regard to the impact of ideology on EM, the LINEE findings point towards a monolingual ideology underlying the national language policies in Switzerland, Spain and the UK, where the overriding objective is to measure the degree of integration of economic migrants through their knowledge of German, Castilian and English (cf. PoPa NL 2009: 13). At the supranational level, the European discourse on multilingualism appears to be strongly informed by the linguistic human rights discourse, although it appears to have become intermingled with socioeconomic ideologies in the more recent past. As a consequence, and against the background of these seemingly contradictory ideologies, stakeholders and policy makers find it difficult to come to terms with human rights and economic capitalisation at the same time (cf. Area Report A 2008: 7). The research results also point to the fact that the equality of languages constitutes an ideological guiding principle in more recent language policy at the European and the national level. At the same time, the principle of language equality also seems to constitute a substantial part of political correctness with little serious content. Furthermore, the LINEE findings suggest that language equality is not a commonly pursued principle, since at the European level, the judgment of the ECJ concerning the Groener case, where a Dutch woman was not admitted to work in an Irish educational setting for lack of adquate competences in Irish, illustrates that languages do not have to be treated equally in all circumstances if language equality runs counter to the socioeconomic realities in place. At the national level, and particularly in contested linguistic spaces where immigrant minorities live together with regional minorities, for example, in Catalonia, Wales or in Switzerland, it is, however, only the regional minorities which enjoy 'parital' status to a certain extent. Here, the language policies are directed towards the promotion of bilingualism among the regional minorities while the bi- and multilingual resources of the immigrant minorities are widely ignored and neglected (cf. Area Report B 2009: 41).

In the education area, ideology, although it appeared rather covert at first sight, proved to impact upon acquisition policies and attitudes concerning the learning and teaching of languages. The research findings reveal that the European school system remains by and large invested by monolingual ideologies, which proceed from the assumption that languages have to be acquired, as it were, native-speaker like. These ideologies are shared by headteachers, teachers, school staff, and partly also by the students themselves, while they contradict the ideologies that combine with the concept of multicompetence and of multilingualism in general (cf. Area Report C 2009: 40). Moreover, and particularly with regard to the students' use of ELF, the results point to ambiguous attitudes: young Europeans orientate positively towards ELF communication and consider it a useful and successful tool of multilingual communication while at the same time articulating a feeling of guilt when using English instead of other languages in multilingual situations. The LINEE findings also indicate that speakers of ELF evaluated fluent English very positively, which may be interpreted as referring to an underlying 'native speaker' ideology. Surprisingly, they also commented positively on their foreign accent in English since they considered their ELF primarily as a means to achieve their communicative goals (cf. Area Report C 2009: 15).

In the minority contexts of German and Hungarian in Transylvania, or of Ladinian in South Tyrol, the working of ideologies appears to be of a complex nature. Here, the so-called 'mother tongue' ideology stresses the importance of maintaining the minority language as a first language whereas the second language is generally seen as a prerequisite for social mobility and competitiveness in the economic spheres. The attitudes towards the languages are nevertheless dependent on the specific political context currently in place. In the German-speaking community in Transylvania, both languages – German and Romanian – are perceived as important and receive equally positive judgements, be it as first or as second language. In the context of the Hungarian Szekler Land (Transylvania), however, Romanian is closely related to the symbolic power and the dominance of the majority group, and is hence less positively evaluated. Here, the findings suggest that the discourse on the powerful state language triggers repulsive ideologies (cf. Area Report C 2009: 39).

Within the economy area, ideology figures as a component of the language management process and is thus closely related to language policy (cf. Area Report D 2009: 6). The findings at the European level suggest that profit-oriented multinational companies – as already mentioned in Section 3.2.3 – are interested in finding the most effective medium of communication, which is often assumed to be English. English is, ideologically speaking, mostly considered to be the language of business communication which moreover, and in contrast to other languages in these contexts, for example, Czech, German or Hungarian, appears to be used as an emotionally neutral variety (cf. Area Report D 2008: 14).

Comparing the four thematic areas, it is obvious that ideology connects very closely with LPP (cf. Section 3.2.6). In both the education and economy area, the link between these two variables is particularly evident. In the identity area, in contrast, general questions of power are paramount which are associated with the occupation of geographic units through the discursive reconfiguration of social spaces. Generally, the working of ideology is closely interrelated with other key components of multilingualism in all thematic areas.

Conclusion

From what has been said, it can be concluded that ideology is a component which participates in the theoretical frameworks of the thematic areas in various manners and degrees. The LINEE findings also highlight the multiple working of ideology in the intersection with other variables, and particularly in the relation with power and conflict. The close relationship between ideology and power in society may be derived from the fact that ideology provides for the particular meanings and assumptions which are explicitly or implicitly directed to the production or maintenance of specific power relations. More precisely, the ideologically loaded assumptions are mostly geared towards specific interests, which in turn are related to the respective positioning of the individuals and groups concerned, and hence to their access to power in society (cf. Rindler Schjerve & Vetter 2003; Woolard 1992: 242). The LINEE research also revealed quite a range of diversified and sometimes competing ideologies, such as the ideology of language equality, towards which particularly European language policy is oriented, or national monolingualism ideologies, which are primarily applied in national pedagogies or with regard to the multilingualism of minorities. The articulation of these ideologies brings about contested linguistic spaces in which the language concerned are entangled in competition with each other, or where certain less 'potent' languages are subordinate to others or even suppressed. It goes without saying that in these contexts, conflicts are likely to arise. Tourism management or the multilingual classroom are just two examples of such contested linguistic spaces in which competing ideologies have been identified within LINEE.

The LINEE findings also confirm that ideologies are articulated, reproduced and eventually transformed through discourse. Thus, the political speeches by the Commissioner for Multilingualism can be considered as a particular site for ideological investments (cf. Area Report B 2009: 16). Another important point is that the actual European language policies do not only result from the top-down working of official ideological discourses but also from bottom-up activities, such as those developed, for example, by teachers and schools when they delegate home language maintenance to the immigrant families as their exclusive responsibility. Thus, the findings concerning the promotion of multilingual repertoires in multilingual schools in Austria, Italy and the UK show that despite the willingness to encourage immigrant students to maintain their home language in all three countries, the teaching practices very rarely make adequate use of the existing multilingual competences of the immigrant students (cf. Area Report C 2009: 28–30).

The LINEE results also point to the intersection between ideology and culture, which at the same time implies some involvement of knowledge (cf. Section 3.2.1 and 3.2.5). Investigating, for example, tourism as a field of ideological struggle indicates that new power relations may evolve from the strategies of reformulating the history of the European past. These strategies imply the generation of knowledge according to which the given characteristics of a specific tourist site are accommodated to match the image of the desired pan-Europeanness. In this specific context, the ideological impact upon identity is more than evident since cultural tourism has strong effects on the formation of new regional and local identities. As to the formation of regional and local identities, the example of the Italian minority in Pula gives a detailed account of how the altered political situation and the changing ideologies associated with the dismay of ex-Yugoslavia and the constitution of a democratic Croatian state impact on the different ways in which the older and the younger generation experience their attachment and belonging to the city (cf. Area Report A 2009: 21).

As to the themes and topics which connect with ideology in the LINEE research, we can say that ideology is at play in all kinds of thematic foci that combine with multilingualism. The focus on the question of how ideology impacts on EM shows that the major topics defining the phenomenon of EM are ideologically invested. This holds true for the wide range of policy manouvres as they evolve from the European, national and local spheres. Ideologies also constitute a driving force in promoting multi-competence in the educational sphere, particularly when it comes to the promotion of multi-competence in the different contexts of the old and new minorities. Beyond this, ideology plays a decisive role in the controversial debates on citizenship. A major point is that the concept of EM lacks as yet a clear-cut definition. This opens the door to heterogeneous practices associated with ideologies that suit the interests and goals of the groups and actors involved in managing linguistic diversity. This is particularly evident when the ideology of social cohesion and democratisation clashes with the ideology of economic efficiency, or when the dominant ideology of cultural homogeneity at the national meets with the existing linguistic and cultural heterogeneity at the local level, or when under the impact of Europeanisation local and regional identities are reconfigured in order to live up to the ideological framework of 'unity in diversity'.

From the LINEE research, it can thus be concluded that ideology is a frequently hidden but nevertheless crucial component when conceiving of multilingualism and linguistic diversity. The LINEE findings indicate that ideology can be integrated into the conception of multilingualism in many different ways. Thus, it can be analysed in terms of a discursive reconfiguration of the social space in relation to governance or it can be seen as a prerequisite for language management and may be elaborated as a top–down or bottom–up force in displaying specific LPPs, and, most importantly, it must be considered as intrinsically related to attitudes. The different perspectives from which ideology can be approached in multilingualism research clearly show that from a theoretical point of view, ideology constitutes a tissue of diversified conceptual strands, which is also the reason why, in terms of a theoretical concept, ideology remains rather vague. The insights gained in the LINEE research concerning the theorisation of this concept, however, suggest that it is only through the relationship with the other variables that the working of ideology can be adequately assessed.

3.2.5 Knowledge

Theoretical concepts of knowledge

Within recent research, the notion of knowledge is strongly associated with models conceptualising society in terms of information and knowledge society. In this context, the concept of knowledge has been assuming increased importance particularly since the millennium. It cannot be overlooked, however, that knowledge is more than just a constitutive component of the knowledge society since, as Stehr (2005: 114) puts it, '[s]ocial groups, social situations, social interaction and social roles all depend on, and are mediated by, knowledge'. In this sense, knowledge constitutes an anthropological constant which forms the basic grounds of all social interaction and social order, and as such closely relates to power and social reproduction. Moreover, knowledge has become a major societal resource in more recent years, as is underlined by the notion of the knowledge society (cf. Stehr 2005: 117). This is most clearly expressed in the Lisbon strategy (cf. Lisbon Conclusions 2000), where the European Union has committed itself to the transition towards a KBS. In this framework, multilingualism and linguistic diversity have come to be seen as a valuable resource and a capital from which the evolving European KBS and its economy would derive their benefit.

Knowledge per se is a rather vague concept as there is actually no common agreement on how to conceptualise this term within the social sciences. Early approaches to knowledge stress its importance as an economic factor (cf. Drucker 1959) and point to technology, science and theoretical knowledge as a source of innovation (cf. Bell 1973). Within the scope of the knowledge society emerging in the past two decades, it has been stressed, however, that knowledge should be conceived as a multifaceted concept since it closely relates to all spheres of social life. Besides the conception of knowledge as an economic factor, it is increasingly associated with the constitution of authority and consequently with political and social struggles (cf. Stehr 2005).

At this point, a distinction needs to be made between knowledge society on the one hand and information society on the other hand. Whereas the term 'information society' is more closely related to information evolving from communication technologies, the term 'knowledge society' takes into consideration the complex social context including individual, emotional and cultural components (cf. Seiler 2008). Among the many attempts to conceptualise knowledge, Stehr (2005: 112) provides a relatively clear-cut and comprehensive definition by describing knowledge as a capacity to act. Most theoretical approaches to knowledge further stress the strong relation to language and discourse. Particularly, the relationship between knowledge and language is of relevance when it comes to multilingualism. In Foucault's terms, knowledge and language are dialectically interrelated since 'there is no knowledge without a particular discursive practice; and any discursive practice may be defined by the knowledge that it forms' (Foucault 2005: 197). According to Seiler (2008: 85), knowledge is articulated through language and cannot be approached otherwise, as it is through language that knowledge is materialised, stored and transferred.

Another important point that has been highlighted in recent research on knowledge is that knowledge mediates between the individual and the social domain, as individual knowledge is bound with social interaction and communication in so far as personal construction and activities involve collective and cultural knowledge in order to be socially meaningful (cf. Seiler 2008: 10).

Another salient issue in theorising knowledge concerns the relationship between explicit and tacit knowledge, which has been introduced by Polanyi (1966). Here, explicit knowledge refers to transmittable know-how which does not require direct experience, whereas implicit knowledge concerns direct experience which, however, cannot be communicated in any direct or codified way. According to Polanyi, explicit and tacit knowledge are nevertheless closely related since explicit knowledge requires tacit knowledge for its interpretation.

With a view to the EU, we can say that due to the EU's commitment to the KBS, knowledge has developed into a key concept with respect to the various processes of Europeanisation. As the recent investigation of this concept in the social sciences shows, knowledge as a capacity to act clearly exceeds the concept of information. Moreover, research is also closely investigating the interrelation of knowledge with language, discourse and the creation of power (cf. also Heller 2011). Important aspects of the current understanding of knowledge furthermore point to the mediation between individual and social components of knowledge, as well as to the link between implicit and explicit knowledge. As we will see, these relationships prove to be particularly relevant with regard to research on multilingualism.

Knowledge within LINEE

Within the LINEE project, knowledge is of major importance as a concept since LINEE was commissioned under the overall objective of priority 7 (European Commission's Work Programme 2004–2006), which comprised of mobilising European research capacities in order to develop an understanding of the European KBS (cf. LINEE Annex I 2006: 10). Hence, it is not surprising that knowledge came to figure more or less as an umbrella term in LINEE. Here, it appeared to be relevant in two ways: on the one hand, in the form of the knowledge that was required to develop an understanding of how multilingualism fosters the emergent KBS and how it impacts on the EU integration process and, on the other hand, in terms of the knowledge referred to when conceptualising EM as a complex process involving the implicit or explicit interaction of diverse individual, lingua-cultural, political, social and economic components.

Within LINEE research, knowledge is a category that both frames and at the same time intervenes into the engineering of multilingualism in the EU. It is obvious that the kind of knowledge investigated in LINEE is mostly associated with language, that is, as knowledge of languages or knowledge about language and language learning. In this respect, knowledge generally relates to multi-competence, which in turn represents a specific type of knowledge. Beyond this scope, LINEE research is also concerned with other kinds of knowledge, such as cultural knowledge in terms of 'shared memory', which is being created via cultural programmes, for example, the cultural routes programme. It is the goal of such a 'shared memory for all Europeans' to offer a new projection of the supranational society which assists in dealing with the wounds inflicted by history. This form of knowledge does not directly relate to language, although it is articulated through language (cf. Area Report A 2009: 11). Further manifestations of knowledge in terms of 'shared memories' which are investigated in LINEE include local knowledge sets associated with context-bound beliefs that facilitate or restrict certain multilingual practices, as this is, for example, the case in the traditionally multilingual and multicultural city of Pula (cf. Area Report A 2009: 39). Although questions relating to the constitution of power are not paramount in the LINEE sub-projects, they are nevertheless present in the results: Questions of power are involved if, for instance, certain histories are omitted in the 'shared memory for all Europeans' or if the local, context-bound knowledge in Pula accepts only certain predetermined forms of multicultural and multilingual practice while there is no room for other forms, like those resulting from immigrant practices.

The LINEE project thus adopts quite a clear position within research focusing on knowledge. It draws on a conceptualisation of knowledge which exceeds that of information by giving special attention to the social context including the individual, emotional and cultural components.

Various aspects which are central to the scientific debates are reflected in LINEE, such as the close connection between explicit and implicit knowledge, the link between the individual and the social component of knowledge or the close relationship between knowledge and discourse. Furthermore, it is particularly obvious that knowledge is associated with questions of power. Overall, we can observe that, regardless of the respective theoretical approaches and focuses advocated in LINEE, the project research makes reference to a common basis founded in the recent understanding of knowledge.

Knowledge in the thematic areas

Against the background of what has been said, it comes as no surprise that the specific kinds of knowledge investigated within LINEE call for different theoretical approaches. Within the identity area, knowledge is defined as pertaining to the *habitus* in the sense of Bourdieu (1986, 1990) since habitus is interpreted as the basic system of knowledge normally used by people in their daily lives, that is, knowledge which refers to the habituated practices of individuals. According to Bourdieu, the habitus is structured, and in turn also structures, social fields as spaces of conflict and competition since in these fields power is generated through the accumulation of various 'legitimate' forms of capital that are valued within the fields (cf. Area Report A 2009: 22). In other words, habitus in terms of durable, transposable, structured and structuring dispositions of individuals works together with the legitimate capital in a given social field. Thus, the LINEE research in the social urban space of Pula shows that the Pulezan habitus is, amongst other dispositions, also defined by the understanding of the *convivenza*, that is, the knowledge about the historical coexistence of Croatian and Italian citizens. In the urban social space, the habitus associating with *convivenza* appears to be critical since it is constructed through forms of capital including linguistic everyday practices that act in a form of symbolic domination. In Pula, these everyday language practices involve the varieties of Istro-Venetian, Chakavian and the urban Pula Croatian vernacular, while they exclude the languages of the immigrants into Pula such as Macedonian, Albanian, Hungarian and so on. At the same time, the everyday practices neither include standard Italian, which is the officially recognised minority language, nor standard Croatian as the state language; both standard Italian and Croatian are used only in very official and formal contexts (e.g. school). As a consequence, public spaces such as shops and even streets are appropriated by the dominant linguistic practices of the Pulezan habitus, whereas the habitus associated with languages of the other social actors is not represented in the multilingual space of the city (cf. Area Report A 2009: 23). From this it can be concluded that the officially proclaimed multiculturalism of Pula is perceived by the local population as *convivenza* between Pulezan Italians and Croats exclusively since these two communities share a traditional local knowledge. Thus, the many voices which are actually present in the city without, however, sharing the *convivenza* are silenced or marginalised. The example of the multilingual urban space in Pula illustrates that knowledge, in terms of Bourdieu's habitus, is closely related to issues of power and may thus produce conflicts caused by symbolic domination and inequalities.

Another example for the salience of knowledge within the Identity area is cultural tourism (see also Section 3.2.1). As the results of the first LINEE phase have shown, cultural tourism encourages European citizens to be active participants in the world of consumer-citizenship, where 'shared memory' is offered as a form of knowledge that could be experienced in new and attractive ways, emptied of specific historically charged meanings and refilled with new meanings in an endless play of difference and commonality (cf. PoPa EL 2008: 12).

In the second phase of the LINEE research, these findings were further elaborated within the governance approach (cf. Rose 1999). In this scope, governing European added value in terms of an ideally mixed set of cultures that convey the sense of 'unity in diversity' implies mobilising shared memory in order to create new ways of seeing and producing new governable spaces. On the one hand, the new governable space positions European citizens as consumers of history, of European values and of European lifestyles through the process of neutralising traumatic and conflicting aspects of the European history (cf. PoPa EL 2009: 9). On the other hand, the funding and application procedures enabling partners to cooperate within European cultural tourism highlight the difficulty of approaching the required knowledge at the appropriate time in the appropriate place. As there is a growing awareness that specialists are called for in order to deal with EU funded projects of this kind, a new category of professionals in the field of knowledge is actually in the making (cf. PoPa EL 2009: 17). These people require a specific kind of knowledge which includes language competences, that is, particularly English as the most widely used language, but they also need to 'speak the language of the EU bureaucracy' in order to secure funds (cf. Area Report A 2009: 12).

Throughout the policy area, knowledge in terms of a theoretical concept was not explicitly theorised, although knowledge figures in an implicit way in the various manifestations of multilingual management and planning, for example, whenever knowledge of language, knowledge about EM or knowledge about languages and culture is at stake. The implicit working of knowledge is particularly evident in the context of migrants in German-speaking Switzerland. Here, the diglossic situation between Swiss and standard German shows discrepancies concerning citizenship and integration of immigrants since there is no clear definition as to the degree of German language knowledge required on the part of applicant immigrants. Another example would be the knowledge transmitted concerning EM through the national print media in Austria and Switzerland. Here, only a small section of the EU discourse on multilingualism was perceived in Austria, where the print media focused primarily upon the appointment of L. Orban as EU Commissioner for Multilingualism, whereas the focus in Swiss print media, in turn, was primarily on educational issues of language policy (cf. Area Report B 2009: 21). Yet another example refers to the conflicts raised about public language signage in the regional minority contexts of the Czech Republic, Wales, Hungary and Croatia, where different sets of knowledge are at work as the specific minority–majority relationships in the respective countries vary from place to place. In contrast to the conflicts articulated in the Czech, English and Croatian contexts, bilingual signage in Hungarian Békéscsaba appears to be less conflicting. This can be explained against the background of Hungary's liberal minority policy and the commonly shared public opinion that the Slovak minority has the right to commemorate their important historical figures, and to install street signs and memorial sites in their own language (cf. Area Report B 2009: 36).

It goes without saying that knowledge figures prominently within the education area since education concerns the transfer and acquisition of knowledge. Moreover, there appears to be a strong relationship between knowledge and acquisition policies on the one hand and attitudes on the other (cf. Area Report C 2009: 4). In the educational context, attitudes are of major interest since they are a largely decisive factor in determining which languages are learned and how these are transmitted and acquired. Thus, investigations of pedagogic cultures in foreign language education indicate that despite the references made to the meaning of EM in influential policy documents, this perspective, and the knowledge it relates to, is not clearly implemented in practice in the context of teaching German in Italy, the UK and Hungary (cf. Area Report C 2008: 8). Another example would be teachers' beliefs, according to which the frequent use of the home language of immigrant pupils delays the learning of the host language and constitutes a source of confusion for the learners. At the same time, pupils do not, however, seem to share this belief since they make frequent reference to other languages in exploiting their multilingual repertoires, especially when comparing the different resources of their linguistic repertoires in the multilingual classroom (cf. Area Report C 2009: 23–25). These findings show that attitudes derive from specific forms of knowledge categorisation, and that they are basically of an evaluative nature as they explain differences and similarities between social groups creating and sustaining all kinds of ideologies. From this, it follows that attitudes may be seen as an instance in which the intersection of knowledge and ideology becomes particularly evident (cf. also Section 3.2.4).

Returning to the area-specific conceptualisation of knowledge, we see that within the economy area, knowledge is explicitly conceptualised as part of the KBS. It thus relates to the New Economy, which is defined as 'one that encourages its organisations and people to acquire, create, disseminate and use (codified and tacit) knowledge more effectively for greater economic and social development' (Dahlman & Andersson 2000: 32). Research within the economy area was strongly inspired by Williams (2005), who argues that knowledge and/or creativity may be maximised in contexts of linguistic diversity. Investigations carried out in Departments of Research and Development in large multinational companies show that the company personnel were most commonly composed of international teams and that due to their reporting, they used the languages based on the need at any given moment. This confirms that in contexts of this kind, the use of different languages appears to be regulated through implicit knowledge of how to appropriately correspond to the functional needs of specific interactions (cf. Area Report D 2009: 8–9).

The attempt to summarise the conceptualisations of knowledge in the LINEE perspective shows that the four thematic areas contained a clear focus concerning the explicitness of knowledge. In the identity area, knowledge is viewed in the framework of cultural tourism as an explicit prerequisite for the tourist consumption of European consolidated culture. In relation to the dynamics in multilingual cities, in contrast, it plays a rather implicit role in the habitus of the competing ethnic groups. In the other thematic areas, explicit knowledge is particularly paramount in terms of 'knowledge about languages', with implicit knowledge, however, taking effect especially in combination with attitudes and knowledge concerning the regulations of language usage. Despite the different priorities in the thematic areas, the LINEE research shows that the explicit and implicit components of knowledge are tightly interwoven, which is why these components and their combination require due attention.

Conclusion

Against the background of the KBS, knowledge is to be viewed as a process which, in a more or less covert way, contributes to the shaping of EM. As knowledge constitutes an important premise for the working of other salient key variables of multilingualism, it has to be taken into account in this function throughout the process of analysing EM.

Owing to the fact that knowledge is largely accessible through discourse, its intersection with discourse has to be carefully investigated in order to sound out the implications arising from multilingual knowledge and knowledge about multilingualism in discursive actions. The discussion of multilingualism implies knowledge of languages, knowledge about languages and knowledge of how to teach and to learn languages. From this, it follows that knowledge also intersects with multi-competence as it impacts on the way multi-competence is shaped through learning and teaching on the one hand, and through the attitudes individuals and collectives display when involved in the development of multi-competence on the other hand (cf. Section 3.2.7).

Furthermore, knowledge is also involved in the formation of identities since identity formation presupposes knowledge about the relation between the self and others while it also requires the knowledge of collective experiences concerning shared cultural spaces of belonging. This also explains why culture is a construct that relies heavily on knowledge in terms of commonly acquired knowledge sets and learned skills that provide for the knowledge how to act. In the LINEE research, this is particularly evident in the context of identity building and Europeanisation on the European level, where selected knowledge sets are produced in order to promote 'unity in diversity', or on the local level, where identification with the local setting in multilingual cities derives from the experience of being or not being included into the shared cultural spaces of the respective city.

Since discourse – as mentioned before – is so central to knowledge, it also constitutes a link which connects knowledge with ideology and with power and conflict. Ideology and power work through the creation of common sense in day-to-day routines, that is, they are based on shared cultural beliefs and on knowledge which derives from these routines. Knowledge produces power, and its power-generating nature is particularly evident when knowledge comes to be naturalised and is thus presented as something naturally given. This is best reflected in the national language ideologies, where the power these ideologies display is generated through common-sensical knowledge implying that the national language is a primordial and naturally 'given' entity which provides for the state's cultural and political unity. Moreover, power-generating knowledge is also included in all kinds of language political actions. Here, the knowledge may be either of a rather explicit or of a more tacit nature, depending on the focus to which the relative language political action is being directed. This is best illustrated in the case of Polish signage in the Czech border region with Poland. Here, explicit knowledge about political standards concerning regional minorities in Europe has led to a positive campaign for Polish signage. The compliance achieved with this policy among the Czech majority was largely influenced by their awareness of the ever-closer European integration and the important role conflict appeasement plays in this process.

As to the themes in which knowledge emerges with particular salience, we can say that in terms of a variable, knowledge figures explicitly within the context of multilingual classrooms, sociocultural integration and citizenship, or economic participation in the labour market, where 'knowledge of languages' represents a primary thematic concern. In other contexts, knowledge appears to remain rather implicit, for example, in those cases where knowledge refers to shared memories, cultural spaces and belonging like in multilingual cities, or in contexts where knowledge plays a role in terms of common beliefs and attitudes, such as in teachers' opinions about the immigrants' home languages or in policy makers' discrepant discourses on EM.

Moreover, the LINEE findings strongly support the distinction between tacit and explicit knowledge since it helps to uncover the hidden dimensions in the working of multilingualism. Here, for example, CoPs appear to play a significant role since they provide for the interactional grounds on which tacit knowledge is best produced and transferred. Thus, schools may figure as CoPs because they constitute a setting which fosters implicit or informal knowledge acquisition among teaching staff and students while at the same time these settings provide for formal education. The case of immigrant children of the first generation, for instance, shows that their coming into contact with teachers and classmates helps them in acquiring the basic prerequisites for participation in the host society. Erasmus students using ELF would be another example for CoPs. Here, the students interacting with one another with a specific aim develop rules for communication, such as code-switching and mixing, that do not comply with the rules of English native speakers (cf. Section 3.2.7). The tacit knowledge developed through these non-compliant rules results from the use of the diverse multilingual repertoires of the ELF speakers, who primarily strive for successful communication.

Against the background of the European KBS, LINEE research has hinted at the management of knowledge in the EU institutions and its implications which have so far hardly been recognised. At the same time, LINEE has shown how knowledge takes effect both on a local and on a supranational level. Furthermore, the LINEE results clearly indicate that the different dimensions in which knowledge becomes operative have to be closely investigated and that the power relations staged under the impression of a certain type of knowledge demand special attention.

In conclusion, we may say that the particular kind of knowledge that emerges from the LINEE research refers first of all to knowledge concerning languages and to components like experiences, awareness, beliefs, attitudes, know-how and knowing, or shared memories, which combine with language in different measures and degrees. As to knowledge concerning language(s), the LINEE findings underline that, while implicit and explicit knowledge of languages is an essential component within the KBS, the strength of these kinds of knowledge appears to be strongly dependent on the identity-specific ideological, political and economic aspects that impact upon the respective multilingual context. As to the implicit dimensions of knowledge, which mostly refer to 'knowledge about languages' in a very broad sense, the LINEE findings suggest that this kind of knowledge, which acts as a rather hidden but powerful force, requires particular attention. Overall, we can conclude that the effects of the interaction between implicit local knowledge sets and explicit knowledge management represent a large research desideratum since the implementation of the programme of EM will depend significantly on the successful interaction of these knowledge dimensions.

3.2.6 Language policy and planning

Theoretical concepts of LPP

Since the 1960s and particularly in the past two decades, LPP has been increasingly studied in the social sciences, where it has come to constitute a special research focus in various disciplines such as sociology of language, anthropology or political and legal sciences. LPP refers to a highly complex set of activities, and in terms of a concept it appears to be rather heterogeneous with respect to thematic focalisation, theorisation and terminology (cf. Spolsky 2004: ix; Wright 2004: 1). The growing interest in LPP and the various approaches related to LPP are to be seen in close relationship with the changing societal conditions over the past decades.

Whereas in the 1960s and 1970s, the focus was set on the issues of decolonisation, independence and nation-building connected with codification and language spread, and on acquisition policies, in the 1980s and early 1990s, the changes induced through globalisation, migration, and an increased awareness concerning linguistic diversity led to a critical analysis of the seemingly neutral LPP approaches. The critical stances taken in this context were mostly inspired by the work of Critical Theory and French cultural theorists. From the mid-1990s, the LPP endeavour concentrated both on the increased information flows and on the spread of English as a global language, and it also accounted for major geopolitical developments, for example, the demise of communism in the former Soviet Union and the subsequent processes of renationalisation and new nation-building.

In the early LPP phase, linguistic diversity was generally seen as an impediment to integration and to nation-building. However, in the 1990s, the LPP stance changed in that diversity came to be seen as something to be promoted, protected and preserved, particularly in relation to minority and endangered languages originating from indigenous peoples' or regional minorities' contexts and from migration. Here, the interest in aspects of power asymmetries, social disparity, inequality and discrimination combined with the issue of linguistic human rights in more recent years (cf. Ferguson 2006: 2–12; Wright 2004: 8–12; Skutnabb-Kangas 2008).

Given the wide range of thematic scopes, a common characteristics of LPP can be seen in that policy making and planning always connects with problems resulting either from tensions within or among speech communities or from conflicts caused through inadequate management of the language policies themselves.

LPP research focuses on the relationship between language practices in terms of agreed rules concerning appropriate language use, on the effort to modify or influence these practices and on the beliefs or ideologies that derive from or that influence these practices (cf. Spolsky 2004: 5). Ricento (2000 in PoPa NL 2009: 13), in adopting an even broader view of LPP, defines it as being 'concerned not only with official and unofficial acts of governmental and other institutional entities, but also with historical and cultural events and processes that have influenced, and continue to influence, societal attitudes and practices with regard to language use, acquisition and status.'

This shows that LPP is conceptualised in a variety of different ways, which again gives rise to considerable terminological heterogeneity. In many studies, a differentiation is made between 'language policy' in terms of the enactment of language political measures (e.g. legal, administrative and governmental), 'language politics' referring to the conceptual and ideological framing of language political measurements, and 'language planning', which points to the implementational aspects of language promotion (cf. also Haarmann 1988: 1666; Labrie 1996: 827–830). There is, however, no common agreement as to the relationship between 'language policy' and 'language planning' since in some studies 'language policy' is used as an umbrella term covering all dimensions of the policy and planning manouvres, whereas in others the inverse position is held, namely, the 'language policy' rather constitutes a subordinate field of the 'language planning' processes (cf. Paulston 2003: 475).

LPP can be defined as any activity that is explicitly or implicitly directed towards maintaining or transforming communicative practices in the interest of specific groups or of a polity. LPP is to be seen in close interaction with a complex set of social, economic, demographic, educational and cultural factors that determine how and why specific communicative practices are being maintained or transformed. Language policies of an explicit kind generally relate to regimes that derive from language legislation or from institutional or state intervention. Here, political management is targeted towards regulating the use and the status of specific languages within multilingual communities whereas in monolingual communities the respective regime mostly aims at spreading or promoting a specific standard variety or at regulating and controlling discursive orders in the case of totalitarian regimes. Language policies of an implicit kind are far more complicated in that the boundaries between active intervention and laissez-faire practices are blurred with ideology coming into play as a major driving force (cf. Rindler Schjerve & Vetter 2003: 48–49). Ideology in terms of both language ideologies and larger scale ideologies (cf. Section 3.2.4) plays an important role in all kinds of language political activities since ideologies impact upon how status and functions of specific languages are transformed or maintained in a community (cf. Rindler Schjerve & Vetter 2008). Since it impinges on communication, LPP also plays a crucial role with respect to the distribution of linguistic power and resources since the use of, and the value assigned to, a specific language generally reflects the power and resources to which its speakers have access in a community. The access to power and resources through language, which is explicitly or implicitly regulated, is particularly evident where two or more languages are bound up in asymmetrical or hierarchical relationships of status and function, as is the case in minority–majority settings in multilingual communities, in historically submerged multi-ethnic state societies or in the European institutional settings.

LPP within LINEE

Within the LINEE research, LPP appears to be a comprehensive category which, unlike the other key variables, points first and foremost to the pragmatic dimension of planning and managing EM. Here, LPP represents a major driving force which explicitly or implicitly impacts on the existing linguistic diversity in the EU and which intrinsically pervades all thematic areas. The LINEE WPs conceptualise LPP in different ways and manners depending on their specific research focus. Thus, LPP is, for example, designed as a dynamic and personalised approach when policy makers at the EU level are under investigation or the theoretical framing draws upon Bugarski (1992) and Blommaert (1999) when immigrants' cultural inclusion is at the focus or alternatively LMT (cf. Nekvapil 2006) is used in order to illustrate how problems concerning public signage in multilingual cities are managed and resolved or in order to show how multinational companies solve their communication problems. Although the individual LINEE approaches are not entirely compatible, they share some characteristics. Thus, LPP is generally seen as a discursive process which integrates different levels of aggregation (macro–meso–micro) by operating bottom-up and top-down, and which is intrinsically related to ideology and to power and conflict.

Conceiving of LPP as a discursive process implies that LPP is a multi-layered phenomenon (cf. Section 3.2.2) and that the specific context from which LPP evolves has to be taken into due account. This was particularly evident within the policy area, where at the European level, with a focus on the social actors who engaged in language planning or policy making, the specific LPP context appeared to steer people's conceptualisations about language policy and hence their contributions to language planning. Thus, the concept of European citizenship and conflicting discourses on multilingualism viewing it as an economic capital, on the one hand, and as a human rights issue, on the other hand, reveal that there are inherent contradictions and unresolved tensions within the EU policy-making bodies which render the planning of multilingualism inconsistent and incoherent. In the scope of LMT, LPP is also focused on when discursive processes are concerned since LMT foregrounds the negotiation of problems concerning language at both the level of discourse and the level of the linguistic system. That is to say, from the LMT point of view, the outcome of an LPP process represents a fairly complex adjustment design which results from a language management process targeted towards solving a language-related problem. The management process starts when the participants not only begin to pay attention to language but also evaluate language phenomena. Management also includes further phases as the participants may deal with the problems both by designing solutions to these problems and by implementing these solutions.

The investigation of the signage language policies in the multilingual cities of Český Těšín in the Czech Republic, Békéscsaba in Hungary, Llanelli and Cardiff in the UK and Pula in Croatia shows that, for example, in Český Těšín (CZ), social conflicts provoked by the signage policy of the Polish minority were successfully negotiated through internal policy-oriented communication and learning, and through communicating adjustment and implementation problems to the appropriate authority. Although Polish signage had largely been perceived as a waste of municipal money on the part of the Czech tax-payers, it became the object of bilingualisation in compliance with the ongoing Europeanisation process, in the course of which the standards as laid down in the *European Framework Convention* (cf. Framework Convention 1995) and the *Minority Charter* (cf. Charter RML 1992) were implemented in the Czech Republic (cf. Area Report B 2009: 34–35).

Furthermore, conceptualising LPP as a discourse-based and multi-layered phenomenon entails that the different activities which contribute to LPP correlate with different levels of aggregation. From the empirical results in all four thematic areas, we may conclude that LPP operates dialectically as a top-down and bottom-up phenomenon. Research carried out on foreign language education policies in Italy, Serbia and Romania underlines that this type of LPP results from the interplay between top-down national policy making and bottom-up forces on the regional or local level (cf. Area Report C 2008: 8). At present, it is assumed that the top-down dimension involves measures and activities which evolve at a highly aggregated macro-sociological level, whereas the bottom-up aspect relates to individual or small-group interactions that are generally identified with the sociological meso- or micro-perspective. Although the macro–meso–micro distinction in LPP has been a strongly debated issue not only within LINEE but also elsewhere (e.g. at the Sociolinguistic Symposium 17 'micro and macro connections', Amsterdam April 2008, cf. Rindler Schjerve & Vetter 2008), it cannot be ignored that the multilevel approach appears to be a useful analytical tool since each of these levels is negotiated differently and serves different goals. While the macro-LPP approach allows for a large-scale comparative perspective, the meso- and micro-approach focuses on contextually bound activities. Within LINEE, all approaches to LPP integrate different levels of aggregation, although, depending on their research goals, they tend to foreground certain levels.

Thus, the study of multilingualism policy at the European level stressed the macro-dimension of LPP during the first LINEE phase, whereas the policy scope in the second LINEE phase focused on the nature and construction of spontaneous or informal language political activities in public contexts. Here, investigations concentrated on lay constructions of individuals' positions in relation to multilingualism within focus groups and on the reception of EU language political efforts in national print media in Bern, Vienna and Prague.

Similarly, the LMT approaches emphasised management at a number of levels, such as the individual level, or the level of associations, social organisations, media, economic bodies, educational institutions, and local or central governments in different countries. The language management cycle (Micro Macro Micro) is supposed to originate from the micro-dimension, that is, from particular interactions as simple management. The language problems can then be transferred to the macro-level, that is, to various institutions in terms of organised management. Finally, the results of organised management may in turn have a bearing on particular interactions at the micro-level. Thus, the LINEE study of how multinational companies negotiate and manage linguistic diversity in the light of the Knowledge Economy shows that most large companies do have an official corporate language although it is a matter of common sense when and with whom it is used (cf. Area Report D 2009: 8).

Concerning the different levels of aggregation, the results gained in the area-specific research seem to sustain that the bottom-up and top-down LPP processes go along with the shaping of different identities. Thus, identities that are constructed in top-down LPP processes, such as the European identity, generally involve interaction contexts which differ from those in which the target groups of the top-down LPP normally evolve their local identities. The separate sites of identity formation may be one reason why the top-down policies are eventually perceived by the target groups at the bottom as something that is imposed or ordained by the higher state or the EU (cf. Rindler Schjerve & Vetter 2008). Therefore, it comes as no surprise that in the Istrian context of identity formation, the local varieties have become a powerful means of resistance against identification patterns as they are commonly propagated by national and European policy making (cf. Area Report A 2008: 8). Yet another example would be the fact that European cultural policies, in selecting the elements that are promoted in cultural tourism, are not free from antagonisms as they reflect the discrepancies between the demands on the local level and those established at the European level. Thus, in the bilingual city of Pula, the Italian language does not even figure on the tourist website, and similarly in one of Gdansk's largest museums, no translation into German is provided (due to the city's historical background), although multiculturalism and tolerance figure prominently as European values in the city's cultural promotion of tourism (cf. Area Report A 2009: 11–13).

From the LINEE research, it can also be derived that LPP is intimately linked to ideology and power and conflict. Regarding ideology, it has already been mentioned that two dimensions of ideology generally appear to be merged when it comes to LPP, namely, larger scale ideologies that are connected with more taxing relations of social power pertaining to modernisation, market-driven freedom, nation building and so on, on the one hand, and language ideologies which guide communicative behaviour in general on the other hand. Here, it was argued that the discursive layering of ideological representation would be identified through the articulation of discourses on language since these discourses derive from deeper ideological positions on specific social issues or from competing interests of social groups (cf. Section 3.2.4).

Concerning the working of ideologies in LPP, one of the most prominent language ideologies inspired by structuralist thinking argues in favour of all languages being equal. In this sense, the EU's institutions espouse the fundamental principle of equal treatment of official and working languages. The investigation of how the meaning of EM is shaped through policy making shows that the ideology of 'language equality' does indeed shape the political discourse at the EU level. However, the implementation of the ideology of 'language equality' as designed in the law in books (prominent documents, legal texts, etc.) fails due to the socioeconomic barriers, that is, the lack of political and economic power of the many less widely used European languages which do not fulfil the status and function of the major languages like English or French. An apt example in this respect is provided by the already mentioned action of Christina Kik against the Office for Harmonisation in the Internal Market (Trademarks and Desings) (cf. Section 3.2.2). Kik argued that the language regime of this Office, where a distinction was made between the languages of the Office and the other languages, was unlawful. The LINEE investigation concerning the judgement of the ECJ on language use in the Kik case confirms, once more, that languages do not have to be treated equally in all circumstances (cf. Area Report B 2009: 13). Thus, the ideological stance of 'language equality' is at the same time confronted with discrepant socioeconomic inequalities. The results derived from the LINEE research hence underline that the transfer of the fundamental principle of equal languages from the structuralist paradigm into the socioeconomic reality of EM policy is not entirely possible.

The ambiguities of the ideological principle of 'language equality' are also reflected in the impact of 'new' migration on contested linguistic spaces and its implications for national language policies in Spain (Comunitat Valenciana), the UK (Wales) and Switzerland (Grisons). Contested linguistic spaces have been referred to above as regions in which immigrants come to live together with the historical regional minorities. In all three cases, the dominant ideology underlying national language policies in these countries was directed towards valuing the languages equally. However, when dealing with minority languages, language policy in this respect appeared to concern itself overwhelmingly with regional minority languages rather than the languages of the immigrant minorities, and indeed constructed them as belonging to distinct and differing categories. Here again, the principle of language equality is not reflected within the *de facto* policy measures (cf. Area Report B 2009: 41). On the other hand, the results obtained from the investigation of conflicting language signage policies in the European cities mentioned above showed that the LPP measures concerned with the management of multilingual landscapes are not always based on one and the same ideology. In this context, it appears that in some cases, pursuing the equality of languages can be a motivational basis of the political management while in other cases, granting ethnic minority rights are to the fore – always depending on the socioeconomic and political background of the city under investigation.

As to the influence of larger scale ideologies on LPP, the LINEE results show that national and regional policies are implicitly driven and constrained by the economic, social and cultural priorities of dominant political constituencies. Thus, for example, the so-called 'mother tongue +2' strategy is embedded in a wider discourse on the mobility and employability of European citizens and is presented as a key instrument in promoting economic integration (cf. Research Area Report B 2008: 7–8).

The last point to be mentioned is the highly conflicting nature of LPP. Here, it can be concluded that European policy is devised to avoid or to solve inter-ethnic conflicts, while at the same time it may also bring about new conflicts.

This is the case when national minority policies are sustaining the survival and promotion of regional minorities while, at the same time, neglecting the multilingual and multicultural demands of the migrant communities who have settled down in the historical minorities' regions. The economic migrant communities examined in the Valencian community, in Wales, and in Chur, Ilanz and the Surselva regions are residents in areas in which the use of more than one language is sanctioned by national legislation. Research showed, however, that support for the home languages is fairly weak in all three research locations. Regional language policies have a simple binocular approach looking only at the interrelation of the dominant and regional languages rather than at the relationships of a number of languages that coexist in the territory. The overriding objective of language policy in all three countries is to facilitate the integration of the economic migrants into the host community by means of encouraging them to learn the languages which effectively form the dominant languages in these areas: Castilian, English and German. Language becomes the prime tool of the integrative process since a certain level of competence in the dominant language is considered a guarantee of integration and acceptance of sociocultural norms on the part of the migrants. Nevertheless, the premise of bi-directionality, that is, mutual accommodation between migrant and receiving community, appears to be rarely followed up. Integration is thus so one-sided that it can resemble assimilation. The conclusion of the research conducted is that current language policies have great difficulty in adapting to newly emerging patterns of migration (cf. PoPa RLL 2009: 21).

On the other hand, research conducted within the Vietnamese community in the Czech Republic shows that in some cases, there might even be no LPP concerning migrants at all. Although the Vietnamese community in the Czech Republic is the third largest immigrant community in the country and the largest non-European immigrant community, the policy makers have so far paid little attention to its integration into the Czech society. Although the second generation is doing extremely well on the path of integration, the unwanted consequence of this process is, however, a partial, or in few cases even total loss of the Vietnamese mother tongue (cf. PoPa RLL 2009: 21).

Moreover, the study of the communication efforts relating to language policies in the EU and their reception in national print media in Austria and Switzerland indicates that there is a gap between the discourses on multilingualism at the supranational level and their reception in the national media. At the level of the EU, multilingualism is dealt with in association not only with social issues such as economy, education or translation/interpreting but also with issues concerning other macro-topics such as culture, the internet, or migration. Interestingly, it is only a small section of the current EU discourse on multilingualism that is actually perceived in Austrian and Swiss media (cf. Area Report B 2009: 21).

LPP within the thematic areas

As to the salience of LPP within the thematic areas of the LINEE research, it can be said that LPP interferes in variable degree and measure in the building of European, national and regional identities. Identity building on these levels always relates to either explicit or implicit political action of a specific kind; it takes place, for example, when cultural policy programmes are enacted, when promotional strategies of cultural tourism are at stake or when repulsive identification patterns evolve from the tension between the global and the local.

Apart from the policy area, where LPP forms the primary theme, LPP also figures prominently within the education area since second and third language learning appears to be strongly influenced by language policies on all the European, national and regional levels. This is particularly evident when it comes to the discrepancy between European educational programmes which promote multilingualism in terms of a mainstreamed policy and national pedagogic cultures which mostly keep retaining the traditionally monolingual pedagogy in their foreign language learning strategies (cf. PoPa NL 2008: 8–9).

In the economy area, LPP impacts implicitly and explicitly on the management of linguistic diversity in the multinational companies. It also has a bearing on the integrational efforts of migrant communities into the Knowledge Economy, for example, in the case of Vietnamese immigrants in the Czech Republic, where there is still no effective language acquisition policy for immigrants. The same applies to the African and French speaking sub-Saharan immigrants in Germany, where the learning of the language of the host country is mostly left to the initiatives of the individuals, with the result that these people end up in low-level jobs in which their multilingual resources are not in demand (cf. Area Report D 2008: 11–12). Furthermore, we cannot fail to notice the influence of LPP on the economic sphere, particularly in cases where problems are concerned that relate to linguistic diversity and are relevant to the free movement of workers, goods and know-how throughout Europe. This is clearly verified by the judgements on language use by the ECJ concerning language as an employment criterion for certain positions, for instance, in the already mentioned case of the Groener lawsuit (cf. Section 3.2.4), or as a medium for labelling products launched in the single market, as in the Goerres and the Piageme cases, in which the court prohibited fining the product sellers for not using the national languages German and Flemish, respectively (cf. Area Report D 2008: 10).

Conclusion

As the above discussion has shown, LPP is an important dimension with regard to the preservation of linguistic diversity and to the promotion of multilingualism. However, the LINEE findings also clearly indicate that the evolvement and analytical development of LPP have to be seen in close relation to the core variables of multilingualism identified in LINEE. In this context, discourse, ideology, and power and conflict appear to be strongly correlating factors in the management of linguistic diversity (cf. Sections 3.2.2, 3.2.4, 3.2.8). Identity, it has been said, is another important force which directly interrelates with LPP. Since identity is intimately intertwined with language, it can be assumed that specific language political actions are associated with the production of specific identities (cf. Section 3.2.3). Given the intimate relationship between culture and language, the LINEE findings suggest that there is also a strong connection between LPP and culture. This is primarily reflected in the ambiguities that tend to exist between the monolingually focused LPPs at the national level and European LPP, which is targeted towards multilingualism (cf. Section 3.2.1). Moreover, LPP implies knowledge in diverse forms and guises, for example, explicit and transferable knowledge when it comes to acquisition policies, or tacit knowledge in the form of attitudinal or ideological patterns which impact upon the selection and use of specific languages (cf. Section 3.2.5). LPP related to multilingualism also presupposes multi-competence, particularly when acquisitional strategies are addressed through which the multilingual repertoires of the European citizens are to be fostered and enhanced (cf. Section 3.2.7).

As to the thematic focalisation of LPP, it can be said that the policy-making processes at the European, national and regional level form a major theme within the LINEE research. These processes are of primary interest when it comes to the integration of minority language communities into the diverse national and regional contexts. Here, the focus is on regional and immigrant minorities and on the different strategies which these minorities develop in order to cope with the policies in place. The LINEE findings show, however, that these policies prove to be rather discrepant and ambiguous in defining their standards: There is a clear divide between the regional minorities policies in the old and the new member states resulting from the conditionality for accession formulated in the Copenhagen Criteria (cf. Section 1.2.2). At the same time, as regards integrative management, these policies prove to be discriminating against migrants when it comes to language equality and to the right of these minorities 'to speak or to have voice'. It goes without saying that in the context of immigrant minorites, citizenship is a key issue.

LPP is also at the focus when identity and language negotiation, for example, in the case of public signage, are investigated in the context of multilingual cities. Moreover, second and third language acquisition in diverse national and regional school settings appears to be strongly influenced by LPP since in many cases the objective of promoting EM appears to be hampered by monolingually oriented pedagogies. LPP of a more implicit and bottom-up nature is of relevance when linguistic diversity is managed in the contexts of large multinational companies and immigrant labour forces since, in general, the actors in these marketplaces adapt their multilingual repertoires to the communicative requirements of the contexts they are working in.

Against the background of what has been said, it can be concluded that LPP is to be considered a salient variable which intimately intersects with all kinds of themes that relate to EM. This, it may be argued, comes as no suprise since EM as a manifestation of the existing linguistic and cultural diversity and as a promotional goal is the object of political planning which originates from different actors on diverse levels, and is supported by partly varying sociocultural circumstances and interests. From the LINEE perspective, LPP can be defined as a complex variable which appears to be entrenched in multi-layered discursive practices which come to be operative on different levels of societal aggregation.

As the LINEE findings show, these different levels of aggregation represent a particular challenge for EM policy since the policy making at the different levels is not always compatible with regard to their varying interests and requirements. In that sense, the goal of policy making on a supranational level could run counter to the objectives and needs on the national and local level. Thus, EU policy is frequently perceived as a top-down process imposed from above and largely ignoring the reality of the people concerned. The results also indicate that the local and national level only takes note of EU language policy to a limited extent and that identifying with European diversity is accompanied by fears relating to the loss of one's own identity. The insights gained in LINEE regarding the focus on LPP confirm that an integrative policy of diversity – as successful as it may intend to be – is not defined by coexistence but by the dialectics of top-down and bottom-up processes, with particular consideration being required for the factor of different identifications combining with the top-down and the bottom-up design, respectively.

The centred investigation of LPP furthermore shows that on all levels, European language policy appears to be quite sustainably governed by ideological factors influencing policy making in the most diverse ways. Here, it emerges that the discrepancies looming in supranational politics basically arise from the ideological contradictions of the objectives of the EU, which are educationally egalitarian on the one hand and economically market-oriented on the other hand. However, it also becomes apparent that the resistance which the naturally practised multilingualism of minorities frequently meets in the member states can be explained by the adherence to the traditional ideology of the nation state, in which multilingualism is perceived as a threat or disruptive factor of the existing unity.

The final point which should be included in the inferential evaluation of LPP is the fact that LPP plays a crucial role with respect to the distribution of sociolinguistic power since LINEE has shown that both the political activities and the objectives and values thus transported always have a bearing on the function and the status of the languages concerned and their speakers. This is particularly evident in the example of the signage policies in the context of regional minorities. Furthermore, LPP is also constantly associated with tensions and conflicts, on the one hand, because the political activities intervene in existing conflicts and tensions and, on the other hand, because they can also cause or reinforce these through inadequate measures. The practical implementation of the language regime in the EU institutions provides a striking example in this context.

Concluding, we can say that the centred view of LPP in the LINEE research once more shows that in the face of the diverse and partly also antagonistic interests and objectives controlling the present EM policy, it needs to be kept in mind that particularly those aspects of LPP which fundamentally contribute to shaping it (such as ideology, identity or power and conflict) have to be taken into account in the respective process of planning and designing EM policy. This is most essential if this policy is to comply with its mission of establishing 'unity in diversity'.

3.2.7 Multi-competence

Theoretical concepts of multi-competence

In contrast to the other key concepts, multi-competence is very new. The term 'multi-competence' was coined by Vivian Cook to refer to 'the compound state of a mind with two languages' (Cook 1991: 112). In defining multi-competence, Cook (1993) argues that persons who know two or more languages are fundamentally different from monolingual speakers. In his view, '[t]he L2 user's mind is different as a whole' (Cook 1993: 3) in at least four respects. According to him, multi-competent people differ from monolinguals in their knowledge of the first language in that two languages are stored in their minds rather than one. Thus, it can be assumed that the coexistence of two languages affects the first language. The second point is that the knowledge of the second language is also assumed to differ from monolingual knowledge of this language. Third, the language awareness of multi-competent speakers is supposed to be different from the one of monolingual speakers. And the fourth point is that the cognitive processes within the multilingual mind differ from those in the monolingual mind (cf. Cook 1992: 557; Cook 1993: 3–4). In Cook's terms, the relationship between L1 and L2 can be viewed as an 'integration continuum' (Cook 2003: 10) which ranges from the total separation of the language systems to interconnection and to total integration into a single mental super-system.

Cook, however, is not the first to point to the kind of phenomena associated with multi-competence. In referring to Weinreich's (1953) research on language contact and to Bailey's (1973) polylectal grammars, he identifies 'multi-competence overtones' (Cook 1993: 6), and in pointing to early research in second language acquisition, he puts forward that in some approaches, such as that of Corder's (1967), language learning has already been detached from striving for native speaker's language knowledge. The impact of Cook's approach to multi-competence is that it has challenged the monolingual bias by conceiving of multilingual speakers as distinct language users in their own right who differ substantially from monolinguals. Thinking of multilinguals as multi-competent rather than failed native speakers allows for a more positive view on them (cf. Hall et al. 2006: 222). Following Jessner (2007), there is a tendency to integrate the main conceptual strands of multi-competence into multilingualism research, although the actual impact of the concept on teaching and learning contexts remains low.

However, Cook's model of multi-competence is not the only one to challenge the monolingual bias. There are many other models which, in one way or another, familiarise with multi-competence as they question the monolingual norm (cf. Hufeisen 2005). Within the wide range of different approaches, some studies figure with particular salience, such as Grosjean's (1982, 1985) work on bilingualism and on the language mode or the dynamic model of multilingualism (DMM) developed by Herdina and Jessner (2002).

Grosjean, for example, objects to conceptualising bilingualism in terms of double monolingualism and describes the state of activation of the languages in the multilingual speaker as a continuum that goes from the monolingual to the multilingual mode. With the DMM, Herdina and Jessner provide a holistic view in which 'the presence of one or more language systems influences the development not only of the second language but also the development of the overall multilingual system' (Herdina & Jessner 2002: 5).

Moreover, the model proposed by Cook has not only inspired most recent research but has also been taken up and developed further by other scholars. Thus, Hall *et al.* (2006), in criticising Cook for not having questioned the notion of language as a discrete and separate system, propose a usage-based approach to multi-competence. This approach conceives of 'language knowledge as provisional, grounded in and emergent from language use in concrete social activity for specific purposes that are tied to specific communities of practice' (Hall *et al.* 2006: 235). Kecskes (2010), on the other hand, criticises the strong focus on usage. In his definition of multi-competence, structure and usage are equally important and multi-competence is seen in terms of a dynamic combination of conceptual changes, bidirectional influences and of up and down movements within the developmental continuum (cf. also Kecskes & Cuenca 2005; Kecskes & Papp 2002).

From this perspective, we can thus say that the term 'multi-competence' encompasses a debate on the specific features of the linguistic repertoire of multilingual individuals. Although this debate has only recently gained momentum, it supplies a range of different concepts. All these concepts share the assumption that due to the manifold relations between the languages of multi-competent language users, their language use should not be measured against the standards applying for native speakers.

Multi-competence within LINEE

The contribution of the LINEE project to the debate on multi-competence follows on from the scientific debate mentioned and leads to an enhancement of the concept. It is particularly within the education area that major efforts were undertaken to reconceptualise multi-competence. Starting out from Cook's work, the research within the education area suggested developing a broader definition of multi-competence (cf. Franceschini 2010). Conceptualising multi-competence within this context went beyond the understanding of multilingualism as a mere agglomeration of several languages, as the conceptualisation developed a culturally, historically and dynamically determined scope for multilingual communication. Thus, Cook's definition of multi-competence with a primary focus on psycholinguistic aspects was broadened by integrating sociolinguistics and educational aspects that embrace the embedded and contextualised adaptive abilities of multilingual speakers in their daily interactions. The definition elaborated within LINEE points to the fact that '[...] multi-competence, i.e. the knowledge of more than one language in the mind, is part of the individual capacity of the person and develops in interaction with his/her social or educational environment. Multi-competent individuals make use of their linguistic knowledge when interacting within a range of linguistic settings, including both multilingual and monolingual situations. Multi-competence, or multilingual competence, is thus at the same time a tool and a state and relates to the complex, flexible, integrative and adaptable behaviour which multilingual individuals display. A multi-competent person is therefore an individual with knowledge of an extended and integrated linguistic repertoire who is able to use the appropriate linguistic variety for the appropriate occasion' (definition given in RePa WP8 2008: 7 taken up in Area Report C 2008: 5–6).

In this definition, which resembles the concept of 'languaging' as developed by Jørgenson (2008a) and Phipps (2007), the knowledge of multi-competent language users is dynamically grounded in the actual linguistic practices in which they engage. Following Dewaele and Pavlenko (2003), the studies within the education area suggest that multi-competence should be conceived as a dynamic, ever evolving system which is useful for describing the linguistic processes and the linguistic behaviour of learners who exhibit competences in more than one language. In accordance with Hall et al. (2006), multi-competence is concerned with the expansion of managing the variability potentially offered by the linguistic repertoire and is linked to language use in CoPs (cf. Area Report C 2009: 3). The LINEE research within the education area strongly underlines that simply adding languages does not fulfil the claim of multi-competence since the focus within multi-competence is on the ability of the multi-competent speaker to take advantage of a wide range of interconnections between the languages. As Area Report (cf. Area Report C 2009: 42) puts it, one can be multilingual without having the ability of adaptation with respect to the linguistic, interactional and cultural aspects pertaining to specific communication settings. This means that one can be multilingual without being multi-competent at the same time.

It can thus be concluded that the approach to multi-competence which has been developed within the education area clearly accounts for the educational and sociolinguistic dimension of multi-competent speakers and learners. As the theoretical focus developed in LINEE concentrates on communicative behaviour which includes the dynamic and flexible use of the multilingual resources, it may be concluded that in contrast to the conception of multi-competence as coined by Cook, multi-competence in LINEE is mainly directed towards a usage-based approach to multilingualism.

Multi-competence in the thematic areas

As mentioned above, it is particularly the education area that was concerned with the concept of multi-competence within LINEE. However, the stance taken in this area remained, as it were, isolated since it did not entirely correspond to the research focus in the work of the other areas. In these contexts, notions such as 'plurilingual repertoire', 'plurilingual competence' or 'bilingualism' were widely used instead since the ability of adaption, which is particularly pertinent to multi-competence, was not at the very focus of these studies. At this point, it should be stressed, however, that the results attained in these areas suggest that multi-competence might be taken as a valuable framework for interpreting the findings in a more flexible and dynamic way.

Within the identity area, for example, notions such as 'plurilingual competence' or 'bilingualism' were used when the command of two or more languages in individuals was referred to. However, from the perspective of multi-competence, the example of Polish immigrants in Szeged shows that in adapting to local Hungarian, these speakers perceive the need to learn the local language. The interesting point is that whereas their Polish accent appeared to be a matter of concern at the very beginning of their stay in Hungary, at a later stage they had come to accept it as a main feature pertaining to their Polish identity. This suggests that these speakers implicitly share the main assumption of multi-competence, that is, in adapting to Hungarian they still remain speakers of Hungarian in their own right (cf. Area Report A 2009: 29).

Within the policy area, the 'plurilingual repertoire' is at the centre of the political discourse. It is so to speak a widely acknowledged and therefore more or less tacit prerequisite for the EU citizens' multilingual achievement and for their participation in the KBS. The debate about the 'legitimate' plurilingual repertoire raises the question from which pool of languages citizens should make their choices. Here, the LINEE findings reveal that the lacking consensus with respect to the 'plurilingual repertoire' gives rise to contradictions when talking about multilingualism within the EU language policies, and particularly in those contexts where integrating the existing multi-competent resources of the immigrant and regional minorities is at the centre of the debate (cf. Area Report B 2009: 17).

Within the education area, the study of ELF speakers in an Erasmus community showed that these speakers are multi-competent communicators who use various strategies for communicating and learning, such as code-switching, repetition and paraphrasing, to ensure smooth communication, to maintain social relations, or to signal membership in a community of multilingual speakers. Multi-competent ELF speakers also conduct a substantial amount of negotiation work to support each other's contributions and acknowledge the co-participants' sociocultural backgrounds. The ELF speakers thus proved to be multi-competent multicultural speakers who invest in sharing, learning and expanding their plurilingual repertoires (cf. Area Report C 2009: 11–15).

Moreover, the research on multilingual immigrant students in England, Italy and Austria revealed that multi-competent students are more aware of their sociolinguistic environment and more interested in learning languages than monolingual students. While the multi-competent immigrant students seem to be well aware of how the languages they know may help them in the learning process, teachers, however, do not seem to be sufficiently informed about the role of prior language knowledge in the learning process. As a consequence, references to students' already existing multilingualism during language classes are rather sparse. The research findings concerning the attitudes in this sample complement this result: the interviewed students project themselves as predominantly open towards the use of other languages in the school context and do not see any problem if their colleagues are using different languages. In contrast to this, teachers, when asked about their students' attitudes towards the home languages, report presumed shame on the part of these students (cf. Area Report C 2009: 16–30). The findings of the investigation of language use and the values accorded to the languages in minority schools in Italy, Hungary, Romania, Serbia and Slovakia revealed that concerning the teaching of English in the multilingual classrooms, teachers support an 'English Only' monolingual attitude. This is in contrast with approaches to multi-competence, and it also contradicts the students' tendency to avoid English for explanation in the classroom where, instead, those languages are preferred in which the students are more proficient or to which they are most frequently exposed (cf. Area Report C 2009: 39–40).

To a certain degree, multi-competence also figures within the economy area, where it relates to the multilingual repertoire when the requirements of the single market in general, and of specific economic settings in particular, raise the demand for a flexible use of foreign languages. The findings in this area suggest that the multilingual scope should be widened beyond Europe since globalisation linked with huge migration flows calls for increased management of linguistic diversity within the EU. Research findings within the economy area underline that increased language diversity due to migration and heightened flexibility on the labour markets do not per se pay in terms of an added value as long as diversity is not sustained by strategies of increasing language multi-competence. The Area Report critically states that linguistic and economic processes are discrepant in that the economy is driven by rapid changes whereas linguistic contexts such as the promotion of multilingualism develop more slowly. This discrepancy makes flexibility and mobility based on multilingual competence a necessary condition for the migrants' survival, as they may stay in the host country or be pushed back to their home countries or even be pushed or pulled to other countries within or outside the European Union (cf. Area Report D 2009: 18–19).

From what has been said, it can be concluded that the concept of multi-competence as developed within the education area turns out to be of an explanatory value for interpreting specific findings in the other areas, where multi-competence does not figure as an explicit component in the theoretical frameworks of the projects under investigation.

Conclusion

Multi-competence is an exceptional category within the theoretical framework of LINEE. Although this variable was only conceptually refined in the area of education, it is nevertheless in accordance with the focus of the research in the other thematic areas. Despite the lack of an overarching perspective on multi-competence in the LINEE research, this variable plays an essential role in the theoretical framework since it is more or less implicitly present in all projects, interacts with all other variables and is relevant for specific topics in all thematic areas.

As to the relationship between multi-competence and the other key variables, we can say that multi-competence constitutes a specific type of knowledge that appears closely connected with LPP since in the European context, language policy reflects the dimension in which multilingualism is actually being shaped as a political goal. As language policy is closely linked to discourse, which, in turn, is associated with ideology and power and conflict, it goes without saying that multi-competence also intersects in various ways and degrees with these variables. The LINEE findings clearly reveal that conflicts may arise when multilingualism in terms of multi-competence is subject to language policies which pay lip service to the principle of equality of languages while in reality sustaining communicative practices which are headed towards maximising economic profit. The tensions reflected in the official discourse of policy makers and stakeholders show that multi-competence of the desired European kind is unlikely to be achieved since equality as a major principle for the building of EM cannot be upheld when, at the same time, the economic laws of supply and demand call for multi-competence in a restricted range of powerful and selected languages (cf. Area Report B 2009: 13). The non-viability of the language equality principle is also reaffirmed on the national level where national language policies, instead of exploiting the naturally given multi-competence of immigrant minorities, increasingly insist on their competence in the national language as a measure of integration (cf. Area Report B 2009: 47). It goes without saying that policies of this kind will generate specific kinds of speakers who may be multilingual without being multi-competent, and that particularly in the case of immigrants, linguistic competence might be eventually degraded to semi-lingualism and insufficient learning of both the heritage and the host language.

Whereas at the European level multi-competence appears as something that is shaped through politically and ideologically invested discourses, at the local level it seems to connect more directly with identity and culture-specific issues. As has already been pointed out, the case of the Polish-speaking immigrants in Szeged shows that multi-competence relates to identity since it is through the use of their linguistic resources that these speakers construct their multiple identities (cf. Section 3.2.3). Beyond this, multi-competence is also relevant when it comes to the promotional efforts of cultural tourism since European cultural tourism also aims at 'selling' the multicultural identity of specific sites and, hence, the multi-competence of the individuals or groups living in these places, for example, in the case of multilingual Pula (cf. Area Report A 2009: 12). Interestingly enough, the findings concerning a 'Szegedi' identity put forward that belonging is not a matter of speaking or not speaking the local language but rather a matter of cultural and social practices (cf. Area Report A 2009: 26). This suggests that the intersection between multi-competence and local, regional or national identities is a multi-faceted and complex process which has to be taken into further consideration.

As to the major themes that relate to multi-competence within the LINEE research, it can be said that multi-competence connects strongly with the question of migrants' economic and social integration. The examples from Vietnamese immigrants in Cheb (CZ) and from sub-Saharan Africans in Germany confirm that multi-competence can be useful for various options concerning immigrants integrating into the host society. In the case of Vietnamese immigrants in Cheb, the lack of possibilities for the second and third generations to be formally educated in Vietnamese, particularly with regard to technical vocabulary, reading and writing skills as well as the ability to translate from Czech into Vietnamese and vice versa, turns out to be a problem since learned knowledge of this kind would give these individuals a competitive advantage in looking for jobs both in international and in Czech companies (cf. Area Report D 2009: 11). Hence, these results bring to the fore that there is a need for educational support of the already existing multi-competence. As to the African immigrants, first-generation parents continue to speak French as their official national language at home with their children in order to guarantee that their children have an excellent command of another European language besides German. The kind of multi-competence to be developed in this context is supposed to be favourable not only for the children's school career in Germany but also for their prospects on the job market in Germany or elsewhere (cf. Area Report D 2009: 14).

Beyond migrants, the context of multilingual classrooms also figures as a prominent topic within the LINEE project since contexts of this kind constitute important sites for the development of multi-competence. Moreover, and contrary to current positions on multilingualism according to which ELF would undermine or impede multilingualism, ELF speakers proved to be multi-competent language users as they adopted a wide range of multilingual strategies in obtaining their communicative goals. Another point is that ELF-speaking groups of students formed CoPs in which they negotiated their different lingua-cultural background with the common aim of successful communication.

Concluding, we can say that multi-competence within the LINEE research is a concept that was developed and adopted within the education area, although there also appears to be some relationship between multi-competence and specific topics in the other thematic areas. Within the education area, the theoretical conceptualisation of multi-competence has broadened the scope from an initially psycholinguistically centred perspective into a wider sociolinguistic and educational understanding. In this scope, multi-competent individuals are seen as language users who dispose of an extended and integrated linguistic repertoire with regard to their knowledge of languages and their ability to adapt the processes of learning and using languages. The LINEE results show that EM has to be primarily conceived in terms of flexible scenarios in order to fulfil the claims resulting from diversity and Europeanisation. In this respect, multi-competence in its dynamic scope offers a perspective in which this multilingualism can be adequately reflected and grasped. Viewed in this light, multi-competence appears as an important category which, however, calls for more precise and further elaboration.

3.2.8 Power and conflict

Theoretical concepts of power and conflict

Power and conflict are two notions which are to a large extent concomitant variables, particularly in those cases where the power relations between specific groups, while they serve the interests of one group to the detriment of another, give rise to social dominance and subordination. Power and conflict are a central issue to the social sciences and there are quite different attempts at theorising the aspects that combine with both notions, although the conceptualisation of power appears to be far more precisely elaborated than that of 'conflict'. Conflict evolves from power and is thus more or less implied in the relative power relations of a social setting. The intersection between the two variables also explains why conceptualising 'conflict' is largely combined with the way power is approached in the social sciences.

The concept of power is clearly related to interests, that is, the manner in which these interests are negotiated and enacted to the advantage or detriment of specific groups. Power is seen to be inextricably linked to discourse, as discourse provides for the basic grounds on which power is generated and negotiated.

In the social sciences, two traditions of power research can be identified (cf. Mayr 2008: 12–14). On the one hand, power is regarded as a static phenomenon associated with conscious and explicit decision making and domination. On the other hand, a more critical and dynamic stance elaborates on the implicit or hidden working of power. Following the stances taken by Gramsci and Foucault, power is mainly conceived in terms of persuasion and consent, in which language is given a central role. Here, power is accounted for in terms of diffused and dispersed processes characterised by continuously evolving social and discursive relations (cf. Foucault 1977 1980). In this perspective, power is not 'held' by any person or institution but is developed through interaction. Discourse is accorded a central role in the generation of power since the relations of power are produced and enacted through disourse. At the same time, discursive orders which in a way reflect the social order are themselves constituted and shaped by the respective power relations (cf. Section 3.2.2). It is in this scope that Fairclough (2001: 36) differentiates between 'power in discourse' and 'power behind discourse'. Beyond discourse, knowledge is also considered an indispensable factor in the production of power. Knowledge, it is argued, produces power and vice versa, and it is again through discourse that power-generating knowledge is put to work to control or regulate social behaviour (cf. Foucault 1977: 27).

Gramsci (1971) adopts the notion of 'hegemony' to highlight the hidden or covert operation of power. Hegemony implies the control of rule by dominant groups through winning consent from subordinate groups. The point is that the arrangements achieved through consent are perceived as legitimate, common-sensical and 'natural' by the subordinate group while, in reality, they suit the interests of the dominant group. Accordingly, power is not enforced through coercion or repression but through the creation of common sense in the day-to-day routines.

Yet another influential contribution to theorising power in relation to language is Bourdieu's notion of symbolic capital. Here, language is conceived in terms of symbolic power which, among others, determines the positioning of the individual in the social markets. Bourdieu (2005: 20–22) argues that individuals dispose of a socially structured linguistic habitus which they acquire in specific fields of the markets and which constitutes a kind of symbolic capital. In this perspective, specific markets generate specific linguistic productions associated with particular social values. The point is that the values assigned to the markets are conferred to the linguistic productions. Concerning the linguistic/symbolic capital, however, individuals or social groups are not equally well equipped since their linguistic habitus is generally acquired in different social fields. Fields such as education, administration and the legal system legitimise a specific linguistic order within society which does not always map the habitus of social groups who derive their linguistic habitus mainly from fields which do not provide sufficient capital for these areas, such as the fields in which minority languages or also dialects are paramount. Following Bourdieu, the conflict between French and the regional languages in France can thus be seen as a struggle for symbolic power which implies social hierarchies and inequality among the speakers.

The different perspectives on power show that power is constituted in different contexts and in different ways operating through diverse social divisions, for example, ethnicity, where social class, gender and generation intersect. Therefore, many contemporary theorists insist on not only privileging one but also taking into account different power dimensions at the same time in order to adequately assess the complex dynamics involved in the generation of power (cf. Talbot et al. 2008: 2).

Now, returning to the linkage between power and conflict, it has already been stated that it is the asymmetrical distribution of power which gives rise to conflicts. Unfortunately, the term 'conflict' itself lacks a precise definition (cf. Rindler Schjerve 2007), although in social theory it is generally conceptualised in terms of diverging group interests and the struggle over power. Functional differentiation, social inequality and diversified social norms appear to be the main constitutive forces of the conflict. The manifestation of the conflict may be of a rather latent kind as long as the inconsistencies and controversies defining the conflict are not communicated. Communicating these aspects implies that the antagonism between the conflicting parties is elaborated and eventually escalated through controversial discourses which, again, show that the antagonism has turned into a manifest conflict (cf. Dahrendorf 1961: 217–218). According to Dahrendorf (1957: 203), conflicts are positive and useful elements as long as they are regulated and transformed by institutional forces since institutions assist in diverting aggression and, in regulating the conflict, also provide ways of debating on the legitimacy of existing power structures. Following Coser (1972), conflicts force the conflict parties into mutual interaction and as such contribute to reactivating and reinforcing the integration and the identities of the conflicting groups.

Within Critical Theory (cf. Habermas 1981, 1984), conflicts can also arise from communication within the life-world dimension of specific groups. Here, it may occur that cultural peculiarities or specific symbolic orders of one group give rise to identities and lifestyles which clash with the identities and lifestyles of the other group(s). In this context, communication appears to form the main source of the conflict since the cultural differences are communicated in a way that threatens or endangers the design and the functional operation of a group-specific life-world (cf. Habermas 1981: 575–583).

Language conflicts are special cases of interethnic conflicts which arise from ethnolinguistically differentiated plural societies, and are therefore associated with antagonistic interests and struggle over social power in these societies. It is also widely known that in these contexts, language as such is not the primary source of the conflict. Rather, this source is provided by diverging group interests associated with unequal power potentials that give rise to the conflict while language works as a symbol over and through which the conflict may escalate (cf. Rindler Schjerve 2007).

Language conflicts are intimately associated with the rise of the nation state in Europe since in the national and single-state context, groups speaking other languages are generally under pressure to assimilate into the dominant single or national language. In those cases where the groups refuse the pressure by continuing to adhere to their language, the inter-group relation is frequently conflict prone. This conflict arises in so far as adhering to another language is mostly interpreted as an expression of deviant identity and as a disruptive factor for national integrity.

From research in multilingualism, it may be derived that unequal power relations are a general and conflict-ridden characteristic of European multilingual societies. In these societies, the power asymmetries result from the diversified status assignments to which the different linguistic groups and their languages are subjected. The different statuses themselves originate from the respective power resources at the disposal of the linguistic groups (cf. Rindler Schjerve 2001, 2007). Here, we can see that in multilingual nation-state societies in which majorities and minorities live together, there are pronounced differences in the access to and the disribution of resources. In the case of regional minorities, there have repeatedly been conflicts in the more recent past which resulted from the tension between the socioeconomically potent majorities at the centre and the marginalised minorities at the periphery. However, conflicts also loom in the case of multilingual immigrant minorities living in the larger cities due to the fact that, socially deprived and living in ghettos, these minorities remain excluded from the networks of the majority society. In this context, language proves to be a significant non-material resource since it regulates access to societal power. That is to say, the language of the dominant group, that is, the national or state language, is used in the public domains of power and enjoys the highest status and prestige whereas the languages of the non-dominant groups – particularly when excluded from the public domains – are functionally degraded and have a socially stigmatising effect on the speakers.

Power and conflict within LINEE

As to the LINEE research, power and conflict are operative throughout all thematic areas, although from a theoretical point of view the intersection of both variables often remains implicit and lacks thorough theoretical elaboration. Within LINEE, conflict, in particular, is not explicitly conceptualised although the LINEE findings point to all sorts of conflict potentials and tensions that emerge from the thematic areas. Power, however, is largely conceptualised by drawing upon Bourdieu's notion of 'symbolic capital', while Gramsci's concept of 'hegemony' and Foucault's 'institutional power' are also integrated in order to make the hidden working of power more visible. In rare cases, LINEE also adopts models such as the governmental approach following Rose (1999) and Bennett (2005), which seeks to understand the forms of action and relations of power that aim to guide and shape (rather than enforce, control or dominate) the action of others or of oneself. In this scope, the focus is on how authority and rule are enacted rather than why (cf. Area Report A 2009: 6; Hawkins 2001: 179). Alternatively, approaches such the Advocacy Coalition Framework (cf. Sabatier & Weible 2007) are used to investigate changing political power generated by coalitions of people from various governmental, public and private organisations who share a set of normative and causal beliefs and engage in a coordinated activity over time using available political, financial and knowledge resources to achieve their goals (cf. PoPa RLL 2009: 8).

Power and conflict within the thematic areas

In the LINEE findings, power is a salient variable in a wide range of contexts. In the identity area, the so-called 'language subordination process' is a theme which reaffirms that power asymmetries are closely linked to ideology and identity. This is particularly evident in the context of decentralisation measures in former socialist countries, where the local self-government also goes hand in hand with strengthening the local identity and language. The findings concerning the role of language in the formation of multiple identities in Istria (Croatia) and Silesia (Czech Republic) show how the changing power relations combine with the change of identities, where regional varieties may stand for resistance to symbolic domination of the national languages or may provide for 'alternative identifications that subvert and contradict officially imposed identities' (PoPa RLL 2009: 25). This shows that the ideology of the 'language subordination process', according to which the standard language and national culture are valorised while the non-standard varieties and associated cultural forms are devalued, has lost in power. At the same time, the naturalised unity of language, nation and identity disperses into a structure of complementing and also complementary identities (cf. Area Report A 2008: 6).

Power issues may also happen to be repressed, as in the context of European cultural policies, where official European narratives on culture are purified, thus repressing the memory of the European colonial past, as well as power relations between different member states or power relations between different groups within member states (cf. Section 3.2.1; Area Report A 2008: 5).

In the policy area, investigations focus on more or less powerful discourses. In this context, tensions may arise from discursive power asymmetries, such as unresolved discrepancies between multilingualism as economic capital and as a human rights issue within the discourses on LPP circulating at the highest EU levels. The law in books (laws, EC regulations, directives, textbooks, journals, acts, etc.), which reflects the true political power in the EU, puts a strong emphasis on language equality (cf. Section 3.2.6). At the same time, however, multilingualism has been increasingly constructed as an economic issue which, in terms of efficiency and competitiveness, calls for regulating linguistic diversity. The ambiguities concerning the language equality principle are best revealed in the analysis of the discriminatory interpretation of language rights in the judgement of the ECJ. Here, it was confirmed that languages do not have to be treated equally in all circumstances, such as in the already mentioned Groener case (cf. Section 3.2.4; PoPa EL 2009: 10). From the LINEE findings, it can be derived that multilingualism policy at the EU level is actually at a difficult transitional stage, as policy makers seek to reconcile the competing perspectives of language equality and economic efficiency (cf. Area Report B 2008: 8).

Another point is that the power conveyed through the promotion of EU multilingualism in terms of cultural benefit and enrichment, as in the case of the minority languages, also conflicts with the language policies at the national level. These policies, it appears, tend to be devoted to supporting the languages of the old minorities while institutionalising migrants' multilingualism as a deficit. Regional minorities have been subjected to longstanding assimilation policies on the part of the states in which they live. However, the hierarchical relationship between national languages and minority languages is now about to change in accordance with the political stance taken by the EU and its power to urge national governments to ratify the *European Minority Charter* (cf. Charter RML 1992) and the *Framework Convention* (cf. Framework Convention 1995) (cf. Section 1.2.2). As to the conflicts that may arise from this change, the above-mentioned bilingual signage in multilingual cities in the UK, the Czech Republic, Hungary and Croatia represents an interesting example in this respect (cf. Section 3.2.6). In general, bi- and multilingual signs are an intrinsic part of the city landscape and can be socially significant in that they symbolise the presence of various groups, while at the same time signalling the assertion of linguistic minority rights. The LINEE findings show that support provided to a bilingual signage which is being contextualised as a requirement of an ethnic minority tends to provoke conflict in settings where there have been tensions in the ethnic majority–minority relations in the past, for example, in Ceský Tesin at the Czech–Polish border. The study also reveals that in the more recent past, the power generated through the Europeanisation of minority protection combines with changing attitudes and a more positive behaviour on the part of the Czech majority population towards the Polish minority in place. Yet another interesting point is that the signage bilingualisation policy in Pula faces less resistance since Italian is supported through its prestige and the contacts with Italy, whereas it appears more conflicting in the Welsh localities where this support is missing (cf. PoPa RLL 2009: 8).

Interestingly, power directly relates to multilingualism in the education area in scenarios where different people and groups of people, for example, citizens, teachers, or state majority members, possess more or less power with respect to the learning and teaching of languages. Thus, investigations of multilingual schools demonstrate that in addition to power inside the school, teachers also have considerable power outside the school context, as they frequently advise parents on issues of relevance to home language maintenance (cf. PoPa RLL 2009: 25). In the case of the Hungarian minority in Romanian Szekler Land, for example, power asymmetries impact upon language learning attitudes and indicate a close relationship with culture, ideology and knowledge. It is shown that in the Szekler Land, the Romanian language sometimes receives a less positive interpretation that appears closely related to the symbolic power and the dominance of the state majority group (cf. Section 3.2.2 and 3.2.4). As understood by the subjects, this attitude was and is still being transmitted from generation to generation. Even though in most of the cases it is articulated unconsciously, the discourse on the state language suggests a distant attitude and, even more, the dominance of repulsive ideologies. Although Romanian is interpreted as an instrument for succeeding in life, on the labour market or in education, its acquisition as a second language is considered to be something obligatory, imposed from above. In this case, resistance to the symbolic domination of the state language seems to be intertwined with the culture and the social group for which this language stands (cf. Area Report C 2009: 38).

The LINEE findings concerning language use and language values among multilingual immigrant students in England, Italy and Austria furthermore indicate that multilingual communicative competence is experienced as one of the many resources of power. Thus, language shift within the Albanian community in Bolzano creates power asymmetries in the families when children or adolescents have more competence in the host language/s than their parents and act as linguistic mediators between their families and the host society. In this case, the linguistic asymmetries endow the young people with a power they are usually not entitled to in other contexts (cf. Area Report C 2009: 16).

The issue of language as a resource of power closely connects with the question as to which languages provide their speakers with what degree of power. At the European and also at the national level, there is a clear ranking among the European languages regarding their actual use and their presumed utility (cf. also Special Eurobarometer 243 2006). This is also confirmed by the study of language attitudes among Hungarian and Ladin minority students in Romania and Italy, who indicate high value and prestige for English and, in comparison, lower values and prestige concerning standard Hungarian and Italian (cf. Area Report C 2009: 31–32; PoPa RLL 2009: 10).

In the economy area, the LINEE results largely confirm that the power asymmetries between the more and the less widely used European languages are strongly reflected in the way language issues are managed and negotiated within multinational companies, particularly concerning economic and other relationships between the EU's old and new member states. Here, the power of ELF as an international trading language makes it a preferred language for business communication, whereas in smaller subsidiaries, the languages in place are selected according to the functional and emotional requirements of specific communicative events (cf. Section 3.2.3; Area Report C 2008: 14–15; PoPa RLL 2009: 12).

Moreover, studies investigating how the Knowledge Economy impacts on the language acquisition of African immigrants in Germany and Vietnamese immigrants in the Czech Republic highlight that these people end up in menial jobs which do not require quality knowledge of the host country's language. Thus, these immigrants remain excluded from participating in the knowledge-based economy because of their socioeconomic status. This status derives from the lack of symbolic power of their immigrants' languages and at the same time from the lack of cultural capital which connects with knowledge of the host country's languages (cf. Section 3.2.7). Interestingly, the case of the sub-Saharan Africans in Germany who continue to speak French as their home language shows that French as a powerful European language does not figure as symbolic capital facilitating the socioecnomic integration of these migrants (cf. Area Report D 2009: 13–14).

In contrast, the investigation of language practices of Italian migrants in Vienna indicates that Italian, being assigned high cultural status and prestige in the city and thus constituting a source of power, is economically beneficial in the job market since in the economic domain, the existence of Italian elements is demanded explicitly by the host society. Thus, the owners of Italian restaurants and Italian ice-cream parlours use their mother tongue in varying degrees and measures in order to cultivate, promote and communicate an Italian 'trademark' (ice-cream or good Italian food) so to say as a marker of collective identity. In doing so, they distance themselves from pseudo-Italian competitors in this domain since many Italian restaurants, for example, are run by North African or Turkish owners (cf. PoPa RLL 2009: 26).

Turning now to 'conflict' within the LINEE project, it can be said that different kinds of tensions may be identified as constituting conflicts, although a theoretical perspective of conflict, as already mentioned, has not been explicitly elaborated in LINEE. The reason for this may also be seen in the fact that the conflicts arising from the management of linguistic diversity at the European, national and local level within the LINEE research mostly emerge in a latent rather than a manifest way.

Conflicts of this kind were identified in relation to the political concept of multilingualism, which in itself gives rise to tensions simply because it is still unclear what multilingualism exactly refers to. The conflicting nature is particularly obvious when it comes to the definition of the multilingual repertoire as put forward within the official political discourse on multilingualism, where it remains unclear which languages would be 'legitimate' part of this repertoire. Moreover, the vagueness of the multilingualism concept gives rise to conflicting discourses as these may be related either to multilingualism as an economic capital or to multilingualism as an issue of human rights and equality (cf. PoPa RLL 2009: 27). Another point of conflict is ELF, which constitutes a widely used practice that apparently seems to undermine the learning of other languages and therefore conflicts with the EU's multilingualism strategy. Here, the findings of the education area, however, appease this tension. Whenever ELF is part of the multilingual repertoire, it represents a powerful means of engaging in multilingual and multicultural contexts while, at the same time, the speakers' interest in other languages remains untouched (cf. PoPa RLL 2009: 8).

Apart from this, there are other kinds of conflicts which relate to the management of citizenship. Conceiving of citizenship as a unitary, national privilege bound up with proficiency in the national language may be in conflict with more innovative models, such as 'cultural citizenship'. The notion of cultural citizenship emerges from the conflicting debates on migration and appears to be particularly problematic in contexts where regional and migrant minorities reside in the same localities. Here, the LINEE findings from Spain, Switzerland and the UK show that cultural citizenship with a focus on the 'right to speak and to have voice' would be more appropriate when talking about minorities and their 'rights' (cf. Section 3.2.1). Results indicate that regional minorities are supported in maintaining their ethnic language within the scope of the principle of equal rights, whereas immigrant minorities do not benefit from this promotion but are instead required to prove proficiency in the host language (cf. also PoPa RLL 2009: 7).

Identities form yet another conflicting issue when it comes to migrants and their concerns about 'feeling at home' and 'belonging' to the host community (cf. Section 3.2.1). The example of Polish migrants in Southampton and New Jersey points to the fact that the integration of migrants into the language and culture of the host community still continues to be seen as an exclusively one-way accommodation process by the host communities (cf. PoPa RLL 2009: 6). Conflicting identities may also arise when Vietnamese second-generation migrant children lose their ethnic language while they undergo Czech schooling (cf. Section 3.2.6; Area Report D 2008: 12) or when German minority speakers in Lorraine decide to assmilate into French for better advancement in French mainstream society (cf. Area Report B 2008: 10).

Conclusion

From all these examples, we learn that power and conflict are concomitant variables which closely intersect with the working of discourse, ideology, knowledge and identity. In other words, these variables interact dialectically with power in that they generate specific forms of power which in one way or another may give rise to conflict. The generation of power combines with specific discourses, which, in turn, connect with specific ideologies and identities, which again imply specific knowledge sets that are fundamental to the constitution of power. Apart from these major interrelationships, power also intersects with LPP in more or less explicit forms and guises depending on the kinds of ideologies and identities that are involved, as was illustrated in the political discourse on EM and identity planning. The findings also point to culture as a rather covert player which, however, provides for the knowledge sets that inform specific ideologies and attitudes, for example, in the case of Romanian in the Hungarian minority context in Transylvania. Beyond this, the LINEE results also point to a close interaction between power and multi-competence since flexible language use and proficiency constitute symbolic power in the European KBS, as particularly the examples of the economy area show.

As to the conflicts that may arise from these intersections, different manifestations can be observed depending on how the conflict evolves from and how it is handled in the diverse multilingual settings. Here, the findings show that different institutions, such as the groups of experts and policy makers at the EU level, educational settings, and the media or tourism industry at the European and the national level, generate specific power potentials which again imply specific conflict potentials. In some cases, the conflict is overtly communicated, triggering political mobilisation, as in the case of the Polish minority in the Czech Republic, where conflict processing was carried out to appease the escalating polarisation. In the majority of cases, however, conflicts remain latent since the inconsistencies and controversies are not elaborated well enough discursively, as in the case of the multilingualism debate at the EU level, or of citizenship for third country nationals at the EU and the national levels.

As to the range of topics combining with power and conflict, we may say that the public discourse on EM mentioned above constitutes a major theme in which power is at stake in various ways and manners. The LINEE results suggest that different interests, such as human rights, language equality or economic capitalisation and social cohesion, serve the interests of different groups and parties, and that the power displayed in this debate produces or reproduces specific ideologies which again associate with particular identities. The question concerning viable ways of shaping a common European identity through the power of language is a key topic within the EU, and the LINEE findings show that the language ideologies at work in shaping the identities at the different levels of analysis (European, national and local) are not always compatible and may even contradict each other. Moreover, the contentious debates on citizenship in terms of national vs. cultural citizenship may be seen as a result of the power incongruencies that forge the current debate on multilingualism at the European level. Power is also implied in all types of multilingualism, with power incongruencies being particularly evident when it comes to minorities' multilingualism. Here, the 'natural' multiple language competences of the minorities are not always considered as symbolic power that would be capitalised in terms of economic gains. Change appears to be underway, though – at least concerning the old or regional minorities – thanks to the powerful role that civil rights and the language equality principle play in the discourses on European minority promotion. However, the new or migrant minorities' multilingual competences, and particularly those of the second-generation immigrants, still neither figure as symbolic nor as economic asset. Here, it remains to be seen how the EU and the member states will deal with this conflict – all the more as migration flows have come to play an increasingly important role in the European national economies.

Moreover, it is not surprising that schooling and educational policies constitute a major conflicting theme when it comes to EM. Here, the LINEE findings show that the power conveyed through the educational programmes concerning multilingualism at the European level is often undermined by the power of monolingual ideologies which continue to underpin foreign language learning at the national level. Yet another major topic in which the power of language is displayed in different ways and manners is the management of linguistic diversity in the knowledge-driven economy which, by following the rules of supply and demand, privileges selected languages such as English. Minor languages play a subordinate role here, and minority languages, in particular autochthonous regional languages or migrant languages, are virtually excluded from the Knowledge Economy.

As to the power relations and asymmetries relating to EM and linguistic diversity, we may conclude that some of these still continue to exist while others are about to change. New and more flexible fields of communication resulting from the greater mobility within Europe call for a differentiation between the various languages in use since multilingualism appears to be a phenomenon which is not only restricted to traditionally powerful 'big' languages but also includes the regional and minority languages, the migrant languages as well as the newly emergent varieties, that is, mainly ELF. The conflict potentials which associate with the transformation of the power relations manifest themselves in conflicting discourses on multilingualism, linguistic diversity and citizenship, which, again, relate to divergent expectations and visions of the actors involved at the different levels of the multilingual European society.

Against this background, it seems all the more essential to analyse the power-generating aspects, and in particular the implicit and hidden working of power in EM, and to ask ourselves which power relations arise from guided and natural multilingualism for the groups concerned and which interests multilingualism serves. The conflicts resulting from the debate on multilingualism appear to be of a rather latent nature, which can imply that the controversies and antagonisms defining these conflicts have not been adequately addressed and investigated. Thus, it seems to be the order of the day to question in particular those scenarios and opinions which are seemingly 'obvious' with regard to their ideological and power-specific contents, and thereby to contribute to preventing the smouldering conflicts which exist from growing into manifest conflicts.

3.3 Methodological Issues

Apart from the theoretical dimension, the LINEE project was also concerned with methodological issues. The search for scientific defragmentation and multidisciplinary models, which should assure scientific pluralism, also implied the concurrent elaboration of a methodological dimension. Interestingly, methodological issues have gained attention rather only recently within multilingualism research at large (cf. Aronin & Hufeisen 2009; Grosjean 1998; Wei 2008). Furthermore, scientific fragmentation as it derives from different scholarly traditions and perspectives has also given rise to a diversified range of methodological profiles in this research area, and similar developments can be observed within the field of theory building. Thus, for example, Li Wei's distinction between a linguistic, a psycholinguistic and a sociolinguistic perspective (cf. Wei 2008: 16) reflects very well the disciplinary biases and their methodological implications for multilingualism research. Moreover, his plea for a transdisciplinarity of multilingualism methodology also combines with the call for re-conceptualising methodology in multilingualism research by Aronin and Hufeisen (2009). Concerning transdisciplinarity within the LINEE project, it has to be stressed that despite its evidently sociolinguistic background, the LINEE research contributes to transdisciplinary methodology since researchers from different disciplines collaborated within the sub-projects and hence agreed upon a common methodology.

In presenting the LINEE methodology, we will reflect upon the methodological decisions taken at the different stages of the research process. Hence, in line with influential methodological literature, the research process is presented as a range of (interrelated) subtasks, each of which exhibits a logic of its own. These sub-tasks relate to decisions concerning, for example, the research question(s), the research strategy, and the choice of appropriate methods of data gathering and data analysis. Thus, the methodological profiles result from the single decisions taken within the research process. In what follows the presentation of the LINEE methodological platform aims at providing a synopsis of the different methodological decisions taken in the LINEE project and at positioning these decisions within the large spectrum of methodological possibilities that have been generally developed for EM.

Clearly, identifying the decisions which bring about specific methodological profiles is not an easy task. The LINEE platform is therefore embedded in the rich scientific literature on research design, which provides a range of suggestions for systematising the descriptions of the research process (cf. Creswell 2009; Creswell & Plano Clark 2007; Crotty 2003; Kelle 2007; Maxwell 2005; Miles & Huberman 1994; Robson 2002; Tashakkori & Teddlie 1998; Yin 2006).

In the third edition of Creswell's *Research Design*, which appeared in 2009, for instance, research designs are understood as 'plans and the procedures for research that span the decisions from broad assumptions to detailed methods of data collection and analysis' (Creswell 2009: 4). Here, it is suggested that researchers should bear in mind three elements of inquiry when developing a research design: the philosophical world view, the research strategies and the research methods. In Creswell's approach, these three elements are closely interrelated. The first component, philosophical world views, is to be understood as epistemological and ontological assumptions which relate to the general orientations about the world and the nature of research. In this perspective, four world views are distinguished and described: postpositivism, constructivism, advocacy/participatory world views und pragmatism. Strategies of inquiry, in turn, comprise qualitative strategies, for example, ethnography, quantitative strategies, experiments and mixed methods strategies. The third element, research methods, relates to questions, data collection, data analysis and interpretation. Based upon the decisions to be taken within these fields of inquiry, Creswell differentiates between three research designs: the quantitative, the qualitative and the mixed methods design.

This conception of research designs as a series of stages or tasks for planning and conducting research has undergone some criticism, particularly from the perspective of qualitative research (cf. Maxwell 2005). As an alternative to perceiving the research process as a series of decisions to be taken, qualitative researchers have suggested more holistic models which conceive of qualitative research as an ongoing reflective process with closely interconnected components.

Taking the interactive model developed by Maxwell (2005) as an example, the five different design components (goals, conceptual framework, research questions, methods and validity) to which he refers to interact in the following way: the research questions constitute the heart of the model and connect with all the other components. Furthermore, they are clearly related to the goals, and both goals and research questions should be shaped by what is already known about the phenomena under study and by the theoretical concepts and models that can be applied to these phenomena.

Conversely, the decisions about the relevant theory and required knowledge depend on the goals and questions. The relationships between methods, research questions and validity can be described as follows: the methods must contribute to answering the research questions and deal with validity threats to these answers. Maxwell uses 'validity' in a common-sense way to refer to the 'correctness or credibility of a description, conclusion, explanation, interpretation or other sort of account' (Maxwell 2005: 106). Finally, the questions have to take into account the feasibility of the method and the significance of particular validity threats, that is, alternative explanations or rival hypotheses. In Maxwell's model, validity is an explicit component of the research design which addresses the strategies used in order to identify and rule out validity threats.

Overall, Maxwell's qualitative model can be distinguished from Creswell's general approach by its more clearly defined holistic character, and by the differing composition of the components identified as elements of the research design. For a description of the LINEE methodology, both models are used, with the following criteria being applied:

In the first step, the central research question is presented, from which the broad framework of the LINEE research can be derived. Subsequently, the LINEE sub-projects are assigned to the so-called basic models of qualitative research. Another step involves describing the levels of analysis of the LINEE research, which forms part of the 'philosophical world views' in Creswell's model, while it is included in the category 'conceptual framework' in Maxwell's approach. Furthermore, the research strategies of the LINEE sub-projects are presented on the basis of the descriptive criterion of openness. This process is targeted at determining in how far the empirical research aims at confirming or falsifying previously formulated hypotheses and assumptions, or in how far it abstains from hypotheses and approaches the research field openly. In Creswell's approach, this question is discussed under 'selected strategies of inquiry' (Creswell 2009: 5), while Maxwell discusses openness in the component 'methods' (Maxwell 2005: 4). Finally, the combination of different methods in the LINEE sub-projects is described.

3.3.1 Central question and methodological framework

The central research question forms the outset of the research process. Even if the question itself may, at a later stage, be subject to the reflection process regarding the research design, it nevertheless constitutes an initial point of orientation.

Within the qualitative framework (in which there is, however, little general consensus as to the core of qualitative social research), it is generally agreed that an overarching research question does not search for an answer to a pre-formulated hypothesis. Thus, the central questions of the 24 LINEE sub-projects, which are all posed as open-ended questions, situate the overall project in a qualitative framework. This does not imply, though, that the LINEE research would be exclusively committed to qualitative methods.

Yet, another and finer differentiation concerning the research question results from the four macro-questions distinguished in the German sociology of knowledge (cf. Lüders & Reichertz 1986; Reichertz 2007; Reichertz & Schröer 1994). From this perspective, qualitative research can formulate questions concerning (1) the subjective sense worlds of actions, (2) the description of social action and social milieus, (3) the reconstruction of structures generating interpretation and action and (4) the (re)construction of historically and socially pre-typified interpretation (cf. Reichertz 2007: 199).

Assigning the central questions of the LINEE sub-projects to these macro-questions, it can be concluded that the project's profile is founded on the framework of qualitative research. Accordingly, the LINEE project is particularly concerned with describing social action, the subjective sense worlds of actions and the (re)construction of the processes determining how acting subjects find their way in the social world, how they create it and how they change it. To give an example, the subjective sense worlds of action are most evident within the policy area, when investigating 'the thinking and experiences of the social actors involved in the various stages of the policy planning process' (Area Report B 2008: 3). Within the economy area, on the other hand, the description of social action and social milieus appears to be foregrounded as long as the research questions focus upon aspects such as the way the migrants use their previous and newly acquired language skills in making decisions about their future jobs and choices of countries of residence, on aspects like the significance they attach to their language skills when it comes to the job market and to other factors of their social life or on the way the knowledge-based economy manifests itself in the use of languages in multinational companies (Area Report D 2009: 4).

From this, it can be concluded that multilingualism research carried out within LINEE fits into an overall qualitative framework although single research sub-projects may pursue quite different options with respect to the macro-questions.

3.3.2 Basic models of qualitative social research

To date, five basic models have been identified within qualitative social research: case studies, comparative studies, retrospective studies, snapshots (analysis of state and process at the time of the research) and longitudinal studies (cf. e.g. Flick 2007 with reference to Creswell 1998). This distinction is situated on two axes: the distinction between single case and comparative study on the one hand and the distinction on the temporal axis between retrospection and longitudinal study on the other hand. As to LINEE, its position concerning the temporal axis can be roughly assigned to the basic type 'snapshot'. All sub-projects ultimately constituted state and process analyses at the time of research. This is best illustrated by the large amount of data gathered through diverse kinds of interviews (one-to-one, focus groups, etc.) or by data concerning the linguistic landscape of multilingual cities. While it must not be overlooked that in many cases retrospective data were taken into account, or claims for the future were made, LINEE's centre of interest was, however, clearly on the 'here' and 'now' present-day phenomena.

As to the distinction between single case and comparative studies, case studies are concerned with the exact and preferably comprehensive description or reconstruction of a single case, which can be defined as a person, as social communities like families, or as organisations and institutions. Comparative studies, in turn, consider several distinct cases with regard to specific details, and ask questions concerning two primary aspects of the research setup: first, the selection of cases and second, the degree of standardisation of the remaining conditions which are not the object of the comparison. This process, however, proved to be quite problematic in some instances. In order to be able to compare, for example, the significance of multilingualism for the current and future position of the Vietnamese population in the Czech Republic and of the Francophone Africans in Germany, it was necessary to analyse the varying economic conditions of these two groups in detail, although these were not part of the research question (cf. Area Report D 2009: 9).

As to the organisation of comparative research in LINEE, networking between several research groups within a sub-project was employed for carrying out comparative studies. The comparability of cases, which constituted a central topic in all sub-projects, was discussed quite diversely. However, against the background that the emerging approaches exhibited considerable variation, comparability was mainly achieved through the binding character of mutual subordinate research questions and through devising shared guidelines for interviews or text analysis.

Another central aspect of the comparative studies in LINEE concerned the fact that their design process frequently involved the development of a considerable dynamics. Here, an apt example is provided by the investigation into the reception of EU multilingualism discourse at the national level, which was part of the policy area (cf. Dorostkar & Flubacher 2010). For this study, Austria was selected as an EU member state and Switzerland as an associated state, owing to research pragmatic considerations since the project team was composed of members of both countries. At the same time, this selection allowed for comparing the inside (member state) perspective with an outside (associated state) view. After having agreed upon the common research question, some important decisions about the data to be collected were taken: official discourses from print media should be analysed first and in the second step semi-official and private discourses were to be collected. Moreover, three language policy events were selected which should serve as a basis for creating the data corpus, namely, the *Action Plan 2004–2006* (cf. COM(2003)449 final) in 2003, the *New Framework Strategy* (cf. COM(2005)596 final) in 2005 and the inauguration of Leonard Orban as EU Commissioner for Multilingualism in 2007. A first analysis of Swiss media texts revealed, however, that there were not enough articles in Swiss print media focusing on these discursive events. Hence, five supplementary events were chosen for Switzerland in order to allow for compiling a data corpus of Swiss print media texts. This example illustrates in how far decisions which had to be taken during the research process might change the design as developed at the outset. In comparative studies, decisions of this kind are particularly complex and delicate, and thus have to be carefully reflected upon.

3.3.3 Conceptual background: Levels of analysis

Naturally, the investigation of individual action and social structure frequently involves questions both regarding the connection between these two phenomena and regarding the perceptions underlying this connection. This leads to the debate about micro–meso–macro, which is intensively conducted in sociology (cf. e.g. Kelle 2001).

As to the LINEE project, the question concerning the levels to be taken into account was only superficially answered by the structure of the overall project, in which a distinction was made between the European, the national and the regional level since the levels addressed by the individual sub-projects appeared to involve complex interactions. Therefore, the question whether a specific research project investigates persons, groups, organisations or societies had to be posed separately in each sub-project and on each level of analysis. If, for example, actors of language policy were interviewed on the European level and the focus was put on the integration of subject positioning in language planning theory (cf. Area Report B 2008), then micro-processes were involved in a project which at first sight seemed to be situated on the macro-level (European level). This example is typical for the multifaceted interdependence between the levels as it occurred in the LINEE sub-projects.

When analysing the different levels from a sociological perspective, we may differentiate between theories which tend to be situated primarily at one or the other level. This is, for instance, illustrated by the survey of Treibel (2006), who distinguishes between macro-theories and micro-theories. A third category, as Treibel argues, consists of those theories which overcome the macro–micro contrast.

Within the LINEE research, the connection between micro and macro was relevant for two reasons: first, no sub-project operated exclusively on one single level, which made it necessary to reflect on how observed individual behaviour integrated into the social interrelations. Second, it should be possible to make the results of LINEE available to policy makers and stakeholders; thus, the need arose to consider the implications of specific social interrelations for individual behaviour and vice versa.

In the theoretical frameworks of the sub-projects, the relation between macro and micro was to some extent conceptualised explicitly, while it was to a certain degree grasped rather intuitively as well. Furthermore, different approaches of linking the micro and the macro were also observed. All these approaches, which are not to be seen as competitive, may contribute to a framework that mediates between the interdependent levels of analysis. The adoption of the various perspectives largely appeared to depend upon the research questions and the theoretical framework of the single sub-projects. Thus, for instance, in the thematic area of 'identity and culture', knowledge represents a concept that mediates between the social and the individual level. This is due to the fact that knowledge exhibits both a local and strongly context-dependent component, and is linked to structural questions of societal power, as is illustrated particularly in the analyses of European cultural tourism or of the local stocks of knowledge in the multilingual city of Pula (cf. Area Report A 2009). In some sub-projects, on the other hand, discourse as a social practice formed this link, in particular in the economy area, where the perspective of LMT focuses on the explicit effort to integrate both levels through discursive action in order to illustrate how macro and micro interact in the language planning and management process. In the education area, in turn, multi-competence and 'social network' mediate between the individual and the social level. Hence, without agreeing explicitly upon a common frame concerning the micro–macro link, the LINEE research nevertheless acknowledges the importance of linking the different levels of analysis theoretically.

3.3.4 Research strategy: Degree of openness

Starting out from viewing the research process as a range of (interrelated) sub-tasks, it is widely agreed that all decisions taken previously are relevant for further decisions still to be reached. However, while researchers commonly agree that the theoretical approach affects the research strategy and that the strategy, in turn, affects the choice of methods for gathering and analysing data, there are diverging answers to the question in how far the selected research strategy reversely influences the theoretical framework and also the research questions. A hypothetico-deductive strategy would tend to exclude reactive effects, whereas an open procedure which allows for the change of procedure in the course of investigation perceives the research process as circular and exposes itself to a continuous reflection process (cf. Kelle 2007; Maxwell 2005).

Concerning the description of individual research strategies, the recent literature on methodological questions identifies a multitude of possibilities (cf. e.g. Creswell 2009; Kelle 2007; Meinefeld 2007). In this process, pairs of opposites such as confirmation versus exploration, quantitative versus qualitative and deduction versus induction are introduced into the discussion, with the terms confirmation, quantitative and deduction being frequently equated, as is the case with exploration, qualitative and induction. Particularly, the discussion about the integration of qualitative and quantitative methods, however, shows that such equations may fall short of the complex reality of empirical research. As far as the LINEE platform is concerned, we will confine ourselves to more target-oriented individual criteria in defining the research strategies, in order to describe the actual methodological practice as concretely as possible.

As to Creswell's (2009: 4) distinction between qualitative and quantitative research, the LINEE project has already been positioned within a rather qualitative framework. Nevertheless, such a rough description does not do justice to the multitude of research strategies within LINEE. It is true that the focus on exploring and understanding in LINEE was mainly of a qualitative nature, but at the same time, data collection also involved numerically significant data, on the basis of which the characteristics of the examined variables were compared.

Another criterion for the research strategy which is frequently referred to in the literature is the degree of openness (cf. Titscher et al. 2000). An open strategy implies dispensing with standardised instruments or predetermined categories, and researchers pursuing an open strategy are willing to distance themselves from predetermined understanding and to change the mode of procedure in the course of investigation. A reverse strategy, which is also frequently assigned to quantitative social research, would require setting up and testing hypotheses. As regards LINEE, all sub-projects could be positioned between these two poles. Overall, the numerous methodological discussions and re-elaborations of the methodological framework pointed to a relatively open strategy. Research questions were revised, reformulated and partly rejected. Initially, projects could not do without assumptions in which the disciplinary background and the previous knowledge about the object of research were clearly reflected. During the research process, however, the openness of the line of action led to a continuous reflection process in which all decisions concerning research designs were integrated. It was particularly for such open strategies that the course of action was accurately documented, for example, by precisely recording the diverse data obtained from the field studies and all new assumptions based on this data, which in turn formed the basis for further research steps.

3.3.5 Method(s)

An important methodological decision results from the questions as to whether one or several methods (of data gathering and data analysis) should be applied, and how these methods might be combined. Since all LINEE subprojects applied several methods of data gathering and analysis, particularly the second question of combining different methods was of major interest. The description criteria for the forms of method combination practiced within LINEE can be derived from the discussion about the relationship of qualitative and quantitative methods. In this discussion, Kelle (2007: 39–40) identifies three major discursive strands: (1) the paradigm model by Guba and Lincoln (1994), in which a fundamental incompatibility of qualitative and quantitative methods is postulated. (2) Mixed methods designs, which are referred to as third paradigm particularly in Anglo-American research, as it supplements the quantitative and the qualitative approaches (cf. e.g. Denscombe 2008; Woolley 2009). Here, recent developments can be traced (online) in the *Journal of Mixed Methods Research*. (3) Triangulation, which was intensively discussed within LINEE and which refers to the use of various data sources, of different investigators, of different methods and of multiple perspectives to interpret the data (cf. Denzin 1989), the investigators and the theories (cf. Denzin 1970).

Interestingly, these three positions appear to coexist side by side without being substantially linked to one another. As far as the combination of methods is concerned, LINEE adhered to the combinability of different methods and hence implicitly rejected the hypothesis of incompatibility. Thus, the notion of 'pragmatic researcher' (Leech *et al.* 2010: 18, referring to Onwuegbuzie & Leech 2005) fits best to describe the type of researchers engaged in LINEE. This notion refers to researchers who are flexible in their research techniques when collaborating with other researchers stemming from different epistemological backgrounds.

Naturally, the integration of diverse research traditions and schools represented a special challenge. Within LINEE, the integration of the different research traditions in which the partners were rooted clearly had an impact on the selection of the methods applied. This, however, is not to say that it actually restricted the range of methods, as would have been the case if certain methodological traditions had dominated the research process.

Hence, and with particular regard to data gathering, a large number of different methods were generally applied in one and the same sub-project. This can be illustrated by an example from the identity area, where research in the four multilingual urban localities contexts of Szeged (Hungary), Pula (Croatia), Jersey (UK) and Cheb (Czech Republic) started out from the hypothesis that language and culture were two potentially independent phenomena. The selected methods of data gathering were both qualitative and quantitative: semi-standardised interviews with local inhabitants of various ethnic backgrounds and societal positions, questionnaires concerning visitors and persons working in tourism-related professions, textual and multimodal data from websites and promotional material targeting visitors, as well as photographs of signs and places of the localities investigated. Accordingly, data analysis drew upon both qualitative and quantitative techniques in that the qualitative data were subject to CDA whereas the quantitative data were analysed statistically (cf. PoPa RLL 2009).

Another example for the great variety of methods used for collecting data stems from the investigation into multilingualism in minority school settings with a special focus on classes teaching English as a foreign language. Data were collected in several parts of Ladinia (Italy), in Transylvania (Romania), Southern Slovakia (Slovakia) and Vojvodina (Serbia). The methods applied for data gathering included questionnaires for direct inquiry into language attitudes, a Matched-Guise Test, semi-structured interviews with both school staff and students, focus groups with students, the Self-Assessment Grid questionnaire on language skill levels, observations at foreign language (English) lessons, as well as audio and video recordings in these settings. In terms of data analysis, content analysis and CDA were used in order to analyse the transcripts of interviews and recordings of naturally occurring classroom interaction, whereas the questionnaires were statistically processed (cf. Area Report C 2009).

These are just two examples which illustrate the flexible combination of methods applied within the LINEE sub-projects. In applying method triangulation within the single sub-projects, then, it was not the researchers' intention to correct the results gained with one method by means of those stemming from another method, but rather to obtain a more complete picture of the complex realities at stake. And in this scope, it can be said that with respect to the models of triangulation (cf. Denzin 1989: 246; see also Kelle 2007), LINEE was clearly committed to the complementarity model.

3.3.6 Conclusion

From what has been said so far, it can be concluded that the entire LINEE project is to be positioned within a qualitative framework, with the individual sub-projects mainly focusing on describing social action, the subjective sense worlds of actions and the (re)construction of actors' meaningful references in multilingual contexts. As regards the cooperation of different research groups within the projects, this aspect was reflected in the very demanding development of comparative studies or comparative case studies. Concerning the relevance of macro- and micro-level, individual action was at the centre of interest for the most part, and various solutions were targeted in order to aggregate the results into the social structure. Moreover, the research strategy within LINEE was largely open and reflexive, and allowed for a huge variety of method combinations.

In the light of the methodological diversity and complexity, the integration of the research design was a particularly challenging issue. As the combination of methods and the design of comparative studies would exhibit varying degrees of integration, discussions about the degree of integration desired were at the centre of the methodological debate.

It can thus be concluded that due to the plurality of methodological options taken within the qualitative frame of LINEE, the research was not only a unique experience for the 'pragmatic researchers' themselves but also represents a good example of how multilingualism may be approached and assessed within the framework of a large-scale interdisciplinary research focus. Although the LINEE research has not actually developed a methodological profile proper for multilingualism research, it has nevertheless succeeded in revealing the major questions which arise within the field of EM research, and it has shown which strategies can be developed in order to answer these questions.

3.4 Lines of Tension Emerging from LINEE

The findings obtained within the LINEE research platform show that tackling EM calls for knowledge in quite a variety of fields and disciplines since the multiple manifestations which account for EM evolve from the intersection of factors relating to diversified disciplinary fields. Although traditional approaches have generally concentrated on different facets of the complex and multi-layered processes of multilingualism, the larger scale comparative scope of the LINEE research has allowed for assessing the multifaceted phenomena from a broader comprehensive perspective. And furthermore, it eventually opened the door to detecting the more covert facets and tensions which actually characterise the EM dynamics.

A major conclusion that can be derived from the LINEE scope is that as a concept EM remains vague and, as yet, not clearly enough defined. What we see is a range of competing discourses. On the one hand, multilingualism is conceptualised within the scope of human rights and the language equality principle, whereas, on the other hand, it has come to be seen in terms of economic capital which should enhance mobility, market efficiency and competitiveness. The LINEE findings show that these contradictory trends give rise to unresolved tensions and a lack of coherence in the perception of policy efforts by stakeholders of the EU and member states alike. The empirical data reveal the difficulty, if not impossibility, of reconciling the principle of equal languages with the reality of socioeconomic inequities as they are actually reflected in the distribution of languages in education, business and the EU institutional contexts, from which smaller national languages and especially minority languages remain largely excluded.

Another inconsistency is that the cause of linguistic human rights and equality is not well served by the weak implementing power of the EU language policies. As a consequence, EM is in danger of being interpreted simply as a noble aspiration remote from the reality of existing socioeconomic discrepancies and the market preferences that are at stake. In this light, EM raises scepticism since it may be understood as a mere catchword promoting European integration with little serious content. All the more as the indeterminacy of EM policy may give licence to political groups and actors of various kinds to interpret them in their own terms, which are contrary to the intended aims of the policy. And finally, since the equality of languages is a guiding principle of the EU politics of diversity, it may at times be instrumentalised as a substantial part of political correctness. In this function, however, it would be further reduced to an empty wording merely promoting politically correct talk about the diverse languages.

Another serious discrepancy relating to EM is reflected in the lack of consensus concerning the 'legitimate' plurilingual repertoire. Within the political scope of EM, European citizens are increasingly required to acquire a plurilingual repertoire. It remains, however, an as yet unanswered question, from which pool of languages citizens should make their choices in developing this repertoire. At the European and the national level, a clear ranking already exists with respect to the use and presumed utility of the European languages, in which the autochthonous and immigrant minority languages are not included. This shows that the principle of language equality as officially advocated by the EU language policy cannot be upheld as long as the market economy, which heavily impacts on the patterns of language selection, calls for a repertoire of only a few privileged languages.

Another factor which has already been mentioned concerns the weak implementing power of the EU language policies. Here, it is in the first instance the EU subsidiarity principle which causes inconsistencies and contradictions. While the question of linguistic and cultural diversity with its focus on the differences among the official languages is steering the debate at the supranational level, the question of the diversity within the member states, that is diversity caused by regional and immigrant minorities, is regulated by the national policies. At the same time, it cannot be ignored, however, that the national policies prove to be rather discrepant in defining their standards in their attempts to cope with diversity. This is exemplified by the divide that exists between 'old' and 'new' member states in handling regional minority promotion or by discriminating policies when the linguistic diversity of third-country nationals has to be accounted for. Here, it remains to be seen how the plea for EM, which, among other aspects, is also targeted towards ensuring social cohesion, can be politically implemented within the provisions made in the recent Lisbon Treaty.

Beyond these inconsistencies, another manifest line of tension emerges from the traditionally strong bond between language, identity and culture. We have seen that the commitment to linguistic diversity is at the same time a commitment to upholding the diverse national identities and cultures in accordance with the 'unity in diversity' principle. This is an issue that appears to have a bearing on EM, as it raises the question as to whether identifying languages with national identities and cultures would not imply sustaining the conception of multilingualism as a common container of parallel national monolingualisms, rather than in terms of variable plurilingual repertoires as they actually arise from the existing multilingual competences of different groups and speakers. Conceiving of EM as the sum of the national languages is consistent with the still dominant national language ideologies which valorise the standard language as the primary manifestation of the national culture while discriminating against other non-national varieties. The monolingual attitude that continues to ideologically underpin language policies at the national level obviously runs counter to European language policies which are informed by human rights and the principle equality. At the same time, it is also unable to meet the requirements of mobility and market efficiency.

Another critical point is that European cultural and language policies stress diversity as a core value seemingly free from contradictions without taking into account the disparities of power and the traumatic histories that equally combine with this diversity. As a consequence, these policies, which suggest a widely neutralised image of the European 'unity in diversity', do not fulfil the expectations and identification potentials of the target groups and therefore tend not to accord with the way European diversity is actually experienced in the different member states. As a consequence, they fail to implement appropriate strategies to overcome mutual resentments and prejudices among the various languages and cultures. This is particularly true, for example, when it comes to fostering the highly requested knowledge of neighbouring languages in transnational activities.

Moreover, the LINEE findings also point to another factor relevant to this 'unity in diversity ideal', that is, the strong fear of Europeans that the Union is intent on imposing a set of economic rules that might transform their 'ordinary way of life', thus endangering their local heritage and culture. The reason for these fears may primarily be seen in the obvious gap that exists between the discourses concerning EM policy making on the supranational level and their reception on the national levels. Here, the national policies apparently fail to mediate the supranational policies to the citizens, although, and paradoxically enough, it is the national policy makers and stakeholders themselves who decide on the EU policy making.

As has already been indicated, minorities, and particularly immigrant minorities, constitute a major challenge to EM policy since managing linguistic diversity at the EU level appears to experience great difficulty in adapting to minorities and to newly emerging patterns of migration. This is not surprising since it implies coming to terms with the interests of the individual member states, which in general remain targeted towards homogenised national monolingualism. The LINEE findings widely confirm that under the pressure of Europeanisation, there has been a move towards an increased awareness in the member states of the obligation to promote the languages of their regional minorities, whereas immigrants' home languages continue to be mostly institutionalised as a deficit. Thus, the language policies of the member states are supportive of diversity when it has to do with the languages of the regional minorities within their borders while they largely discriminate against the languages of immigrant minorities within the same borders. This shows that the focus of this policy is at best directed towards the promotion of regionally restricted bilingualism rather than towards seriously enhancing societal multilingualism.

From this angle, the contentious debates on immigrants' citizenship, based on proficiency in the host language while suppressing the heritage language, are but one aspect of the tensions that emerge from these policies. It is obvious, however, that migration has come to play an ever important role in the New Economy. Therefore, it still remains to be seen how the national policies will come to terms with multilingualism that originates from immigration – all the more so since the integration of second-generation immigrants calls for regulations that go beyond the one-sided accommodation of the immigrant minorities into the host society.

From this, we can furthermore conclude that there is an immediate need for increased educational support of already existing forms of multicompetence. Here, issues arise about schooling and educational policies, which are a major conflicting theme when EM is addressed. The LINEE findings show that there is very little support for the multicompetent immigrant students in the multilingual classroom, as the responsibility to maintain the heritage language generally remains delegated to the immigrant families themselves. Moreover, the institutional bodies in the member states appear to be rather hesitant about providing for education in the heritage languages of the immigrant children and again leave it to the parents to find ways of enabling their children to acquire literacy skills in the heritage language.

Apart from the question of making provision for immigrant languages, the school system is also heavily challenged when it comes to implementing EM in foreign language learning classrooms. The LINEE results clearly indicate that in the European school system, the EM programmes are very often undermined by monolingual ideologies that continue to inform the foreign language learning practices at the national level. In this scope, native-speaker competences still turn out to be the norms against which foreign language proficiency is measured, since in general teachers do not appear to be sufficiently informed about the role of students' prior or coexistent language knowledge in the learning process. Thus, their practices often contradict the concept of multilingualism as a dynamic phenomenon which implies the continuous activation and interaction between the learned languages.

English – it is well known – is the dominant second language in the context of foreign language education. Again, the LINEE findings show that in this context, the teaching and learning of English is largely targeted towards native-speaker achievement. This, however, contradicts the reality of using ELF, that is, without conformity to native-speaker competence, as a preferred and flexible mode of multilingual communication. The predominant use of English, it is commonly feared, would favor 'English Only' communication, undermining EM and the learning of other languages. The LINEE findings, however, show this fear to be ungrounded since they confirm that English used as a lingua franca is a powerful means of flexibly engaging in multilingual communication without compromising speakers' motivations for learning or using other languages. This indicates that increased mobility associating with more flexible fields of communication includes newly emergent varieties, for example, ELF, which have to be seriously accounted for in the plurilingual repertoire of EM.

What emerges from the LINEE findings is that EM is actually at a difficult stage since it is not clear whether the demand for EM is rather oriented towards economic Europeanisation or indeed towards the ideal of plurilinguistic and -cultural Europeanisation. Competing and contradictory ideologies are at present informing the discourse on EM at the highest EU policy levels. They confirm that the strong bond between language, identity and culture continues to persist at the national level, where institutions still adhere to the traditional practices of linguistic homogenisation, unilateral integration of linguistic heterogeneity and a monolingual habitus. The ideological underpinnings of these practices clearly run counter to EM as a mode of effective Europeanisation, with the consequence that EM is being conceived as an addition of parallel monolingualisms which might be reduced to form a plurilingual repertoire of privileged languages eventually reserved to the mobile and learned European elites. These ideologically driven inconsistencies combine with the weak implementing power of the EU policies, with the effect that these policies seem to pursue some noble aims whereas an awareness of these aims is lacking at the more local national level.

Clearly, the inconsistencies of the EM concept give rise to major problems in handling the existing linguistic pluralism within European society. This is particularly evident in the contradictory trends of multilingual management when the bilingual promotion of the old minorities or the citizenship and integration of the new minorities are at stake. And finally, it is also manifest in education where the EU programes are all too often undermined by the national policies, which instead of fostering functional multilingualism still tend to emphasise conformity to norms of native-speaker correctness in their language learning curricula. From all this, it can be concluded that EM is not a neutral but a highly contentious issue which relates to diverse actors, interests and objectives and which therefore challenges policy makers and academia alike to conceive of new and more flexible ways of communication. Such a reconceptualisation should not be restricted to a few major national languages but should rather include the natural multilingual resources of minorities and migrants and the newly emergent multilingual repertoires such as ELF and other lingua francas.

In conclusion, we may say that due to the large multidisciplinary and comparative approach of the LINEE research, it was possible to discern how EM, as it is at present constituted, actually works and what primary factors are involved in its manifestations. The research yielded specific insights into how the key factors combine and interact in shaping the emergent EM framework, as well as into the critical and conflicting points that actually constitute a serious challenge to its further successful development, and which call for political attention and further scientific enquiry.

4 European Multilingualism Beyond LINEE

In this chapter, we will move from an account of the findings that emerged from LINEE research on the prevailing conception of EM to considering how these findings might lead to a re-conceptualisation of EM, with a view to seeking a solution for some major questions which have remained unanswered within the research platform. We would argue that such a re-conceptualisation is in the interests of both theoretical coherence and political transparency.

Drawing on the theoretical potentials of the single LINEE key variables, we will then adopt a multi-focal approach which should allow for analysing the saliently weak points of the actual concept of EM. The analysis will focus both on the influence of the individual variables and on the interaction between them in the debatable manifestations of EM, thus aiming at revealing the basic contradictions and incoherencies that shape the conception of what EM is supposed to, or could represent. In disclosing these inconsistencies, we are attempting to find new ways for developing greater coherence in planning and promoting EM in the future.

4.1 Re-Conceptualising European Multilingualism

Many of the issues earlier identified as problematic can, as we would argue, be subsumed under four main questions:

(1) How can, or should, the various languages and their coexistence be validly and consistently conceptualised?
(2) What are the major principles that should guide the underlying assumptions and objectives of EM?
(3) What would be the overall linguistic resource or language pool from which Europeans would draw their multilingualism?
(4) How can the linguistic resources of minorities be handled, and how are these to be integrated into the EU's diversity framework?

4.1.1 European multilingualism: Container of national languages

As it seems, EM is widely viewed as a collective container of the official EU languages, apparently since conceiving of it as the sum of all national languages is thought to ensure the desired preservation of cultural diversity in the process of supranational unification. From a practical point of view, policy makers and stakeholders nevertheless appear to be well aware that this way of representing EM is more of a rhetorical exercise in appeasement than a manageable political programme: in reality, multilingual communication, particularly on the EU level and in other transnational encounters, has largely been restricted to the use of a few selected languages.

Paradoxically, this conception of multilingualism as a container of the national languages accords with the inherent monolingual attitude which appears to be ideologically entrenched in the still dominant paradigm of the nation state. From this perspective, Europeanisation thus evolves by the simple addition of the national languages, which are seen as reflecting the entire range of European identities and cultures. However, this conceptualisation of Europeanisation in terms of an additive alignment of the nationally distinct identities, languages and cultures is clearly problematic since it entirely avoids the question of how a, 'unity in diversity' which is dynamic and both linguistically and culturally integrated is to be established if national languages, cultures and identities are to be preserved as distinct and compartmentalised. Moreover, retaining the idea of homogeneous national identities and cultures is all the more questionable since it obscures the fact that identification and cultural practices within the national context are not monolithic and static but rather constitute processes in which locally diversified orientations, norms and values may play an important role (cf. Sections 3.2.1 and 3.2.3).

A particularly critical point of this perception is that within the national framework, culture and identity are generally seen as stable entities that are bound up with one language which provides the common grounds for the identification with a distinct cultural community. However, conceiving of language, identity and culture in terms of a static relationship does not accord with the reality that defines existing multilingual societies. Research conducted in multilingual contexts shows that identity and culture form a historically variable nexus of dynamic and unstable processes which unfold their meaning in discursive interaction and negotiation. In these contexts, language may, but does not necessarily, position speakers' membership in a given culture or determine their identity. First, it cannot be taken for granted that adopting a particular language entails the adoption of all kinds of cultural practices. And second, although language, as is widely acknowledged, plays an important part in the formation of identities, the conflation of language and identity actually masks the plurality of positions which are implied in the notion of identity itself.

Moreover, following post-modern thinking, it appears to be problematic to maintain the idea of fixed and homogeneous identities since both theory building about and research in multilingual societies confirm that the concept of identity comprises multiple and flexible identities, that is, different kinds of identifications which may coexist and interact with one another. European identity, it is commonly argued, would include the possibility of multiple identifications. However, conceiving of the multiple identifications in terms of added layers where the sum of the national identities yields a supranational identity would not do justice to the dynamics unfolding through Europeanisation. Rather than from simply adding the national identities, it may be assumed that a European identity will evolve from the ongoing negotiation of transnational and also transregional interactions which are essentially targeted towards achieving the goal of a common European identity.

Apart from the questionable issues concerning the ideological underpinning of EM politics, another serious issue involves the fact that confining EM to the national languages does not account for the actual degree of diversity in Europe since the huge number of languages spoken by the different minorities in the EU is largely neglected in this concept. On the one hand, multilingualism of the old or regional minorities has, apart from a few exceptions, been traditionally silenced by the nation states, with the consequence that these minorities have largely assimilated into the national languages and cultures. On the other hand, the new or immigrant minorities resulting from migration in more recent times have been and are still being directly forced into assimilation of the host country's language and culture. Although EU policies have attempted to cautiously integrate the regional minority languages into their strategies in more recent times (cf. Section 1.2.2), they have, however, failed to specify the position the minorities would hold within this unity framework. Thus, these minorities still remain excluded from this framework, which to date appears to be restricted exclusively to the diversity resulting from the national languages. The same also holds true for immigrant minorities for which no language political regulations have been implemented so far. We hence have to ask ourselves in how far minorities which are linguistically excluded from 'unity in diversity' also remain excluded from the formation of a common European identity and culture.

As the above remarks show, the conceptualisation of EM in terms of exclusive national languages needs to be seriously revised. The static scope in which national languages are seen as inextricably linked with a stable and homogenised identity and culture clearly ignores post-modern thinking and also turns a blind eye to the actual dynamics of Europeanisation. At the same time, it continues to underpin and, even worse, to legitimise the sociolinguistic subordination process of the non-national and minority languages. Therefore, solutions have to be sought in which EM is conceptualised in more flexible ways that account for the dynamics displayed at the various levels of Europeanisation. Here, it is obvious that the solutions required in transnational encounters differ from those which are appropriate for multilingual management at the national or local level. Furthermore, an important point seems to be that the various languages, that is, national and minority languages, are taken into due account with respect to the various multilingual settings to which they pertain functionally and symbolically. In contrast to prefixed regimes composed of selected national languages, flexible and adaptive multilingual management would leave room for multiple identifications and senses of belonging from which, as we argue, the desired European identity and culture is most likely to emerge.

4.1.2 Language equality principle

Within the current debate on EM, great emphasis is put on the language equality principle since at the EU and the national level it is commonly agreed that all official languages are equal and have to be accounted for in this equality. Most recent official reports and recommendations of the EU continue to reaffirm the relevance of language parity, particularly when the EU institutional language regime is at stake (cf. Section 1.2.3). Following these statements, all national languages must be equally represented since EU citizens should have the right to communicate with the European institutions in their own languages. Although in practice, institutional communication follows a rather selected language regime of English followed by French and some German, policy makers and stakeholders object to the political option of a restricted number of languages since they believe that it would not do justice to the idea of equal languages within equal member states. In fact, the principle of language equality is to ensure the equality of the citizens and at the same time the citizens' democratic participation in the Europeanisation process. Language equality thus constitutes the ideological premises on which the 'unity in diversity' scope is to be developed. This explains why options which account for selected national languages such as English, French or German seem to be inacceptable since they contradict the EU's unity framework. Hence, it comes as no surprise that particularly the 'English Only' option, which nevertheless constitutes a widely used practice in institutional and transnational communication, is officially rejected by policy makers and stakeholders alike.

Although language parity should ensure linguistic diversity on an equal footing, its practical implementation appears to be problematic in many respects. First and foremost, the equality principle seems to concern only the national languages although it does not even ensure an equally balanced diversity among these languages in the EU. The institutional language regime is a good example in this respect: in principle, it should support an integral language use whereas in practice it represents a highly selected regime of languages which, in one way or another, reflects the political power of the member states that stand behind these languages.

Another discrepancy of this kind relates to foreign language learning within the educational systems of the EU. Despite continuous attempts on the part of the EU to induce national policies to widen the range of the languages to be learned, the actual selection of foreign languages remains as yet rather restricted to a few major national languages. Restricting foreign language learning to the privileged large languages, however, is tantamount to furthering a type of elitist and at the same time hegemonic EM which contradicts the ideology of equality and democratic participation.

Apart from education, another most critical point is that managing linguistic diversity within the equality framework can be problematic whenever linguistic equality runs counter to the laws of market-driven economy. In this context, the authoritative judgements of the ECJ have more recently confirmed that languages do not have to be treated equally in all circumstances (cf. Sections 3.2.2, 3.2.4, 3.2.6, and 3.2.8).

Beyond the concerns that relate to inequalities among the national languages, the language equality principle turns out to be even more questionable when it comes to minority languages. The point is that minority languages and particularly immigrant languages largely remain excluded from this principle.

It is true that regional minorities have undergone some changes with respect to their standing within the dominant national communities in more recent times, and especially since the *European Minority Charter* and the *Framework Convention* have entered into force (cf. Section 1.2.2) This cannot, however, obscure the fact that apart from single exceptions, regional minorities are still a long way from being treated equally. In this context, we should not forget that it was the explicit plea for equal treatment which put the member states under pressure to make a move towards their historical minorities. Member states could not afford to keep neglecting the equality principle vis-à-vis these minorities since equality constitutes a fundamental principle to which the EU adheres. According to the decision of the European Parliament and the Council on the occasion of the European Year of Languages 2001 (cf. OJ 2000 L 232), all European languages are considered equal in value and dignity. Regional minorities have come to be subsumed under the principle of European language equality since their languages are classified as European languages – even if it is otherwise unclear which languages actually define the term 'European languages' (cf. Chapter 1). The equality principle also explains why non-discrimination and respect for the 'national' minorities' diversity have been enshrined in the recent Lisbon Treaty (cf. Section 1.1).

The longstanding debate on regional minorities' equal rights has also led to the establishment of half-hearted double standards of protection in connection with the Copenhagen Criteria (cf. Section 1.2.2). Here, it remains to be seen how the member states which have as yet not sufficiently applied the rule of equality to their regional minorities will accommodate their policies to the provisions as foreseen in the *Minority Charter* or the *Framework Convention*. It should not be ignored, though, that notwithstanding the integrative power of these legal instruments, their practical implementation remains fragmentary as long as the monitoring mechanisms remain as weak as they are. At present, monitoring is confined to a simple reporting system in which the states account for the measures they have undertaken in specific domains. However, no significant sanctions are imposed upon those states that have fallen short of their obligations. Moreover, the *Minority Charter* and the *Framework Convention* are legal instruments which, in terms of promotional efficiency, may prove to be discrepant since they allow member states to circumvent highly contentious issues in their promotional efforts. Here, for example, it is the states themselves which are called upon to nominate their minorities and the languages to which the latter pertain, and it is furthermore left to the states to select from a proposed range of options the types of measures they prefer (cf. Section 4.1.2 and Section 3.4; see also Cullen *et al.* 2008: 69 and 91–92). Despite these shortcomings, we can say that the situation of the regional minorities has improved although in their status and standing they are, as yet, far from being on an equal footing with the still dominant national majorities.

Besides the regional minorities, it is the immigrant minorities who make a major contribution to the existing diversity in Europe. The question of how to manage diversity deriving from immigration within a European equality framework is a highly contentious issue. Here, it remains unclear how the immigrants' integration into the host society is to be ensured while manoeuvring their diverse lingua-cultural backgrounds. In this context, a major problem is that immigrant minorities as yet do not benefit from promotional measures as they apply, for example, to the regional minorities. It is true that at times there have been political attempts to consider immigrants' multilingual resources as an added value, especially in those cases where immigrants stemming from EC and EU countries are concerned (cf. Section 1.2.2). In reality, however, the language equality principle does not apply to immigrants, least of all when it comes to immigrants who are third-country nationals (cf. Section 3.4; cf. also Extra *et al.* 2004: 402; Nic Craith 2006: 166).

In view of the fact that immigrants do not figure within the European equality framework, their underprivileged position within the member states and the restricted use of their heritage languages raises the question of fundamental and human rights (cf. Sections 1.2.4 and 1.2.2; cf. also Extra *et al.* 2004: 73–92). Thus, against the background of growing globalisation, it can be observed that most recently concerns about equality and human rights have been combining with an increasing awareness that the naturally given multilingual resources of the immigrants constitute an economic asset rather than an impediment to integration. Interestingly, a growing awareness of the fact that the use of the mother tongue constitutes a human right has solicited a debate (cf. Skutnabb-Kangas 1995) which in recent years has brought about initiatives both on the level of the states and at the grass-roots. Here, an increasing concern about schooling and minority children shows that there is a cautious move towards integrating the immigrant languages into the school curricula, which might indicate that immigrants and their languages can no longer be excluded from the diversity framework of the EU.

The last point in relation to equality relates to the fact that in more recent years, the debate about EM has been strongly informed by two major discourses: on the one hand, the discourse combining language equality with human rights, especially vis-à-vis the minorities and on the other hand, the discourse on EM as a means to foster economic efficiency. It has already been mentioned that policy makers and stakeholders find it difficult to reconcile the diverse objectives pursued by both discourses (cf. Section 3.4; cf. also Cullen *et al.* 2008: 8–10) since policies concerned with equality and human rights are not easily compatible with the principles of market-driven freedom and economic gain. A major factor is that in the economic perspective, multilingualism is ideologically considered to be a marketable skill and a prerequisite for economic development, whereas in the scope of equality and human rights, the focus is on the symbolic power of the different languages, which are seen as systems of social meaning and markers of identities of diverse but yet equal value. A chief concern of the equality debate involves ensuring the right to speak and giving a voice to those who as yet have been excluded from or who are not sufficiently in possession of this right. Quite differently, the economic discourse is targeted towards more flexible communication ensuring economic efficiency. While accommodating the requirements of the market, this discourse promotes a rather selected model of EM accessible in the first instance to those who are in possession of the powerful EU languages. Migrants' languages, although they figure prominently in today's globalised labour markets, are largely silenced and discriminated against in this context since their multilingualism is not seen as contributing to the New Economy.

In conclusion, we may say that equality appears to be a very central issue in conceptualising EM, although it is obvious that the ideological framework which combines with the equality principle deviates from the actual multilingual reality in many respects. The reason for this discrepancy may be seen in various aspects which, as we argue, have hitherto not been seriously enough investigated. A major point concerns the issues of power which have to be clarified when talking about EM. The 'unity in diversity' scope suggests that all languages, diverse as they are, are to be united on an equal footing. Conceiving of diversity in terms of harmoniously balanced and inclusive relationships, however, implies hiding the diversified power and conflict potentials that combine with the European languages and the cultural communities for which the languages still stand. The 'unity in diversity' scope is to conceal the antagonisms which derive from the different status accorded to the languages on the basis of the power displayed by the communities to which these languages pertain. The fear that these antagonisms might endanger the unification framework of the EU explains why policy makers eventually uphold language parity against the existing hierarchies as they actually derive from the status and functions of the different European languages.

Hence, re-conceptualising EM would imply seriously rethinking the ideological grounds on which an equally balanced 'unity of diversity' framework is to be constructed. A starting point might be provided by taking a critical stance towards the major ideological strands that inform the debate about EM and linguistic diversity. Here, a basic rethinking of the equality principle would be required, with a particular focus not only on the lesser used minority and immigrant languages but also on the various less widely used national languages in their relationship with the powerful big languages. In these contexts, equality as an ideological objective is being steadily ruled out by the still dominant national language policies and by the hegemonic power displayed by the prominent and prestigious languages in transnational communication.

Rethinking equality in this respect would involve rethinking the traditional status assignments to the languages as they evolve from the power hierarchies within and among the nation states. This raises the question whether it would be possible to conceive of EM in terms of a postnational framework, that is, without linking the languages to traditionally fixed identities, static cultures and the power hierarchies to which the national paradigm normally gives rise. Could we envisage a multilingual society that is not subject to hegemony, dominance and subordination? Can the divide between linguistic majorities and minorities be retained any longer in a multilingual society? Rethinking equality also implies the question of how the contradictory ideological strands which actually underpin the EM discourse, namely, language equality and market-driven freedom, are to be brought together in a common framework, and particularly in view of the fact that both the economic and the equality discourse appear to constitute vital premises for Europeanisation.

The principle of equality was claimed in order to counteract newly feared inequalities among the national languages at the European level as no single language should dominate over the other, and it was thought to fight longstanding inequalities among the national and the minority languages at the national level. Hence, the question arises whether the equality principle, which has hitherto served as a device to counteract linguistic hegemony in and among the nation states, should be upheld on precisely these terms within a European framework beyond the nation state. This is not to suggest that the language equality principle should be dismissed, it rather underlines that it should be accommodated to the reality of the multilingual dynamics as it actually derives from Europeanisation, economic globalisation and migration. It may also be argued that within a dynamic framework of EM, it actually makes little sense to accord equal weight to all languages. Rather, a framework of this kind should allow for multiple patterns of language use, and it should furthermore account for the plurilingual repertoires as they emerge from the communicative requirements and the symbolic power of the various languages in place and time. Such an open framework would also reduce the inconsistencies which threaten to undermine the EM project in its current version as this project actually tends to convey the impression of pursuing noble aims of little political weight.

4.1.3 The 'legitimate' plurilingual repertoire

Another highly contentious issue within the EM debate is the question of the pool of languages European citizens should make their choices from. EU language policies expect citizens to be competent in at least two European languages besides their mother tongue. However, there is as yet no common agreement concerning the languages that should be part of the citizens' multilingual achievement, as there is no answer to the question of how the already existing multilingual resources of the minorities and migrants are to be managed. Hence, defining the 'legitimate' plurilingual repertoire is a highly controversial issue – all the more as it remains unclear how the different aims and objectives that combine with Europeanisation at large can be handled within the EM project.

Following the official discourse, one might be inclined to believe that it is first and foremost the official European languages from which citizens are supposed to make their choices. However, restricting the plurilingual repertoire to the national languages is likely to bring about new conflicts rather than ensuring the desired 'unity in diversity' (cf. Section 3.2.8). A critical point is that not all national languages are equally powerful, and that consequently the average plurilingual repertoire will mainly be composed of English and French, followed by German and possibly by some Italian and Spanish – as is actually the case. The second point concerns the fact that this kind of repertoire obviously furthers a highly elitist model of EM where citizens having access to the powerful languages will have an advantage over those that do not have the opportunity to acquire the prestigious multilingual competences (cf. Section 3.4). Finally, a third crucial factor is that this model of EM runs counter to the *de facto* multilingual diversity in the EU since it ignores the huge bulk of languages which originate from the many regional and immigrant minorities living in the Union.

The reason for the fact that minority languages are not considered to be part of the repertoire on which to build the EM framework is that on the basis of their presumed minor utility and value they are not seen on an equal footing with the national languages. Here again, it is the national language ideology and its discriminating effect against the non-national languages which constitutes a serious impediment to conceptualising EM as a flexible and open framework. Such a framework should ensure both the necessary multilingual competences for increased communication tasks and the management of natural multilingual resources as they evolve from the minorities' cultural backgrounds. It can be argued that minorities' multilingual resources might equally well feed into the 'legitimate' plurilingual repertoire, provided that EM is conceptualised in terms of flexible resources 'available to members of a community for socially significant interaction' (Gal 1987: 286; for a recent critical account see Blommaert & Backus 2011). As a matter of fact, repertoires of this kind are evolving from the use of languages for communicative and cultural purposes in the multilingual constellations that actually characterise the Europeanisation process. In this context, the range of these repertoires comprises the diversified communication patterns of the globalised and transnational labour market as well as the multilingual practices defining the informal sphere of multilingual communities.

Conceiving of EM in terms of flexible repertoires presupposes that the factors which are of primary importance for the constitution of such repertoires are accounted for, that is, the nature of the multilingual constellation including the actors involved in this constellation, the function and the symbolic power allocated to the linguistic resources, and the communicative requirements set with respect to such constellations. As to the constitution of the plurilingual repertoires, it should not be overlooked that, on the one hand, these repertoires may derive from the interactional routines of specific multilingual constellations while, on the other hand, they may be established through language policy and planning (LPP) at the institutional and educational levels. In this respect, education appears to be the most prominent site of re-/producing and implementing plurilingual repertoires since educational settings provide the necessary grounds on which organised language learning on a larger scale societal level can take place (cf. Section 3.2.6).

Furthermore, grasping EM as flexible repertoire also implies reconceptualising the acquisitional models which have hitherto been in use. In this context, a major question would be whether learning languages occurs in the traditional terms of distinct and separated linguistic entities or whether the languages to be learned rather constitute single components of an overall multi-competence. Multi-competence in this sense would mean that individuals dispose of an extended and integrated linguistic repertoire which includes varying degrees of language proficiency. Individuals use this repertoire in a flexible way in order to appropriately adapt their linguistic behaviour to the communicative requirements of the multilingual encounters they are involved in (cf. Section 3.2.7). Another question in this context would then be to what extent the languages should be learned. Should languages be learned with the aim of achieving native-speaker competences in a restricted range of languages or should they rather be learned in order to cope with the pragmatic requirements in specified communicative settings?

A most crucial point in connection with flexible repertoires would concern the question of how to integrate the naturally existing resources which associate with the diverse life-worlds of the old and the new minorities. Here, the question remains open as to how the 'natural' multilingualism that derives from the background of linguistically diverse life-worlds combines with the educated multilingualism that results from learning and instruction. In this respect, cultural knowledge, which is a necessary prerequisite for appropriately handling the components of the linguistic repertoire, appears to be of primary importance. Even if the boundary between natural and educated multilingualism is blurred, it can be assumed that the kind of cultural knowledge which combines with diversified life-worlds does not map onto the cultural knowledge that is transmitted through instruction. Whereas in the context of the life-worlds, the knowledge concerning cultural norms and practices is acquired through experience, in the context of instruction it appears to be mostly transmitted in a codified way, and thus constitutes knowledge of a different kind (cf. Section 3.2.5). If we now proceed from the assumption that the knowledge sets originating from the life-world constitute a natural resource which is conducive to the expansion of educated multilingualism, it is all the more regrettable that the natural multilingual resources of the minorities have been ignored, suppressed and even stigmatised by schools and society alike. If, however, a policy were provided in which knowledge resulting from minority-related multilingualism is regarded as a resource facilitating rather than impeding the learning of more languages, then an important step would be taken towards a form of multilingualism which, at the same time, contributes to a more inclusive European society.

The last point when talking about the 'legitimate' plurilingual repertoire concerns English as a supranational lingua franca. Clearly, English forms an important part of the plurilingual repertoire since it constitutes a widely used practice in all kinds of multilingual settings. The actual dominance of English suggests, however, that its increased use would be an impediment to the learning of other languages and would thus seriously undermine the multilingualism project of the EU (cf. Section 1.2.3). Yet, this widely sustained fear should not be upheld any longer since from research on ELF we may conclude that this is not the case. ELF appears to be a rather powerful means of engaging in multilingual and multicultural encounters without compromising the speakers' interest in learning other languages (cf. Section 3.2.3 and 3.2.4.; cf. also Seidlhofer 2004, 2007; Jenkins 2007). Investigations of ELF in multilingual CoPs furthermore confirm that ELF is a successful means of intercultural communication (cf. Section 3.2.7) As a matter of fact, ELF speakers are multi-competent communicators (cf. also Jørgenson 2005: 394; Jørgenson 2008a: 169, 170; Jørgenson 2008b: 144) who adjust their language use to the multilingual settings they are being part of. Code-switching and mixing appears to be a preferred strategy through which ELF speakers negotiate their mutual understanding. ELF speakers thus take advantage of their multilingual resources, and it can therefore be hypothesised that ELF is not an impediment to EM but rather opens up to the flexible use of languages other than English. In this perspective, ELF does not sustain a hegemonic 'English Only' repertoire but proves to be an important part of diverse plurilingual repertoires and should therefore be accounted for in this function within a flexible and open framework of EM.

From what has been said, it follows that the notion of linguistic competence has to be revised when talking about the European multilingual repertoire. Instead of being viewed as a set of compartmentalised languages within a pre-established repertoire, EM should be conceived in terms of flexible resources of which multi-competent speakers make use in order to cope with the requirements of multilingual interaction. However, conceptualising and planning the repertoire as flexible resources implies that the different forms of natural and guided multilingualism have to be carefully revised with regard to the resources they provide, particularly in those cases where the integration of minority-related multilingualism is concerned.

In conclusion, we may say that a 'legitimate' plurilingual repertoire simply does not seem to exist. Conceiving of new and more flexible ways of communication that account for the dynamics of Europeanisation and globalisation implies that the foundations of the EM project would be constituted by many repertoires. Policy makers and stakeholders should be well aware of this fact.

4.1.4 European multilingualism and migration

Clearly, reconceptualising EM in the scope of Europeanisation and globalisation cannot dismiss migration since migration has been contributing substantially to increasing linguistic diversity within the EU even further over the past decades. Nevertheless, immigrants' multilingual competences have come to be a matter of political concern only in more recent years.

A serious question in this context relates to how immigrants can be part of the EM framework since their multilingual resources generally do not figure as a valuable asset. Rather, these are seen as an impediment to integration, which is the reason why immigrant language policies keep focusing on immigrants learning the host language. This is particularly evident when political practices concerning citizenship are at stake. Within the member states, citizenship is traditionally associated with language-based belonging and thus with the requirement of proficiency in the national language (cf. Section 3.4). However, this practice proves to be problematic in several respects.

First, by focusing exclusively on proficiency in the national language, the politics of citizenship disregards the immigrants' lingua-cultural backgrounds. It thus runs counter to the active democratic participation and cultural inclusion of these people into the host society. At the same time, it gives rise to severe discrepancies compared to the regional minority policies. It is true that within the framework of national assimilation and after longstanding political claims, regional minorities have generally been accorded the right to difference of cultural belonging based upon their heritage languages – albeit under the premises of becoming bilingual. In the meantime, these languages have come to be seen as constituting an enriching part of the common national heritage and are considered to form the primary grounds for the ethnic identification and cultural belonging of these groups. Quite differently, in the context of citizenship politics, immigrant minorities lack comparable rights and thus cannot lay claim to cultural belonging based upon their heritage language – instead, they are first and foremost expected to acquire proficiency in the respective national language in order to cope with the requirements of integration into the host society. Moreover, they are supposed to abandon their heritage languages and to undergo one-sided assimilation into the host society. The critical point here is that the regional minorities' cultural belonging is seen as intimately related to their heritage languages whereas in the context of immigrant minorities, the bond between the heritage language and the respective cultural belonging is largely ignored or even entirely negated (cf. Section 3.2.1).

Another highly problematic issue that directly relates to the suppression of the immigrants' heritage languages concerns the schooling of the immigrant children, who are in most cases, as yet, being educated in the national host languages only (cf. Section 3.2.6). In this context, a crucial point appears to be that second-generation immigrants do not succeed well enough in primary and secondary education and thus appear to be seriously hampered in their social advancement and mobility. The reason for this may be seen in the fact that the one-sided education in the host language leads to a situation where immigrant children generally lack the learned input and positive feedback concerning their heritage languages, and thus risk ending up with insufficient proficiency in both the host and the heritage language. Hence, member states are increasingly called upon to revise their language educational politics with respect to second-generation immigrants. Political revision is particularly essential with respect to the symbolic and communicative functions of the home languages of these children (cf. also Extra et al. 2004: 402). From research on immigrant children, it can be derived that children who are instructed in both the heritage and the host language prove to be more successful in acquiring the host language (cf. De Cillia 2001; Akkuş et al. 2005). Here, change seems to be underway in some member states, but in general it appears that these developments take place all too slowly if at all.

Within the EU diversity framework, it would therefore be desirable to seriously rethink some crucial issues concerning the language policies with respect to immigrant minorities. An important point would involve reconsidering the inconsistent distinction actually made concerning the languages of the old and the new minorities. Indeed, constructing the minorities as belonging to two different categories is to be questioned since both groups are similar with regard to the fundamental qualities defining minorities at large (cf. also Extra & Yağmur 2004: 17–18). These similarities can be seen first and foremost in the issues of ethnic difference and inequality which come to bear in asymmetrial power relationships between the minorities and their majorities. Similarities can also be observed in the identification patterns of these minorities, which are basically entrenched in diverse manifestations of their cultural heritage, of which in turn their languages form an integral part. It is true, however, that both the old and the new minorities differ with respect to their genesis and formation, and hence in their motivational backgrounds and their desire to be included into the national societies (cf. Rindler Schjerve 2004: 483–485). Despite this difference, it appears, however, to be inappropriate to construct two distinct categories of minorities since this distinction masks the ideological foundations that commonly underpin the minority policies in most of the member states. These policies still appear to be strongly driven by the national language ideologies with the result that member states keep paying lip service to diversity and equality while in reality attempting to minimise their efforts in fostering the existing multilingualism and multiculturalism within their societies.

Hence, the first step towards an integral minority language politics would comprise reconsidering the relations of difference and inequality that combine with the minorities within the national paradigm. This implies revising the notion of minority. In its traditional understanding, the concept of minority is a relational term which implies that minorities are being conceived on the basis of their relating to majorities. This relationship comes to bear in the form of asymmetrical power and hegemony. Reconceptualising this relationship on the grounds of the European diversity framework constitutes a process which might allow for integrating the multilingual resources of the minorities more appropriately into the repertoires of EM instead of upholding them as separate entities which, in different measures and degrees, remain juxtaposed to the lingua-cultural dominance of the state majorities.

Apart from the lack of common grounds on which to tackle the minorities' diversity, European language policies also continue to neglect the ideologically loaded and highly sensitive relationship of language, identity and culture. This is particularly evident in the case of immigrants. Whenever the question of integration and belonging of these minorities is under discussion, the debate focuses upon the requirement of their knowledge of the host language and culture (cf. also Vertovec 2010: 90–91). The critical point is, however, that speaking a language does not automatically entail membership of a specific culture. Therefore, proficiency in the host language – as generally presupposed in citizenship testing – does not reveal anything about immigrants identifying with the cultural spaces of the host society. The belief that language proficiency would be a safe tool for measuring integration simply neglects the fact that immigrants, while moving between the host and the heritage culture, identify in multiple and flexible ways with both cultures. They accommodate their multi-layered identities by positioning the different layers in relation to one another (cf. Section 3.2.1). This, however, raises the question of how the multiple identifications actually match the one-sided concept of immigrant citizenship and integration. Current controversies about integration and citizenship show that new forms of inclusion are required in order to avoid that immigrant minorities be pushed into social closure or politically mobilised re-ethnisation which may occur in cases where the heritage languages are denied the status of a reference framework for the immigrants' identifications and cultural belonging. Hence, sticking to the traditional assumption that knowledge of the host language stands for successful integration runs a high risk of undervaluing the conflict potentials that may arise from the multi-layered dynamics immigrants are faced with when integrating into the host societies.

The last and crucial point when talking about migration and linguistic diversity concerns the fact that the multilingual resources of the immigrant minorities are generally not considered to constitute economic capital and do not count as an added value in the labour markets although immigrants and their skills play a central role in the national economies. The demand for flexible language use in the markets is largely restricted to the big and more widely used European languages and does, apart from a few exceptions, not concern the immigrant languages. In other words, immigrants in most cases do not dispose of the required multilingual repertoire, and in cases where they do, this repertoire is not adequately valued since the immigrants are generally employed in very low niches of the labour market in which competences of this kind are not required as such. The multilingual skills of educated Africans who, besides their home language, also speak French or English are a good example for these discrepancies (cf. Sections 3.2.6 and 3.2.8).

An important point is, however, that in terms of flexibility and mobility there seems to be a considerable difference between the various immigrant groups stemming from inside and outside the EU. These groups differ with respect to their positions within the national labour markets, which begs the question of whether and how the multilingual resources of these people can be integrated into the diversity framework of the EU.

One problem in this context relates to the fact that the tremendous increase of linguistic and cultural diversity brought about by globalisation and market-driven Europeanisation cannot be regulated according to the principles of the New Economy. On the one hand, considering the immigrants' multilingual skills as an exclusively economic resource turns a blind eye to the symbolic capital that immigrant languages may have for their speakers. This is particularly evident in those cases where the immigrant languages assume primary importance in the identity formation and in upholding the ethnic vitality of the groups concerned. On the other hand, the immigrants' multilingualism does not always figure in terms of an economic resource since in most cases it does not match with the linguistic requirements of the respective labour market. Including the multilingual resources of immigrants into the diversity framework of the EU would thus imply accounting for both the economic and symbolic capitalisation and the consequences they may have.

The first step in this direction would involve providing for adequate measures to promote and sustain the multilingual resources. This might occur through institutional support, that is, schooling and training in which immigrant adults and children obtain the necessary learned input in the home and/or the host language in order to adequately exploit their multilingual skills in specific niches of the labour market. At the same time, and given that immigrants will have a bearing on the desired social cohesion within the EU, they should be granted linguistic rights especially in those cases where communication intersects with the issues of human rights, for example, in the case of communication in court or contacts with administrative authorities. Furthermore, it should be borne in mind that immigrant languages, like any other languages, may constitute an important symbolic capital for their speakers and can, thus, play a vital role in the process of a more or less successful social inclusion.

Concluding, we may say that migration constitutes a particular challenge for conceptualising EM within the diversity framework of the EU. First, language-based citizenship, which represents a widely used practice in most of the member states, necessitates a fundamental rethinking with respect to the lingua-cultural consequences connecting with the immigrants' social inclusion and participation in the host society. Here, the question remains how the pressure on the minorities' one-sided integration is compatible with the potentials of these communities of truly identifiying with the language and culture of the host society. The second point is that the divide between regional and immigrant minorities appears to be no longer tenable. Instead, it is the common juxtaposition of linguistic and national majorities which calls for a basic revision within a framework of diversity. As a matter of fact, the languages and cultures of the minorities have been, and are still being, considered as minor and less powerful in the perspective of the national majorities. Although the attitudes towards the regional minorities have changed in some respects (cf. also Cullen *et al.* 2008: 86), it appears that in general, the integrational state policies concerning the immigrant minorities are strongly guided by the dominant national ideologies. Integrating the immigrant minorities into the diversity framework would therefore presuppose a critical rethinking of the power asymmetries on which the concept of minority is founded.

Finally, the third point relates to the fact that, in the meantime, immigrant minorities have come to play a crucial role on the labour markets. Consequently, an answer should be sought to the question of how the immigrants' multilingual resources might be capitalised more efficiently. At the same time, activities targeted towards an economic capitalisation of the immigrant languages should keep an eye on the symbolic power potentials which immigrant languages may display for their speakers, especially when conflicting issues of identity and culture are at the forefront of the migration debate.

4.2 Towards an Integrative View of European Multilingualism

Dealing with EM beyond LINEE necessarily includes dealing with the theoretical issues of the EM framework to which the LINEE research did not provide appropriate answers. In our plea for a partial re-conceptualisation of EM in Section 4.1, we have already returned to the explanatory potentials of the single key variables. In the absence of a relative framework, the potentials of these variables have, however, not been utilised in a correspondingly systematic way. In the following, we will thus develop scenarios which are intended as a potential basis on which EM can be conceptualised as a dynamic phenomenon in the synopsis of the various key variables.

Clearly, the broad scope of the LINEE research allowed for identifying crucial factors which opened the door to viewing EM in diverse ways and manners. In this multifaceted scope it was not possible, though, to go beyond a general itemisation of the single key variables. The LINEE research – it is true – contributed to uncovering the basically intersecting nature of the variables in the various manifestations of EM; nevertheless, it remained, unclear how and to what extent the variables actually interacted with one another. Thus, in some cases, for example, specific variables figured prominently, whereas in others they remained rather vague and blurred. As the phenomena under investigation appeared to combine with the key variables in a highly diversified way, the question arose as to which factors impacted on the salience of the single variables and their clustering. From the LINEE perspective, it seemed obvious that these phenomena correlated with the research theme and, maybe more precisely, with the research focus that guided the respective investigation of EM.

Beyond these questions, it also appeared difficult to arrange the key variables in relation to one another since they stemmed from quite different epistemological and ontological backgrounds, for example, 'knowledge' and 'language policy and planning', which were to be seen as deriving from differing levels of meaning and abstraction.

Another crucial issue concerned the fact that conceiving of the variables in terms of key components of multilingualism appeared to be inextricably linked to the question of their alignment in relation to this concept. Hence, the most challenging question was how to put these variables together in a theoretical framework of multilingualism. At first sight, it seemed as if EM could be viewed in terms of compounded variables. A closer look at the phenomena under investigation suggested, however, that it rather constituted a flexible arrangement of the single variables in the form of unstable relational clusters. Conceiving of flexible relational clusters appeared to match the complexity and dynamics displayed in EM and would, at the same time, be in line with post-modern theory building, which the conceptualisation of the key variables is essentially committed to.

Against the background of the LINEE findings, we will now seek to proceed one step further by developing an exemplary scenario which might shed more light on the still unresolved problems. Starting out from the question of how to align the key variables within a theoretical framework of EM, it was somehow evident that within the established set of key variables, 'knowledge' would represent a kind of umbrella item. The reasons for the overarching position of 'knowledge' compared to the other key variables have as yet not been elaborated sufficiently enough. Therefore, no precise answer can be found at the moment to the question of whether a theoretically overarching role can actually be ascribed to 'knowledge' or whether the prominent position of 'knowledge' is rather related to the LINEE focus, in which multilingualism was investigated in relation to the knowledge-based society. In the absence of more in-depth knowledge, and in view of the apparently all-embracing way in which 'knowledge' intervenes in the various lingua-cultural manifestations (cf. Section 3.2.5), we adhere to the hypothesis that 'knowledge' might constitute a common frame in which the processes connecting with the other key variables could be integrated.

Within the LINEE research, 'knowledge' appeared to be relevant in different ways and manners, that is, in terms of 'knowledge of languages', 'knowledge about languages and language learning', and also in terms of 'cultural knowledge' which results from culturally diversified historical backgrounds, stereotyped validations and attitudes. This cultural type of 'knowledge' was of particular interest as it refers to more implicit forms of 'knowledge' which impact upon the choice, the use and the value accorded to the different languages while also intervening into the construction of identities and belonging. This multifunctional presence of 'knowledge' in the various manifestations of EM appeared to justify defining 'knowledge' in terms of an overarching variable. Thus, if 'knowledge' is actually an all-embracing variable, it could be assumed that a knowledge-based perspective would provide a suitable framework for the coherent conception of the various components of EM.

Now, choosing 'knowledge' as an umbrella term presupposes that multilingualism is founded on specific knowledge sets which relate to language. These knowledge sets derive from the diverse individual, lingua-cultural, political, social and economic processes that constitute multilingualism in general. It can be presumed that the knowledge sets include questions about the status, the function and the value of the various languages, such as the following: what do the languages represent and what do they mean to people? How are these meanings enacted? What kind of power is displayed when people interact through different languages? Furthermore, how do the languages combine within the multilingual individual and how do individuals draw on the specific linguistic resources that are available to them? And finally, a crucial question to ask would be: what is a language (cf. Jørgensen 2008b: 10, 151) and, consequently, what does the concept of multiple languages refer to?

Clearly, conceiving of multilingualism as basically founded on 'knowledge' paves the way for focusing more clearly on the interaction of the various key variables which participate in the manifestations of multilingualism. In this perspective, the issue of 'knowledge concerning languages' may be seen as relating to 'identity' (cf. Section 3.2.3). By this we mean 'identity' based upon the sociocultural knowledge and the shared beliefs to which individuals or groups refer when they identify with specific languages while constructing a sense of affinity or belonging or even a sense of distance towards the languages. This is also the point where 'culture' intervenes (cf. Section 3.2.1). 'Culture' reflects the symbolic orders and value hierarchies, which in their meaning are primarily negotiated through language and which are collectively shared. In other words, language in terms of communicative practices and the norms and values they imply is in itself culturally bound. It is thus subject to the knowledge that is generated through cultural negotiation. This is particularly true in the European context, in which culture and languages have been shaping a historical nexus of meaning since the formation of the nation state. Hence, talking about 'European languages' presupposes that we consider these languages to be founded on the European national cultures. In this perspective, linguistic Europeanisation can be seen as a process in which the meaning of the norms and values traditionally associated with the languages may change as the cultural orders and the knowledge about these orders change.

Furthermore, viewing multilingualism from a knowledge-based perspective cannot ignore that 'identity' and 'culture' relate to 'ideology', that is, ideology in terms of cognitive representations and beliefs serving specific interests and purposes (cf. Section 3.2.4). Multilingualism includes ideology whenever ideologically loaded conceptualisations of language in connection with group membership are at stake or when social inter-group relations or the cultural values and norms assigned to the languages are at the centre of interest. The ideological loading of these phenomena may be seen as deriving from larger ideologies and might therefore point to social and political spheres that go beyond language. An example in case would be EM as an objective to achieve the sought-after European unity in diversity. Ideologies are geared to specific features, as encoded, for example, in languages, or to principles such as the unity framework mentioned above. Issues of this kind form the basis of the ideologically invested beliefs which, again, refer to particular knowledge sets that are shared and reproduced by particular social groups through discursive action. Thus, 'discourse' as a carrier and producer of meaning transmits and also transforms 'knowledge' in that it may construct specific knowledge sets that suit specific interests (cf. Section 3.2.2), for example, when EM is instrumentalised as a strategy to ensure not only the desired unity but also social cohesion and intercultural understanding, or when the discourse on migration endorses the need for language-based citizenship in order to cope with conflict-driven integration. 'Discourse' is a highly salient key variable which – comparably to the all-embracing potential of 'knowledge' – links up with all the other variables as these variables manifest themselves in a more or less explicit way through discursive interaction.

'Discourse' as a transmitter and generator of knowledge generally involves relations between individuals and social groups, which is the reason why 'power' emerges as a major factor in this context (cf. Section 3.2.8). Naturally, 'power' is a variable that connects intimately with the other key variables since despite their diverse nature all these variables originate from discursively bound social interaction. The concept of 'power' relates to issues of social relationships and to the way these relationships are enacted or negotiated to the benefit or the disadvantage of the groups involved. In a knowledge-centred perspective on multilingualism, it may be argued that 'power' is produced through the 'knowledge' generated in relationships in which language constitutes a major functional or symbolic feature and thus co-determines the dynamics of the relationships. More specifically, and with regard to EM, we may conclude that the power generated through this kind of 'knowledge' has an effect on what languages are used, on how they are used by which speakers or groups of speakers, for what purposes they are used, and on what they mean to their speakers, or – in Bourdieu's terms – what symbolic capital they represent for their speakers.

Given that the diverse European languages are more or less powerful – as are their speakers – these asymmetries may come to bear on the speakers' identities, their self-awareness and their social advancement. This also explains why the power characterising the relations among the big and the less widely used national languages, or among the national majority and the minority languages, gives rise to tensions and conflicts which the official EM policy seeks to avoid.

Conceiving of 'knowledge' as an overarching dimension of EM will also take into account the question concerning the kind of 'knowledge' required when languages are learned, produced and received and when they are stored. In this scope, it is obvious that 'multi-competence', which has been conceptualised in terms of speakers' flexible use of more languages (cf. Section 3.2.7), intersects with 'knowledge'. In other words, this intersection comes to bear at least in a three-fold way: one point is that specific knowledge sets are required in order to develop multi-competence when learning or teaching a second, a third or a fourth language. The famous 'mother tongue +2' strategy is but one example in this respect. Moreover, the specific knowledge normally produced in multilingual interaction requires multi-competence to ensure the appropriate interpretation of its meaning. Here, the dynamics generally unfolding in multilingual communities of practice provides an apt example. And yet a third point is that 'knowledge', albeit of a more ideological nature, intervenes when specific languages are preferred and selected at the various institutional levels, that is, EU institutions and educational settings, while others are silenced.

The last and most challenging issue within a knowledge-based framework of EM relates to 'language policy and planning' (cf. Section 3.2.6). Assessing the intersection between 'knowledge' and 'LPP' turns out to be somewhat problematic since LPP, quite differently from knowledge, seems to refer primarily to interventionist issues. Although LPP appears, as it were, as an outsider within the range of key variables, a closer investigation of the workings of LPP shows, however, that these cannot be grasped by exclusively interventionist terms since LPP also comprises other dimensions related to 'knowledge'. Talking about LPP is, as a matter of fact, mostly directed towards official policies in which the deliberately interventionist character of LPP is foregrounded in various top–down activities as they are performed by the state or authoritative institutions, whereas the participation of 'knowledge' in these activities is largely neglected. As the example of promoting official signage in bilingual communities clearly showed (cf. Section 3.2.6), however, the highly sensitive implementation of bilingual place names presupposes explicit knowledge of the political standards and requirements concerning linguistic diversity in place in order to appease or avoid conflicts over these matters. Another point is that the wide range of bottom–up policies which come to bear in the form of individual actions, identifications or ideologically driven knowledge sets is not always accounted for in terms of political action.

Therefore, the knowledge-based dimension which impacts upon policies of this kind remains rather hidden.

Another factor concerning the relation between LPP and 'knowledge' is that on the one hand, LPP relies on 'knowledge' in order to design and implement the language political action, whereas on the other hand, it generates knowledge through the implementation of the language political action. Here, it may happen that the kind of 'knowledge' generated through LPP does not always meet the objectives which LPP was actually targeted at. Thus, for example, EM policies, while fostering content and language-integrated learning focused primarily upon English as a native language, may be risk developing a kind of multilingualism which undermines the current activities displayed by theses policies in order to implement the 'mother tongue +2' strategy.

Discrepancies of a similar kind may occur when the knowledge dimensions of the top–down and the bottom–up policies do not meet but run counter to each other in terms of their respective objectives. Second and third language acquisition in diverse EU school settings is a good example for these opposed LPPs (cf. Section 3.2.4). Here, the teaching and learning strategies mostly remain embedded in monolingually oriented pedagogies at the national level and thus run counter to the EU multilingualism policies targeted towards enhancing EM, which, however, would imply pedagogies of a different kind.

At the same time, the knowledge-based perspective appears to offer an appropriate scenario in which LPP may easily be approached with respect to its ideological and power-specific implications. Since LPP is a primarily discourse-based variable, it intersects with the dimensions of 'ideology' and 'power' through 'discourse'. At this point, it should also be mentioned that LPP cannot be separated from 'discourse' since conceiving of LPP, for example, in the case of European language policy and planning, necessarily implies viewing these policies as a vast stream of discursive strands relating to LPP.

From what has been said, we may conclude that 'knowledge' appears to be a dimension which, as we argue, allows for investigating the major components of EM in a multi-focal and coherent way. This, however, does not imply that a dynamic perspective on EM can exclusively be developed via 'knowledge'. Rather, EM could conceivably be captured in the form of a flexible framework, that is, in terms of fluid and intersecting key variables collocated around a key focus in which, beyond 'knowledge', other key variables might also function as an umbrella.

One example in this context would be 'discourse', and since it may be hypothesised that according to the overarching dimension that defines this variable, a discourse-centred perspective would also allow for assessing the major components of multilingualism in a coherent way. Different from the knowledge-based focus, a discourse-based perspective would primarily concentrate on the meanings that are elaborated or negotiated in connection with multilingualism by various groups and their speakers.

In a similar manner, it would also be possible to conceive of 'power' as an overarching dimension from which to proceed when exploring multilingualism. Investigating multilingualism from a power-centred perspective would imply elaborating on questions which focus on the production and reproduction of power relating to the diverse languages, and to question the meaning and the consequences this power has for the speakers and collectives under investigation.

With respect to EM and on the basis of the particular intersection between multilingualism and politics in this case, it might furthermore be an option to take LPP as a central focus for investigating multilingualism. An LPP-centred perspective would concentrate on the questions of what actors are involved in which political activities at what levels of decision making, and, in turn, would certainly foreground questions relating to discourse, ideology, as well as power and conflict since these variables connect with aspects that have a strong bearing upon LPP. Hence, an LPP-centred focus would be directed towards investigating how the actors intervene in maintaining or transforming specific communicative practices in the interest of specific groups and what beliefs and objectives underpin their political activities.

As 'ideology' appears to play a crucial role in all these scenarios, it might also be hypothesised that 'ideology' could form a central focus from which to analytically construe multilingualism. In this case, research would be directed towards questions which concern the politically and morally loaded ideas about the value and function of languages and the meaning, that is, the symbolic power these languages display in social interaction and group membership.

Moreover, it seems that the argument of flexibly centred focuses would equally well apply to an identity- or culture-based perspective provided that such a perspective suits the focal aspects under investigation. As far as multi-competence is concerned, it seems, however, that a competence-centred focus can only be implemented to a limited extent since 'multi-competence' constitutes a variable with a primary focus on multilingualism in the individual (cf. Section 3.2.7).

Summarising the results as they may be derived from the scenarios outlined so far, we may say that it is the research focus on multilingualism which most likely biases the way and the salience in which the single variables combine with one another. Another conclusion would be that both 'knowledge' and 'discourse' appear to provide an umbrella which, in terms of the overarching and integrative potentials of these two variables, seems to be somewhat different from the other key variables. At the present state of the art, we cannot explain, however, why 'knowledge' and 'discourse' are as all-embracing as they appear when approaching multilingualism in a flexible and multi-focal way.

Against the background of the LINEE findings, it was assumed that the fluid and complex meaning of the key variables would be assessed more precisely through their intersection with the other variables rather than through static variable compounds or an isolated focus on single phenomena. The multi-focal approach has, we believe, also revealed the multi-layered dynamics of the key variables. Unfortunately, neither do we as yet know very much about the kernel factors that regulate the intersections among the variables nor do we know how epistemological and ontological perceptions exert influence upon the intersections. Therefore, several rather substantial blind spots still appear to exist which have to be clarified before we can proceed with further elaborating a coherent framework which adequately grasps the dynamics of multilingualism. Such a framework could, as has been shown, evolve around the axis of 'knowledge' or 'discourse', or of any other key variable, with the particular focus always depending on which specific aspects of multilingualism are at the focus of the investigation.

Conclusion

In the process of working on this book, it was apparent that 'EM' lacks a clear definition, both as a scientific concept and as a political programme. This also explains why the term EM is sometimes applied divergently in politics and science. Moreover, it has become apparent that the goals of politics and science do not always coincide. Hence, it is not surprising that the meaning of EM, which is still in the making, appears contradictory and inconsistent in some respects.

In the public discussion on the topic of multilingualism in Europe – here primarily within the EU – one cannot fail to notice that this topic is closely linked with the will to shape policy. This is especially evident in the debate on European diversity, in which the maintenance of the different languages and cultures in the EU has been particularly emphasised since Maastricht. Maintaining this diversity is based on the primary values and principles on which the EU is founded. Moreover, this aspect is emphasised to guarantee that in view of the increasing European integration, the different national cultures and identities of the member states are preserved. This also explains why the call for multilingualism is progressively developed into a political strategy which is to ensure the regulation of language diversity within the framework of the European unification process.

Furthermore, considerable significance is added to the ideology of 'unity in diversity' by the development of the European KBS and the Lisbon strategy. Here, economic arguments calling for enhanced EM are increasingly introduced. According to the latest documents on European language policy, the topic of EM presents itself as a transversal issue which is to be asserted in other central policy areas of the EU. Hence, policy makers and stakeholders are seeking to establish EM as a cross-cutting policy framework in its own right.

As to the political dimension of EM, the book concentrates upon three areas that have been particularly focal in EM policy making over the past 50 years. These areas are the linguistic minorities, in fact, both the regional and the immigrant minorities, as well as the area of language education policy and the linguistic regime in the institutions of the EU. In these three areas, EU language policy is faced with quite diverse challenges since these policy areas call for different solution strategies.

The focus on EM, however, has not only been directed towards the political dimension since the 1990s but has also been intensified in the area of research. It seems, though, that the scientific debate combines with the political debate to a certain extent, as politics occupies knowledge generated by research while it conversely commissions and initiates research.

The European large-scale project LINEE can be seen as an example for the intersection between politics and research. At the same time, however, it also shows the difficulties resulting from the varying expectations and goals of research and politics. In this context, research cannot always prepare its stocks of knowledge in a form as it is required for implementing political action.

It was the political mission of LINEE to assess the implications of linguistic diversity among European populations and to answer the question of how linguistic diversity relates to the promotion of the knowledge-based society (cf. LINEE Annex I 2006: 11, 21). Against the background of the results obtained in LINEE, it becomes clear that the term linguistic diversity comprises phenomena which are most diverse and multi-layered in their conditions and which in turn contain highly differentiated answers. Science provides a number of theoretical and methodological approaches for investigating these phenomena. At the same time, however, we cannot fail to notice that exploring multilingualism constitutes a rather recent research area which is quite fragmented both in its thematic focus and in its theoretical and methodological approaches. Thus, the results of the LINEE research are to be seen against the background of this discipline in the making, even if considerable efforts were made in LINEE to contribute to the defragmentation of the disciplinary knowledge by developing a research platform.

The central task of LINEE comprised of plumbing the sociopolitical implications of EM by exploiting the scientific potentials available. In this process, it became obvious that the concept of EM in its complexity and vagueness leaves scope for conflicting and inconsistent interpretations. Fault lines can be observed with regard to the ideological localisation of EM. Here, the ideology of the nation state with all its hegemonic and repressive implications continues to prevail, while the step towards multilingualism beyond the nation state has not been taken yet in the diversity framework of the EU.

In the EU's motto 'unity in diversity', the persistence of nation-state ideologies becomes apparent since 'unity in diversity' is based on a severe blending of language, identity and culture. This perspective primarily concerns the maintenance of the national languages and cultures, while the minority languages are largely ignored. Besides, aspects of the European history of conflict, in which the languages and cultures are embedded, are mostly omitted as they do not fit into the concept of harmonious diversity. Another point relates to the fact that against the background of the equation of language, identity and culture, the development of the longed-for European identity and culture in the form of the simple addition of all national languages seems to be warranted. This implies that the concept of EM is reduced to the sum of all languages.

Another fault line which is also related to ideology concerns the fact that the discourse on EM is characterised by conflicting interests. These contradictions become apparent in the great tension resulting from two obviously conflicting conceptions of EM. On the one hand, EM is conceived of as a coexistence of all languages spoken in the EU on the basis of the equality of all languages and of the right to language as a human right, while on the other hand, EM is put to the service of market-based efficiency and capitalisation.

Marked flaws can also be detected in relation to the role ascribed to English. On the one hand, it is feared that English could eliminate the other languages since English plays a more and more dominant role in transnational communication. On the other hand, it is increasingly pointed out that ELF performs an important function in multilingual communication independent of any national bonds, and that it should thus be included in the repertoire of EM.

In this context, it should also be noted that EM constitutes a concept which is subject to major political influence, and which thus raises the question concerning the protagonists of EM policy. When referring to EM, we tend to think primarily of the EU, as it constitutes the leading institution in the conceptual design of EM. In fact, however, the EU's implementing power is limited since the implementation of language policies continues to lie within the responsibility of the member states. The discrepancy of national and supranational language policy is evident in several respects and particularly in those cases where transnational phenomena would call for coordinated language political action. Thus, for example, recent migration in Europe is characterised by short-lived phenomena which require speedy solutions concerning language competence in order to ensure both cultural and economic integration. Furthermore, the long unsolved problems brought about, for example, by the integration of the Roma minority show that no satisfactory solutions can be found on a national level. At the same time, the efficacy of the Copenhagen Criteria illustrates how transnational concepts can take effect at the level of regional minority support on a national level, although there is still a need for uniform measures.

Needless to say, the detailed insights as to the weaknesses and inconsistencies in the conception of EM have been primarily brought about by the academic debate. By adopting a very broad perspective, the LINEE project has created the conditions for focusing on the multi-layered phenomena of EM and – as we feel – for grasping these in their basic dynamics in greater detail.

In dealing with the theoretical aspects of EM within the framework of the LINEE research platform, eight key variables can be defined as main components of this multilingualism, that is, 'culture', 'discourse', 'identity', 'ideology', 'knowledge', 'LPP', 'multi-competence' and 'power and conflict'. Although these variables are continually referred to in the academic debates on multilingualism, it is due to the comprehensive perspective of LINEE that the scientific awareness of the way these variables interact within the scope of multilingualism has been notably increased. In this process, it became apparent that the single variables combined in a flexible manner and that they overlapped and formed variable interactional clusters. Research into EM within LINEE showed that conceptualising EM appeared rather problematic in certain areas – since these seemed too fragile and conflicting. More specifically, focusing on the identified problem areas revealed that the respective variables emerged with variable prominence and cluster formation in these fields. Finally, going beyond the scope of the results of the single LINEE subprojects, a repeated focus on the relevant variables enabled us to capture the complexity of the problem areas more accurately. Here, a multifocal approach was applied, in which the respective domains were viewed from the perspective of several variables at the same time. This enabled us to analyse the problems identified in more detail regarding their complexity, and to find answers to various basic questions closely associated with the current conceptualisation of EM.

One major question concerning this conceptualisation of EM relates to the fact that EM is generally taken to correspond to the sum of the EU's various national languages. If we now seek to find an answer to the question whether this conception is valid from the perspective of the key variables mentioned, a close interaction of 'identity', 'culture' and 'ideology' emerges in this context. In this interplay, it becomes evident that the ideological basis on which the coexistence of the European languages is conceived appears to be highly debatable. On the one hand, it is based on the equation of culture, identity and language. This equation, however, leaves little room for the dynamic realisations of the connections between culture, identity and language as they seem to be conditioned by Europeanisation and globalisation. On the other hand, the equation is restricted to the national languages, which are in turn connected to homogeneous national identities and cultures. The approach of viewing EM as a common container of the national languages thus does not take into account various facets of multilingualism in Europe. The multilingualism of minorities, which accounts for a large proportion of European language diversity, for example, is excluded from this definition. Alternatively, a more flexible approach which is adjusted to the diverse linguistic and cultural possibilities of identification seems to provide a more suitable framework for EM than the present perspective, which is strongly geared to the national languages.

Moreover, investigating the major principles that actually guide the assumptions concerning EM from the perspective of the key variables also reveals that the foundations of the concept of EM are, in fact, ideologically debatable. Here, however, a different constellation of key variables emerges since in this context, 'power' and 'discourse' become particularly operative in interaction with 'identity' and 'ideology'. The principle of maintaining language equality is a fundamental ideological assumption on which EM is based since this principle is assumed to balance the prevailing asymmetries of status and power between the national languages. Furthermore, it involves accounting for the symbolic power of the languages in their significance for constructing identities. This applies particularly to the linguistic minorities, where the principle of language equality aims at ensuring language rights. At the same time, however, the language equality principle is opposed to the discourse on the economic efficiency of EM, which is ideologically located in the market-based capitalisation of languages. Yet, putting EM to the service of economic efficiency might lead to a further intensification of existing power asymmetries or potentially also to the development of new asymmetries.

All in all, the failure of the language equality principle and its incompatibility with the ideological foundations of the New Economy indicate that the great challenges for a future composition of EM can be summarised in terms of the following questions: what is the ideological basis on which the multiple patterns of language use resulting from Europeanisation, globalisation and migration can be adequately accounted for? On which ideological basis can EM be planned and implemented in a Europeanised society beyond the nation state?

Yet another fundamental question to which the multifocal approach yielded sophisticated insights relates to the pool of languages EM is to be composed of. This is a question which concerns the so-called 'legitimate plurilingual repertoire'. In this context, 'power' and 'ideology' are closely related to each other, although 'culture' and 'LPP' also appear to play a role. In addition, the dimension of 'multi-competence' appears to be particularly prominent. Here, conceptualising 'multi-competence' as an extended and integrated linguistic repertoire which includes varying degrees of language proficiency allows for the integration of all languages which fulfill functional purposes. A restriction to specific languages and thus to one or several 'legitimate plurilingual repertoire(s)', in contrast, does not seem to be a suitable solution since it does not account for the diversity of language-related communication needs and acquisition modes.

Furthermore, an approach which focuses on communicative needs also enables us to take into account the relevance of ELF as a successful means of intercultural communication – rather than regarding it as an obstacle to multilingualism. Moreover, the multifocal approach also shows that the diverse life-world- and school-related modes of language acquisition are associated with the acquisition of different stocks of knowledge. These differences should be adequately considered in the conceptualisation of EM in terms of flexible repertoires. From the synopsis of the critical points, it thus becomes clear that we need to search for a dynamic and flexible framework rather than for predefined repertoires.

A final question concerns the minorities' linguistic resources and how these are to be integrated into the EU's diversity framework. The variables featuring most prominently in this context are 'identity', 'culture', 'power' and 'ideology'. Here, the multifocal approach also leads to more detailed results: on the one hand, the language political distinction between old and new minorities obscures the asymmetries of power generally characterising both old and new minorities in their relationship with the majorities. Here, the notion of minority calls for a serious revision. On the other hand, most essential differences between the regional and the migrant minorities can be noted regarding their language political options for identifying with the minority culture. With respect to the immigrant minorities, where the focus is on the linguistic integration into the host society, the close linkage of language and culture should be seen in a very critical light. The requirement of linguistic integration into the host society eventually appears to disregard the various positions of identity which immigrant speakers may assume while moving between the heritage and the host culture. At the same time, it also underestimates the symbolic capital and thus the power that migrant languages constitute for their speakers. At any rate, the question of migrant languages represents a dimension which is of prime importance to the conceptualisation of EM. The heated debates on citizenship in relation to migrants show that alternatives need to be found here that go beyond citizenship, which at present is primarily linked to knowledge of the host language.

As this book shows, the multifocal view on the fundamental questions of conceptualising EM adopted in LINEE and beyond clearly reveals the specific interplay of the key variables. In the last chapter, we have thus attempted to use the key variable 'knowledge' as an umbrella concept and to jointly relate all other key concepts to EM under this umbrella term. It was the aim of this attempt to show which perspectives emerge in relation to the conceptualisation of EM under the central aspect of 'knowledge'. Against the background of the overlapping dynamics of the key variables we eventually realised that besides 'knowledge' other key variables, for example, 'discourse', would also qualify as umbrella terms for grasping EM in its dynamic complexity. With a view to the European context in particular, we cannot fail to notice, however, that 'knowledge' lends itself to being used as a cover variable in the first place since the knowledge-based society forms a central political goal for the Europe of the future.

Proceeding from these remarks, the question could now be raised as to which new insights a 'knowledge'-based perspective yields in relation to the discrepancies concerning the conceptualisation of EM mentioned above. In this context, we could attempt to find answers to questions like the following: what would the focus on the knowledge dimension imply for the lingua-cultural integration of the immigrants? Can the juxtaposition of linguistic minorities and majorities be maintained in a knowledge-based notion of EM? How would the concept of the plurilingual EM-repertoire have to be configured from the perspective of 'knowledge'? What would be the ideological guiding principles of EM if 'knowledge' represented the framework for this EM? Against the background of the knowledge processed in LINEE and beyond LINEE, we feel, by all means, that a central contribution to refining the concept of EM may be expected by answering these questions or questions with a similar focus.

References

Akkuş, R., Bricić, K. and De Cillia, R. (2005) *Bilingualer Spracherwerb in der Migration. Psychagogischer und soziolinguistischer Teil des Schlussberichts*. Wien: BMBWK.
Ammon, U. (2006) Language conflicts in the European Union. On finding a politically acceptable and practicable solution for EU institutions that satisfies diverging interests. *International Journal of Applied Linguistics* 16 (3), 319–338.
Apeltauer, E. (ed.) (1987) *Gesteuerter Zweitspracherwerb. Voraussetzungen und Konsequenzen für den Unterricht*. München: Hueber.
Appadurai, A. (1996) *Modernity at Large. Cultural Dimensions of Globalisation*. Minneapolis: University of Minnesota Press.
Aronin, L. and Hufeisen, B. (2009) Methods of research in multilingual studies: Reaching a comprehensive perspective. In L. Aronin and B. Hufeisen (eds) *The Exploration of Multilingualism. Development of Research on L3, Multilingualism and Multiple Language Acquisition* (pp. 103–120). Amsterdam: John Benjamins.
Auer, J.C.P. (1984) *Bilingual Conversation*. Amsterdam: John Benjamins.
Bailey, C.Y. (1973) *Variation and Linguistic Theory*. Arlington, VA: Center for Applied Linguistics.
Barni, M. and Extra, G. (eds) (2008) *Mapping Linguistic Diversity in Multicultural Contexts*. Berlin/New York: Mouton de Gruyter (= Contributions to the Sociology of Language, 94).
Basch, L.N., Schiller, G. and Szanton Blanc, C. (1994) *Nations Unbound: Transnational Projects, Postcolonial Predicaments and Deterritorialized Nation-States*. Amsterdam: Gordon and Breach.
Bell, D. (1973) *The Coming of Post-Industrial Society*. New York: Basic Books.
Bennett, T. (2005) Civic laboratories: Museums, cultural Objecthood and the governance of the social. *Cultural Studies* 19 (5), 521–547.
Bhabha, H.K. (1994) *The Location of Culture*. London/New York: Routledge.
Blackledge, A. (2009) *Discourse and Power in a Multilingual World*. Amsterdam: John Benjamins.
Blackledge, A. and Creese, A. (2010) *Multilingualism. A Critical Perspective*. London/New York: Continuum.
Blommaert, J. (2005) *Discourse. A Critical Introduction*. Cambridge: Cambridge University Press.
Blommaert, J. (ed.) (1999) *Language Ideological Debates*. Berlin/New York: Mouton de Gruyter.
Blommaert, J. and Verschueren, J. (1998) The role of language in European nationalist ideologies. In B.B. Schieffelin, K.A. Woolard and P.V. Kroskrity (eds) *Language Ideologies. Practice and Theory* (pp. 189–210). New York/Oxford: Oxford University Press.
Bourdieu, P. (1986) *Distinction: A Social Critique of the Judgement of Taste*. London: Routledge and Kegan Paul.
Bourdieu, P. (1990) *The Logic of Practice*. California: Stanford University Press.
Bourdieu, P. (2005) *Was heißt Sprechen. Zur Ökonomie des sprachlichen Tausches*. Wien: Braumüller.

Brah, A. (1996) *Cartographies of Diaspora: Contesting Identities*. London: Routledge.
Brah, A. (2000) The scent of memory: Strangers, our own and others. In A. Brah and A. Coombes (eds) *Hybridity and Its Discontents: Politics, Science, Culture* (pp. 272–291). London/New York: Routledge.
Braunmüller, K. (1995) Semikommunikation und semiotischeSprache. Bausteinezueinem Modell für die VerständigungimNordenzurZeit der Hanse. In K. Braunmüller (ed.) *Niederdeutsch und die skandinavischenSprachen II* (pp. 35–70). Heidelberg: C. Winter.
Bugarski, R. (1992) Language situation and general policy. In R. Bugarski and C. Hawkesworth (eds) *Language Planning in Yugoslavia* (pp. 10–26). Columbus: Slavica Publishers.
Butler, J. (1993) *Bodies that Matter. On the Discursive Limits of 'Sex'*. New York/London: Routledge.
Cameron, D. and Kulick, D. (2003) *Language and Sexuality*. Cambridge: Cambridge University Press.
Castiglione, D. and Longman, C. (eds) (2007) *The Language Question in Europe and Diverse Societies. Political, Legal and Social Perspectives*. Oxford/Portland: Hart Publishing.
Cazden, C.B. (2001) *Classroom Discourse. The Language of Teaching and Learning*. Portsmouth: Heinemann.
Cenoz, J. (2009) *Towards Multilingual Education. Basque Educational Research in International Perspective*. Bristol: Multilingual Matters.
Clifford, J. (1997) *Routes. Travel and Translation in the Late Twentieth Century*. Cambridge: Harvard University Press.
Cook, V.J. (1991) The poverty-of-the-stimulus argument and multi-competence. *Second Language Research* 7, 103–117.
Cook, V.J. (1992) Evidence for multi-competence. *Language Learning* 42 (4), 557–591.
Cook, V.J. (1993) Wholistic multi-competence: jeu d'esprit or paradigm shift? In B. Kettemann and W. Wieden (eds) *Current Issues in European Second Language Acquisition Research* (pp. 3–8). Tübingen: Narr.
Cook, V.J. (2003) Introduction: The changing L1 in the L2 users' mind. In V.J. Cook (ed.) *Effects of the Second Language on the First* (pp. 1–18). Clevedon: Multilingual Matters.
Corder, S.P. (1967) The significance of learners' errors. *International Review of Applied Linguistics* 5, 161–170.
Coser, L.A. (1972) *Theorie Sozialer Konflikte*. Neuwied: Luchterhand.
Creswell, J.W. and Plano Clark, V.L. (2007) *Designing and Conducting Mixed Methods Research*. Thousand Oaks: Sage.
Creswell, J.W. (1998) *Qualitative Inquiry and Research Design: Choosing Among Five Traditions*. Thousand Oaks: Sage.
Creswell, J.W. (2009) *Research Design: Qualitative, Quantitative, and Mixed Methods Approaches*. Thousand Oaks: Sage.
Crotty, M. (2003) *The Foundations of Social Research: Meaning and Perspective in the Research Process*. Thousand Oaks: Sage.
Dahlman, C. and Andersson, T. (2000) *Korea and the Knowledge-Based Economy: Making the Transition*. Washington D.C.: The World Bank, OECD.
Dahrendorf, R. (1961) Elemente einer Theorie des sozialen Konflikts. In R. Dahrendorf (ed.) *Gesellschaft und Freiheit: Zur Soziologischen Analyse der Gegenwart* (pp. 197–235). München: Piper.
Dahrendorf, R. (1957) *Soziale Klassen und Klassenkonflikt in der Industriellen Gesellschaft*. Stuttgart: Enke.
Davies, B. and Harré, R. (1990) Positioning: the discursive production of selves. *Journal for the Theory of Social Behaviour* 20, 43–63.

De Cillia, R. (2001) Sprachliche Menschenrechte und die Bedeutung der Muttersprache im schulischen Spracherwerb. In W. Weidinger (ed.) *Bilingualität und Schule. Ausbildung, Wissenschaftliche Perspektiven und Empirische Befunde* (pp. 246–252). Wien: öbv and hpt.

De Cillia, R. and Wodak, R. (2004) Political discourse. In U. Ammon, N. Dittmar, K. Mattheier and P. Trudgill (eds) *Sociolinguistics. An International Handbook of the Science of Language and Society* (pp. 1638–1652). Berlin/New York: de Gruyter.

De Swaan, A. (1999) The European Language Constellation. In N. Bos (ed.) *Which Languages for Europe? Report of the Conference Held in Oegstgeest, The Netherlands, 9–11 October 1998* (pp. 13–23). Amsterdam: European Cultural Foundation.

Denzin, N.K. (1970) *The Research Act In Sociology. A Theoretical Introduction to Sociological Methods.* London: Butterworth.

Denzin, N.K. (1989) *The Research Act.* Englewood Cliffs, N.J.: Prentice Hall.

Dewaele, J.M. and Pavlenko, A. (2003) Productivity and lexical richness in native and non-native speech: A study of cross-cultural effects. In V.J. Cook (ed.) *Effects of the Second Language on the First* (pp. 120–141). Clevedon: Multilingual Matters.

Dorostkar, N. and Flubacher, M.C. (2010) Europäische Diskurse über Mehrsprachigkeit: EU-Sprachenpolitik und deren Rezeption in österreichischen und schweizer Printmedien. In C. Hülmbauer, E. Vetter and H. Böhringer (eds) *Mehrsprachigkeit aus der Perspektive zweier EU-Projekte: Dylan Meets LINEE* (pp. 135–168). Frankfurt am Main: Peter Lang.

Drucker, P.F. (1959) *Landmarks of Tomorrow.* New York: Harper and Row.

Eagleton, T. (1991) *Ideology. An Introduction.* London: Verso.

Eagleton, T. (2001) *Was ist Kultur?* München: C.H. Beck.

Ehlich, K. (2006) Die Vertreibung der Kultur aus der Sprache. 13 kurze Reflexionen zu einem reflexionsresitenten Thema. *Zeitschrift für Germanistische Linguistik. Deutsche Sprache in Gegenwart und Geschichte* 34 (1/2), 50–63.

Extra, G. and Vallen, T. (1997) Migration and multilingualism in Western Europe: A case study of the Netherlands. *Annual Review of Applied Linguistics* 17, 151–169.

Extra, G. and Gorter, T. (2008) *Multilingual Europe: Facts and Policies.* Berlin/New York: Mouton de Gruyter.

Extra, G., Yağmur, K. and Van der Avoird, T. (2004) Multilingual Cities Project: Crossnational and crosslinguistic perspectives. In G. Extra, and K. Yağmur, (eds) *Urban Multilingualism in Europe. Immigrant Minority Languages at Home and School* (pp. 299–408). Clevedon: Multilingual Matters.

Extra, G. and Yağmur, K. (eds) (2004) *Urban Multilingualism in Europe. Immigrant Minority Languages at Home and School.* Clevedon: Multilingual Matters.

Fairclough, N. (2007) *Analysing Discourse: Textual Analysis for Social Research.* London/New York: Routledge.

Fairclough, N. (2001) *Language and Power.* Harlow: Longman.

Fairclough, N. and Wodak, R. (1997) Critical discourse analysis. In T.A. van Dijk (ed.) *Discourse as Social Interaction* (pp. 258–284). London: Sage.

Ferguson, G. (2006) *Language Planning and Education.* Edinburgh: Edinburgh University Press.

Flick, U. (2007) Design und Prozess qualitative Forschung. In U. Flick, E. von Kardorff and I. Steinke (eds) *Qualitative Forschung. Ein Handbuch* (pp. 252–265). Reinbek bei Hamburg: Rowohlt.

Flick, U., Kardorff, E. von and Steinke, I. (eds) (2007) *Qualitative Forschung. Ein Handbuch.* Reinbek bei Hamburg: Rowohlt.

Foucault, M. (1972) *The Archeology of Knowledge.* London: Routledge.

Foucault, M. (1977) *Discipline and Punish: The Birth of the Prison.* London: Allen Lane.
Foucault, M. (1980) *Power/Knowledge: Selected Interviews and Other Writing 1972–1977.* New York: Pantheon Books.
Foucault, M. (2005) Science and knowledge. In N. Stehr and R. Grundmann (eds) *Knowledge and Society. Forms of Knowledge* (pp. 193–208). London: Routledge.
Franceschini, R. (2010) Mehrsprachigkeit: Forschungsperspektiven. In C. Hülmbauer, E. Vetter and H. Böhringer (eds) *Mehrsprachigkeit aus der Perspektive zweier EU-Projekte: DYLAN Meets LINEE* (pp. 17–39). Frankfurt am Main: Peter Lang (= Sprache im Kontext, 34).
Franceschini, R. (in press) Multilingualism and multi-competence: A conceptual view. *Modern Language Journal.*
Gal, S. (1987) Linguistic repertoire. In U. Ammon, N. Dittmar and K. Mattheier (eds) *Sociolinguistics. An International Handbook of the Science of Language and Society* (pp. 286–292). Berlin/New York: de Gruyter.
Gal, S. (1998) Multiplicity and contention among language ideologies. A commentary. In B.B. Schieffelin, K.A. Woolard and P.V. Kroskrity (eds) *Language Ideologies. Practice and Theory* (pp. 317–331). New York/Oxford: Oxford University Press.
Gal, S. and Irvine, J. (2000) Language ideology and linguistic differentiation. In P.V. Kroskrity (ed.) *Regimes of Language Ideologies, Politics and Identities* (pp. 35–83). Santa Fe, NM: School of American Research Press.
Gee, J.P. (1999) *An Introduction to Discourse Analysis.* London: Routledge.
Gellner, E. (1983) *Nations and Nationalism.* Ithaca, NY: Cornell University Press (= New Perspectives on the Past).
Goebl, H., Nelde, P.H., Starý, Z. and Wölck, W. (eds) (1996) *Kontaktlinguistik: ein Internationales Handbuch Zeitgenössischer Forschung* (Vol. 1). Berlin/New York: Mouton de Gruyter.
Gogolin, I. (1994) *Der Monolinguale Habitus der Multilingualen Schule.* Münster/New York: Waxmann.
Gramsci, A. (1971) *Selections from the Prison Notebooks.* London: Lawrence and Wishart.
Grimm, D. (1995) Does Europe need a constitution? *European Law Journal* 1 (3), 282–302.
Grin, F. (1996) Current problems and dilemmas of language strategies for Europe. An economist's perspective. In P.Ó. Riagáin and S. Harrington (eds) *A Language Strategy for Europe. Retrospect and Prospect* (pp. 27–36). Dublin: Bord na Gaeilge.
Grosjean, F. (1982) *Life with Two Languages.* Cambridge, MA: Harvard University Press.
Grosjean, F. (1985) The bilingual as a competent but specific speaker-hearer. *Journal of Multilingual and Multicultural Development* 6, 467–477.
Grosjean, F. (1998) Studying bilinguals. Methodological and conceptual issues. *Bilingualism: Language and Cognition* 1 (2), 131–47. Reprinted in: Bhatia, T.K. and Ritchie, W. C. (eds) (2004) *The Handbook of Bilingualism* (pp. 32–63). Malden: Blackwell.
Guba, E.G. and Lincoln, Y.S. (1994) Competing paradigms in qualitative research. In N.K. Denzin and Y.S. Lincoln (eds) *Handbook of Qualitative Research* (pp. 105–117). Thousand Oaks: Sage.
Gubbins, P. and Holt, M. (eds) (2002) *Beyond Boundaries. Language and Identity in Contemporary Europe.* Clevedon: Multilingual Matters.
Haarmann, H. (1988) Sprachen- und Sprachpolitik. In U. Ammon, N. Dittmar and K. Mattheier (eds) *Sociolinguistics. An International Handbook of the Science of Language and Society* (pp. 1660–1678). Berlin/New York: de Gruyter.

Habermas, J. (1981) *Theorie des kommunikativen Handelns. Band 1–2*. Frankfurt am Main: Suhrkamp.
Habermas, J. (1984) *Vorstudien und Ergänzungen zur Theorie des Kommunikativen Handelns*. Frankfurt: Suhrkamp.
Hage, G. (1998) *White Nation: Fantasies of White Supremacy in a Multicultural Society*. Annandale: Pluto Press.
Hage, G. (2003) *Against Paranoid Nationalism: Searching for Hope in a Shrinking Society*. Annandale: Pluto Press.
Hall, J.K., Cheng, A. and Carlson, M.T. (2006) Reconceptualising multicompetence as a theory of language knowledge. *Applied Linguistics* 27 (2), 220–240.
Hall, S. (1996) Introduction. Who needs identity? In S. Hall and P. Du Gay (eds) *Questions of Cultural Identity* (pp. 1–17). London: Sage.
Hall, S. (ed.) (2003) *Representation: Cultural Representations and Signifying Practices*. London: Sage.
Hawkins, G. (2001) The ABC radio and rhetorics of choice. In T. Bennett and D. Carter (eds) *Culture in Australia: Policies, Publics and Programs* (pp. 176–193). Cambridge: Cambridge University Press.
Hejl, P.M. (2008a) Kultur. In A. Nünning (ed.) *Metzler Lexikon Literatur- und Kulturtheorie. Ansätze–Personen–Grundbegriffe* (pp. 391–392). Stuttgart/Weimar: Verlag J.B. Metzler.
Hejl, P.M. (2008b) Kulturtheorien. In A. Nünning (ed.) *Metzler Lexikon Literatur- und Kulturtheorie. Ansätze–Personen–Grundbegriffe* (pp. 402–404). Stuttgart/Weimar: J.B. Metzler.
Heller, M. (2007a) Bilingualism as ideology and practice. In M. Heller (ed.) *Bilingualism: A Social Approach* (pp. 1–22). Houndsmill/Basingstoke: Palgrave Macmillan.
Heller, M. (2007b) The future of 'bilingualism'. In M. Heller (ed.) *Bilingualism: A Social Approach* (pp. 340–345). Houndsmill/Basingstoke: Palgrave Macmillan.
Heller, M. (2011) *Paths to Post-Nationalism. A Critical Ethnography of Language and Identity*. Oxford: Oxford University Press.
Heller, M. and Labrie, N. (2003) Langue, pouvoir et identité: une étude de cas, une approche théorique, une méthodologie. In M. Heller and N. Labrie (eds) *Discours et Identités. La Francité Canadienne Entre Modernité et Mondialisation* (pp. 9–39). Cortil-Wodon: E.M.E. Éditions Modulaires Européennes.
Hellinger, M. and Pauwels, A. (eds) (2007) *Handbook of Language and Communication: Diversity and Change*. Berlin/New York: Mouton de Gruyter.
Herdina, P. and Jessner, U. (2002) *A Dynamic Model of Multilingualism: Changing the Psycholinguistic Perspective*. Clevedon: Multilingual Matters.
Hornberger, N.H. and Corson, D. (1997) (eds) *Research Methods in Language and Education*. Dordrecht: Kluwer Academic Publishers.
House, J. and Rehbein, J. (2004) (eds) *Multilingual Communication*. Amsterdam: John Benjamins.
Hufeisen, B. (2005) Gesamtsprachencurriculum: Einflussfaktoren und Bedingungsgefüge. In B. Hufeisen and M. Lutjehams (eds) *Gesamtsprachencurriculum. Integrierte Sprachendidaktik* (pp. 9–18). Tübingen: Gunter Narr.
Irvine, J. (1989) When talk isn't cheap: language and political economy. *American Ethnologist* 16 (2), 248–267.
Jenkins, J. (2007) *English as a Lingua Franca: Attitude and Identity*. Oxford/New York: Oxford University Press.

Jernudd, B.H. and Neustupný, J.V. (1987) Language planning: for whom? In L. Laforge (ed.) *Proceedings of the International Colloquium on Language Planning* (pp. 69–84). Québec: Les Presses de L´Université Laval.

Jessner, U. (2008) Teaching third languages: Findings, trends and challenges. In *Language Teaching* 41 (1), 15–56.

Jørgenson, J.N. (2005) Plurilingual conversations among bilingual adolescents. *Journal of Pragmatics* 37, 391–402.

Jørgenson, J.N. (2008a) Introduction. Polylingual languaging around and among children and adolescents. *International Journal of Multilingualism* 5 (3), 161–176.

Jørgenson, J.N. (2008b) *Languaging. Nine Years of Linguistic Development of Young Turkish–Danish Grade School Students* (Vol. 1). Copenhagen: University of Copenhagen Faculty of Humanities.

Kecskes, I. (2010) Dual and multilanguage systems. *International Journal of Multilingualism* 7 (2), 1–19.

Kecskes, I. and Cuenca Martinez, I. (2005) Lexical choice as a reflection of conceptual fluency. *International Journal of Bilingualism* 9 (1), 49–69.

Kecskes, I. and Papp, T. (2003) How to demonstrate the conceptual effect of the L2 on L1? Techniques and methods. In V. Cook (ed.) *Effects of the Second Language on the First* (pp. 247–265). Clevedon: Multilingual Matters.

Kelle, U. (2007) *Die Integration Qualitativer und Quantitativer Methoden in der Empirischen Sozialforschung. Theoretische Grundlagen und Methodologische Konzepte.* Wiesbaden: VS Verlag für Sozialwissenschaften.

Keller, R. (2004) *Diskursforschung. Eine Einführung für SozialwissenschaftlerInnen.* Wiesbaden: VS Verl. für Sozialwiss.

Kempf, T. (1991) *Aufklärung als Disziplinierung. Studien zum Diskurs des Wissens in Intelligenzblättern und gelehrten Beilagen der zweiten Hälfte des 18. Jahrhunderts.* München: Iudicium.

Kenner C. and Hickey, T. (eds) (2008) *Multilingual Europe: Diversity and Learning.* Stoke on Trent/Sterling: Trentham Books.

Klein, W. (ed.) (1975) Sprache *Ausländischer Arbeiter.* Göttingen: Vandenhoeck und Ruprecht.

Kraus, P.A. (2008) *A Union of Diversity: Language, Identity and Polity-Building in Europe.* Cambridge: Cambridge University Press.

Kremnitz, G. (ed.) (1979) *Sprachen im Konflikt. Theorie und Praxis der katalanischen Soziolinguisten. Eine Textauswahl.* Tübingen: Narr.

Kremnitz, G. (ed.) (1982) *Entfremdung, Selbstbefreiung und Norm. Texte aus der Okzitanischen Soziolinguistik.* Tübingen: Narr.

Krumm, H-J. (1994) Mehrsprachigkeit und interkulturelles Lernen. Orientierungen im Fach Deutsch als Fremdsprache. *Jahrbuch Deutsch als Fremdsprache* 20, 13–36.

Krzyżanowski, M. (2009) Discourses about enlarged and multilingual Europe: Perspectives from German and Polish national public spheres. In J. Carl and P. Stevenson (eds) *Language, Discourse and Identity in Central Europe. The German Language in a Multilingual Space* (pp. 23–47). Basingstoke: Palgrave Macmillan.

Krzyżanowski, M. and Wodak, R. (2010) Hegemonic multilingualism in/of the EU institutions: An inside–outside perspective on European language policies and practices. In C. Hülmbauer, E. Vetter and H. Böhringer (eds) *Mehrsprachigkeit aus der Perspektive zweier EU-Projekte: DYLAN Meets LINEE* (pp. 115–133). Frankfurt am Main: Peter Lang.

Labrie, N. (1996) Politique linguistique. In H. Goebl, P.H. Nelde, Z. Starý and W. Wölck (eds) *Kontaktlinguistik: ein Internationales Handbuch Zeitgenössischer Forschung* (pp. 826–833). Berlin: de Gruyter.
Laclau, E. (1980) Populist rupture and discourse (trans. Jim Grealy). *Screen Education* 34, 87–93.
Laclau, E. (1990) *New Reflections on the Revolution of Our Time.* London: Verso.
Laclau, E. and Mouffe, C. (1985) *Hegemony and Socialist Strategy: Towards a Radical Democratic Politics.* London: Verso.
Leech, N.L., Dellinger, A.B., Brannagan, K.B. and Tanaka, H. (2010) Evaluating mixed research studies: A mixed methods approach. *Journal of Mixed Methods Research* 4 (1), 17–31.
Lefebvre, H. (1974) *La Production de l'Espace.* Paris: Anthropos.
Lo Bianco, J. (2010) The importance of language policies and multilingualism for cultural diversity. *International Social Science Journal* 199, 37–67.
Lüders, C. and Reichertz, J. (1986) Wissenschaftliche Praxis ist, wenn alles funktioniert und keiner weiß warum: Bemerkungen zur Entwicklung qualitativer Sozialforschung. *Sozialwissenschaftliche Literaturrundschau* 12, 90–102.
Mackey, W.F. (1987) Bilingualism and multilingualism. In U. Ammon, N. Dittmar and K. Mattheier (eds) *Sociolinguistics. An International Handbook of the Science of Language and Society* (pp. 699–713). Berlin/New York: de Gruyter.
Mamadouh, V. (1999) Concluding remarks. In N. Bos (ed.) *Which Languages for Europe? Report of the Conference Held in Oegstgeest, The Netherlands, 9–11 October 1998* (pp. 155–171). Amsterdam: European Cultural Foundation.
Martin-Jones, M. (1989) Language, power and linguistic minorities: The need for an alternative approach to bilingualism, language maintenance and shift. *Sociological Review Monograph* 36, 106–125.
Martin-Jones, M. (2007) Bilingualism, education and the regulation of access to language resources. In M. Heller (ed.) *Bilingualism: A Social Approach* (pp. 161–182). New York: Palgrave Macmillan.
Maxwell, J.A. (2005) *Qualitative Research Design: An Interactive Approach.* Thousand Oaks: Sage.
Mayr, A. (2008) Introduction: Power, discourse and institutions. In A. Mayr (ed.) *Language and Power. An Introduction to Institutional Discourse* (pp. 1–25). London: Continuum.
Meinefeld, W. (2007) Hypothesen und Vorwissen in der qualitativen Sozialforschung. In U. Flick, E. von Kardorff and I. Steinke (eds) *Qualitative Forschung. Ein Handbuch* (pp. 265–275). Reinbek bei Hamburg: Rowohlt.
Meisl, J.M. Clahsen, H. and Pienemann, M. (1983) *Deutsch als Zweitsprache. Der Spracherwerb Ausländischer Arbeiter.* Tübingen: Verlag Gunter Narr.
Miles, M.B. and Huberman, A.M. (1994) *Qualitative Data Analysis: An Expanded Sourcebook.* Thousand Oaks: Sage.
Miller, T. (2006) *Cultural Citizenship: Cosmopolitism, Consumerism, and Television in a Neoliberal Age.* Philadelphia: Temple University Press.
Mills, S. and Kriest, U. (2007) *Der Diskurs. Begriff, Theorie, Praxis.* Tübingen: Francke.
Nekvapil, J. (2006) From language planning to language management. *Sociolinguistica* 20, 92–104.
Nekvapil, J. and Sherman, T. (2009) Pre-interaction management in multinational companies in Central Europe. *Current Issues in Language Planning* 10 (2), 181–198.

Nelde, P.H. (1980) *Sprachkontakt und Sprachkonflikt*. Wiesbaden: Steiner.
Nelde, P.H. (1987) Research on language conflict. In U. Ammon, N. Dittmar and K. Mattheier (eds) *Sociolinguistics. An International Handbook of the Science of Language and Society* (pp. 607–612). Berlin/New York: de Gruyter.
Nelde, P.H. (1989) *Historische Sprachkonflikte*. Bonn: Dümmler.
Nelde, P.H., Strubell, M. and Williams, G. (1996) *Euromosaic: Produktion und Reproduktion der Minderheiten – Sprachgemeinschaften in der Europäischen Union*. Luxemburg: Amt für die amtliche Veröffentlichung der EG.
Nic Craith, M. (2006) *Europe and the Politics of Language: Citizens, Migrants and Outsiders*. Hampshire: Palgrave Macmillan.
Onwuegbuzie, A.J. and Leech, N.L. (2005) On becoming a pragmatic researcher: The importance of combining quantitative and qualitative research methodologies. *International Journal of Social Research Methodology: Theory and Practice* 8, 375–387.
Parsons, T. (1976) *Zur Theorie Sozialer Systeme. Herausgegeben und Eingeleitet von Stefan Jensen*. Opladen: Westdeutscher Verlag (= Studienbücher zur Sozialwissenschaft 14).
Paulston, C.B. (2003) Language policies and language rights. In C.B. Paulston and R.G. Tucker (eds) *Sociolinguistics. The Essential Readings* (pp. 472–483). Malden/Oxford/Melbourne/Berlin: Blackwell.
Pavlenko, A. (2005) *Emotions and Multilingualism*. Cambridge: Cambridge University Press.
Pavlenko, A. (2008) *Research Network Symposium Russian Diaspora. Multilingualism in Post-Soviet Countries*. AILA Essen, Germany, August 2008.
Pavlenko, A. (2009) Multilingualism and democracy. Plenary address at the Third Language Acquisition Conference, Bozen-Bolzano, Italy, September 2009.
Phillipson, R. (2003) *English-Only Europe? Challenging Language Policy*. London/New York: Routledge.
Phillipson, R. (2009) *Linguistic Imperialism Continued*. London/New York: Routledge.
Phipps, A. (2007) *Learning the Arts of Linguistic Survival: Languaging, Tourism, Life*. Clevedon: Channel View Publications.
Polanyi, K. (1966) *The Tacit Dimension*. Garden City, NY: Doubleday & Co.
Reckwitz, A. (2006) *Die Transformation der Kulturtheorien. Zur Entwicklung eines Theorieprogramms. Studienausgabe*. Weilerswist: Velbrück.
Reichertz, J. (2007) Qualitative Sozialforschung – Ansprüche-Prämissen-Probleme. *EWE* 18(2), 195–208.
Reichertz, J. and Schröer, N. (1994) Erheben, Auswerten, Darstellen. Konturen einer hermeneutischen Wissenssoziologie. In N. Schröer (ed.) *Interpretative Sozialforschung. Auf dem Weg zu einer hermeneutischen Wissenssoziologie*. (pp. 24–55). Opladen: Westdt. Verlag.
Ricento, T. (2005) Considerations of identity in L2 learning. In E. Hinkel (ed.) *Handbook of Research in Second Language Teaching and Learning* (pp. 895–910). London: Routledge.
Ricento, T. (ed.) (2000) *Ideology, Politics and Language*. Amsterdam: John Benjamins.
Rindler Schjerve, R. (1998) Sprachkontaktforschung und Romanistik: Theoretische und methodologische Schwerpunkte. In G. Holtus, M. Metzeltin and Ch. Schmitt (eds) *Lexikon der Romanistischen Linguistik. Bd. VII* (pp. 14–31). Tübingen: Niemeyer.
Rindler Schjerve, R. (2001) Languages in contact and competition: Lessons from diglossia. In C. De Bot, S. Kroon, P.H. Nelde, H. Van der Velde (eds) *Institutional Status and Use of National Languages in Europe* (pp. 77–90). St. Augustin: Asgard (= Plurilingua XXIII).
Rindler Schjerve, R. (2007) Language conflict revisited. In J. Darquennes (ed.) *Contact Linguistics and Language Minorities (Kontaktlinguistik und Sprachminderheiten. Linguistique de Contact et Minorités Linguistiques* (pp. 37–50). St. Augustin: Asgard.

Rindler Schjerve, R. (2004) Minderheiten. In V.U. Ammon, N. Dittmar, K.J. Mattheier and P. Trudgill (eds) *Sociolinguistics. An International Handbook of the Science of Language and Society* (Vol. 1) (pp. 480–486). Berlin/New York: Mouton de Gruyter.
Rindler Schjerve, R. (ed.) (2003) *Diglossia and Power: Language Policies and Practice in the 19th Century Habsburg Empire*. Berlin/New York: Mouton de Gruyter.
Rindler Schjerve, R. and Vetter, E. (2003) Historical sociolinguistics and multilingualism: Theoretical and methodological issues in the development of a multifunctional framework. In R. Rindler Schjerve (ed.) *Diglossia and Power: Language Policies and Practice in the 19th Century Habsburg Empire* (pp. 35–66). Berlin/New York: Mouton de Gruyter.
Rindler Schjerve, R. and Vetter, E. (2008) Language Policy and Social Power: Some Open Questions. Unpublished manuscript. Sociolinguistic Symposium 17: 'Micro and Macro Connections', Amsterdam April 2008.
Robson, C. (2002) *Real World Research: A Resource for Social Scientists and Pracitioner-Researchers*. Oxford: Blackwell.
Rosaldo, R. (1994) Cultural citizenship in San Jose, California. *POLAR Political and Legal Anthropology Review* 17 (1), 57–63.
Rose, N. (1999) *Powers of Freedom. Reframing Political Thought*. Cambridge: Cambridge University Press.
Sabatier, C.M. and Weible, P.A. (2007) The Advocacy Coalition Framework: Innovations and clarifications. In P.A. Sabatier (ed.) *Theories of the Policy Process* (pp. 189–220). Boulder: Westview Press.
Said, E. (1994) *Kultur und Imperialismus: Einbildungskraft und Politik im Zeitalter der Macht*. Frankfurt am Main: S. Fischer.
Schiffrin, D. (2004) Discourse. In U. Ammon, N. Dittmar, K. Mattheier and P. Trudgill (eds) *Sociolinguistics. An International Handbook of the Science of Language and Society* (pp. 597–604). Berlin/New York: de Gruyter.
Schloßmacher, M. (1997) *Die Amtssprachen in den Organen der Europäischen Gemeinschaft. Status und Funktion*. Frankfurt am Main/Berlin/Bern/New York/Wien: Peter Lang.
Seidlhofer, B. (2004) Research perspectives on teaching English as a lingua franca. *Annual Review of Applied Linguistics* 24, 209–239.
Seidlhofer, B. (2007) Common property: English as a lingua franca in Europe. In J. Cummins and C. Davison (eds) *Kluwer Handbook of English Language Teaching* (pp. 135–150). Dordrecht: Kluwer.
Seiler, T.B. (2008) *Wissen zwischen Sprache, Information, Bewusstsein. Probleme mit dem Wissensbegriff*. Münster: Monsenstein und Vannerdat.
Sercu, L. (2004) Researching the acquisition of intercultural communicative competence in a foreign language. A state of the art of research findings. In O. St John, K. van Esch and K. Schalkwijk (eds) *New Insights into foreign Language Learning and Teaching* (pp. 131–156). Frankfurt am Main: Peter Lang.
Sercu, L., Bandura, E., Castro, P., Davcheva, L., Laskaridou, C., Lundgren, U., Del Carmen Méndez Garcia, M. and Ryan, P. (2005) *Foreign Language Teachers and Intercultural Competence. An International Investigation*. Clevedon: Multilingual Matters.
Shore, C. (2000) *Building Europe: The Cultural Politics of European Integration*. London: Routledge.
Silverstein, M. (1979) Language structure and linguistic ideology. In R.P. Clyne, W.F. Hanks and C.L. Hofbauer (eds) *The Elements: A Parasession on Linguistic Units and Levels* (pp. 193–247). Chicago: Chicago Linguistic Society.

Silverstein, M. (1998) The uses and utility of language ideology: A commentary. In B.B. Schieffelin, K.A. Woolard and P.V. Kroskrity (eds) *Language Ideologies. Practice and Theory* (pp. 123–145). New York/Oxford: Oxford University Press.
Skutnabb-Kangas, T. (ed.) *Multilingualism for All*. Lisse: Swets and Zeitlinger.
Skutnabb-Kangas, T. (2008) *Linguistic Genocide in Education-Or Worldwide Diversity and Human Rights*? New Delhi: Orient Longman.
Smit, U. (2011) *English as a Lingua Franca in Higher Education: A Longitudinal Study of Classroom Discourse*. Berlin/New York: De Gruyter.
Spolsky, B. (2004) *Language Policy*. Cambridge: Cambridge University Press.
Stavrakakis, Y. (2004) Antinomies of Formalism. *Journal of Political Ideologies* 9 (3), 253–267.
Stehr, N. (2005) The texture of knowledge societies. In N. Stehr and R. Grundmann (eds) *Knowledge and the Economy* (pp. 112–135). London: Routledge (= Knowledge, Vol. 3).
Straub, J. (2004) Identität. In F. Jaeger and B. Liebsch (eds) *Handbuch der Kulturwissenschaften* (Vol. 1). *Grundlagen und Schlüsselbegriffe* (pp. 277–301). Stuttgart/Weimar: J.B. Metzler.
Talbot, M., Atkinson, K. and Atkinson, D. (2008) *Language and Power in the Modern World*. Edinburgh: Edinburgh Univ. Press.
Tashakkori, A. and Teddlie, C. (1998) *Mixed Methodology: Combining Qualitative and Quantitative Research*. Thousand Oaks: Sage.
Thompson, J.B. (1990) *Ideology and Modern Culture*. Cambridge: Polity Press.
Titscher, S., Wodak, R., Meyer, M. and Vetter, E. (2000) *Methods of Text and Discourse Analysis*. Thousand Oaks: Sage.
Toggenburg, G.N. (2003) Cultural diversity at the background of the European debate on values: An introduction. In F. Palermo and G.N. Toggeburg (eds) *European Constitutional Diversity* (pp. 9–23). Bolzano: EURAC Research (= EURAC Arbeitshefte/Quaderni, 43).
Treibel, A. (2006) *Einführung in soziologische Theorien der Gegenwart*. Wiesbaden: VS Verlag für Sozialwissenschaften.
Van Dijk, T.A. (1998) *Ideology: A Multidisciplinary Approach*. London: Sage.
Van Dijk, T.A. (2003) Discourse as interaction in society. In T.A. van Dijk (ed.) *Discourse as Social Interaction* (pp. 1–37). London: Sage.
Van Dijk, T.A. (2006) The study of discourse. In T.A. van Dijk (ed.) *Discourse as Structure and Process* (pp. 1–34). London: Sage.
Van Els, T.J.M. (2001) The European Union, its institutions and its languages. Some language political observations. *Current Issues in Language Planning* 2 (4), 311–360.
Van Els, T.J.M. (2005) Multilingualism in the European Union. *International Journal of Applied Linguistics* 15 (3), 263–281.
Vertovec, S. (2010) Towards post-multiculturalism? Changing communities, contexts and conditions of diversity. *International Social Science Journal* 199, 83–95.
Warren, J. and Benbow, H.M. (eds) (2008) *Multilingual Europe: Reflections on Language and Identity*. Newcastle upon Tyne: Cambridge Scholars Publishing.
Weber, P. (1999) *Contact and Conflict*. Bonn: Dümmler.
Wei, L. (2008) Research perspectives on bilingualism and multilingualism. In L. Wei and M.G. Moyer (eds) *The Blackwell Guide to Research Methods in Bilingualism and Multilingualism* (pp. 3–17). Malden: Blackwell.
Wei, L. (ed.) (2010) *Bilingualism* (4 Volumes). New York/London: Routledge.
Wei, L. and Auer, P. (eds.) (2009) *Handbook of Multilingualism and Multilingual Communication*. Berlin / New York: de Gruyter.
Wei, L. and Moyer, M. (eds) (2008) *The Blackwell Guide to Research Methods in Bilingualism and Multilingualism*. Malden: Blackwell.

Weinreich, U. (1953) *Languages in Contact: Findings and Problems*. The Hague: Mouton.
Weiss, G. (2002) Searching for Europe. The problem of legitimisation and representation in recent political speeches on Europe. *Journal of Language and Politics* 1 (1), 59–84.
Williams, G. (1987) *The Sociology of Welsh*. The Hague: Mouton.
Williams, G. (2005) *Sustaining Language Diversity in Europe: Evidence from the Euromosaic Project*. Basingstoke: Palgrave Macmillan.
Wodak, R. (2001) The discourse: Historical approach. In R. Wodak and M. Meyer (eds) *Methods of Critical Discourse Analysis* (pp. 63–94). Thousand Oaks: Sage.
Wodak, R. (2007) Pragmatics and critical discourse analysis: A cross-disciplinary inquiry. *Pragmatics and Cognition* 15 (1), 203–225.
Wodak, R. (2009) *The Discourse of Politics in Action: Politics as Usual*. Basingstoke: Palgrave Macmillan.
Wodak, R., De Cillia, R., Reisigl, M. and Liebhart, K. (1999) *The Discursive Construction of National Identity*. Edinburgh: Edinburgh University Press.
Woolard, K.A. (1992) Language ideology: Issues and approaches. (Special Issue) *Pragmatics* 2 (3), 235–249.
Woolard, K.A. (1998) Introduction. Language ideology as a field of inquiry. In B.B. Schieffelin, K.A. Woolard and P.V. Kroskrity (eds) *Language Ideologies. Practice and Theory* (pp. 3–47). New York/Oxford: Oxford University Press.
Woolley, C. (2009) Meeting the mixed methods challenge of integration in a sociological study of structure and agency. *Journal of Mixed Methods Research* 2009 3 (1), 7–25.
Wright, S. (2000) *Community and Communication. The Role of Language in Nation State Building and European Integration*. Clevedon: Multilingual Matters.
Wright, S. (2004) *Language Policy and Language Planning. From Nationalism to Globalisation*. Basingstoke: Palgrave Macmillan.
Yin, R.K. (2006) Mixed methods research: Are the methods genuinely integrated or merely parallel? *Research in the Schools* 13 (1), 41–47.

Online Documents – Varia:

2003/2057(INI): *European Parliament resolution with recommendations to the Commission on European regional and lesser-used languages: the languages of minorities in the EU – in the context of enlargement and cultural diversity (2003/2057(INI))*. (2003) Online document: http://www.europarl.europa.eu/sides/getDoc.do?type=TA&reference=P5-TA-2003-0372&language=EN#BKMD-2 (13.07.2010).
2008/2225(INI) EP 2009: *European Parliament resolution of 24 March 2009 on Multilingualism: an asset for Europe and a shared commitment (2008/2225(INI))*. - Online Document: http://www.europarl.europa.eu/sides/getDoc.do?pubRef=-//EP//NONSGML+TA+P6-TA-2009-0162+0+DOC+PDF+V0//EN (07.07.2010).
2008/2225(INI) Report 2009: *Report on multilingualism: an asset for Europe and a shared commitment (2008/2225(INI))*. Online document: http://www.europarl.europa.eu/sides/getDoc.do?pubRef=-//EP//NONSGML+REPORT+A6-2009-0092+0+DOC+PDF+V0//EN (14.07.2010).
Asia-Europe-Meeting: *The Asia–Europe Meeting's lifelong learning initiative*. Online Document: http://www.asia-europeinstitute.org/ASEM-LifeLong-Learning/lllcontent.htm (29.11.2010).
Blommaert, J. and Backus, A. (2011) Repertoires revisited: 'Knowing language' in superdiversity. *Working Papers in Urban Language & Literacies*. Paper 67. Online document: www.kcl.ac.uk/projects/ldc/.../67.pdf (07.10.2011).

Barcelona Conclusions 2002: *Barcelona European Council 15 and 16 March 2002. Presidency conclusions*. (2002) Online document: http://www.consilium.europa.eu/ueDocs/cms_Data/docs/pressData/en/ec/71025.pdf (12.07.2010).
Bogdandy, A. von (2007) Die Europäische Union und das Völkerrecht kultureller Vielfalt – Aspekte einer wunderbaren Freundschaft. *European Diversity and Autonomy Papers: EDAP* 1, 1–66. Online document: http://www.eurac.edu/en/research/institutes/imr/activities/Bookseries/edap/Documents/2007_edap01.pdf (23.08.2010).
Bull. 12-1973: Declaration on European identity. In *Bulletin of the European Communities* 12, 118–122. Online Document: http://www.ena.lu/declaration_european_identity_copenhagen_14_december_1973-2-6180 (12.07.2010).
Bull. 6-1985: Milan European Council (28 and 29 June 1985) Conclusions of the Presidency In *Bulletin of the European Communities* 6, 13–16. Online document: http://www.ena.lu/conclusions_milan_european_council_28_29_june_1985-2-7656 (13.07.2010).
Bull. Supp.7-1985: Report by the Committee on a People's Europe In: *Bulletin of the European Communities*, Supp. 7, 18–30. Online document: http://www.ena.lu/report_committee_peoples_europe_submitted_milan_european_council_milan_june_1985-2-7674 (12.07.2010).
CEFR 2001: *Common European Framework of Reference for Languages: Learning, Teaching, Assessment*. (2001) Online Document: http://www.coe.int/t/dg4/linguistic/Source/Framework_EN.pdf (13.07.2010).
Charter RML 1992: *European Charter for Regional or Minority Languages: Strasbourg, 5.XI.1992*. Online document: http://conventions.coe.int/Treaty/EN/Treaties/Html/148.htm (13.07.2010).
CILT 1999: *Foreign languages in primary and pre-school education: context and outcomes. A summary*. (1999) Online document: http://ec.europa.eu/education/languages/pdf/doc531_en.pdf (11.08.2010).
CILT 2006: *Effects on the European economy of shortages of foreign language skills in enterprise (ELAN)*. Online document: http://www.cilt.org.uk/home/research_and_statistics/research/cilt_activities/idoc.ashx?docid=fc2dd2c9-1193-4b57-8a1f-737ca3fdd6b7&version=-1 (12.07.2010).
Code of Conduct 2006: *Code of Conduct on Multilingualism adopted by the Bureau on 4 September 2006*. Online document: http://www.europarl.europa.eu/pdf/multilinguisme/code_conduct_multilingualism_en.pdf (14.07.2010).
COM(2003)449 final: *Communication from the Commission to the Council, the European Parliament, the Economic and Social Committee and the Committee of the Regions. Promoting language learning and linguistic diversity: an action plan 2004–2006*. (2003) Online document: http://ec.europa.eu/education/doc/official/keydoc/actlang/act_lang_en.pdf (12.07.2010).
COM(2004)508 final: *Communication from the Commission to the European Parliament, the Council, the European Economic and Social Committee and the Committee of the Regions. First Annual Report on Migration and Integration*. (2004) Online document: http://eur-lex.europa.eu/LexUriServ/LexUriServ.do?uri=COM:2004:0508:FIN:EN:PDF (14.07.2010).
COM(2005)356 final: *Communication from the Commission to the European Parliament and the Council. The European Indicator of Language Competence*. (2005) Online document: *http://eur-lex.europa.eu/LexUriServ/LexUriServ.do?uri=COM:2005:0356:FIN:EN:PDF* (13.07.2010).
COM(2005)596 final: *Communication from the Commission to the Council, the European Parliament, the European Economic and Social Committee and the committee of the Regions.*

A New Framework Strategy for Multilingualism. (2005) Online document: http://eur-lex.europa.eu/LexUriServ/LexUriServ.do?uri=COM:2005:0596:FIN:EN:PDF (12.07.2010).

COM(2006)236 final: *Amended proposal for a Decision of the European Parliament and of the Council establishing an integrated action programme in the field of lifelong learning.* (2006) Online document: http://eur-lex.europa.eu/LexUriServ/LexUriServ.do?uri=COM:2006:0236:FIN:EN:PDF (14.07.2010).

COM(2007)184 final: *Communication from the Commission to the Council. Framework for the European survey on language competences.* (2007) Online document: http://eur-lex.europa.eu/LexUriServ/LexUriServ.do?uri=COM:2007:0184:FIN:EN:PDF (13.07.2010).

COM(2007)554 final: *Commission working document. Report on the implementation of the Action Plan 'Promoting language learning and linguistic diversity'.* (2007) Online document: http://eur-lex.europa.eu/LexUriServ/LexUriServ.do?uri=COM:2007:0554:FIN:EN:PDF (13.07.2010).

COM(2007)773 final: *Communication from the Commission to the Council, the European Parliament, the European Economic and Social Committee and the Committee of the Regions. Mobility, an instrument for more and better jobs: The European Job Mobility Action Plan (2007–2010).* (2007) Online document: http://eur-lex.europa.eu/LexUriServ/site/en/com/2007/com2007_0773en01.pdf (12.07.2010).

COM(2008)865 final: *Communication from the Commission to the European Parliament, the Council, the European Economic and Social Committee and the Committee of the Regions. An updated strategic framework for European cooperation in education and training.* (2008) Online document: http://ec.europa.eu/education/lifelong-learning-policy/doc/com865_en.pdf (27.07.2010).

COM(2008)566 final Accomp.doc.: *Accompanying document to the Communication from the Commission to the Council, the European Parliament, the European Economic and Social Committee and the Committee of the Regions. Multilingualism: an asset for Europe and a shared commitment. An inventory of community actions in the field of multilingualism and results of the online public consultation.* (2008) Online document: http://ec.europa.eu/education/languages/pdf/com/inventory_en.pdf (13.07.2010).

COM(2008)566 final: *Communication from the Commission to the Council, the European Parliament, the European Economic and Social Committee and the Committee of the Regions. Multilingualism: an asset for Europe and a shared commitment.* (2008) Online document: http://ec.europa.eu/education/languages/pdf/com/2008_0566_en.pdf (12.07.2010).

COM(95)590: *White Paper on Education and Training. Teaching and Learning. Towards the Learning Society.* (1995) Online document: http://europa.eu/documents/comm/white_papers/pdf/com95_590_en.pdf (12.07.2010).

COM(96)462: *Education – Training – Research. The obstacles to transnational mobility. Green Paper.* (1996) Online document: http://aei.pitt.edu/1226/01/education_mobility_obstacles_gp_COM_96_462.pdf (11.08.2010).

Copenhagen Conclusions 1993: *European Council in Copenhagen 21–22 June 1993. Conclusions of the Presidency.* (1993) Online Document: http://www.consilium.europa.eu/ueDocs/cms_Data/docs/pressData/en/ec/72921.pdf (13.07.2010).

Cullen, J., Cullen, C., Maes, V. and Paviotti, G. (2008) *Multilingualism: between policy objectives and implementation.* Brussels: European Parliament. Online document: http://www.pedz.uni-mannheim.de/daten/edz-ma/ep/08/EST23219.pdf (27.09.2011).

Delanty, G. (2003) *Citizenship as a learning process: disciplinary citizenship versus cultural citizenship*. Online Document: www.eurozine.com/articles/2007-06-30-delanty-en.html (04.10.2011).

Denscombe, M. (2008) Communities of practice: a research paradigm for the mixed methods approach. *Journal of Mixed Methods Research* 2008/2. Online document: http://mmr.sagepub.com/content/2/3/270.full.pdf+html (30.11.2010).

DeSeCo 2005: *The Definition and Selection of Key Competences. Executive Summary*. Online document: http://www.oecd.org/dataoecd/47/61/35070367.pdf (24.11.2010).

Diaz-Bone, R., Bührmann, A., Gutiérrez Rodríguez, E., Schneider, W., Kendall, G. and Tirado, F. (2007) The field of Foucaultian discourse analysis: structures, developments and perspectives. *Forum Qualitative Sozialforschung/Forum: Qualitative Social Research* 8 (2). Online document: http://nbn-resolving.de/urn:nbn:de:0114-fqs0702305 (28.09.2010).

DYLAN Online: Homepage of the *DYLAN*-Project - http://www.dylan-project.org (04.10.2011).

ECJ C-361/01: *European Court of Justice Case C-361/01 – Judgement of the Court: 9 September 2003 (Regulation (EC) No 40/94 - Article 115: Rules in force governing languages at the Office for Harmonisation in the Internal Market (Trade Marks and Designs) (OHIM) - Plea of illegality - Principle of non-discrimination)*. Online document: http://curia.europa.eu/jurisp/cgi-bin/gettext.pl?lang=en&num=79969090C19010361&doc=T&ouvert=T&seance=ARRET (27.04.2011).

Education and Training 2010: *Implementation of 'Education and Training 2010'. Work Programme. Working Group B 'Key Competences', Key Competences for Lifelong Learning. A European Reference Framework* (2004). Online document: http://ec.europa.eu/education/policies/2010/doc/basicframe.pdf (24.11.2010).

Euromosaic III 2004: *Euromosaic III. Regional and minority languages in the new Member States. Synthesis*. Online document: http://ec.europa.eu/education/languages/archive/languages/langmin/euromosaic/synthesis_en.pdf (23.11.2010).

European Cultural Convention: http://conventions.coe.int/Treaty/Commun/QueVoulezVous.asp?NT=018&CM=2&DF=13/12/2005&CL=ENG (19.04.2011).

Europublic 2009: *Study on the Contribution of Multilingualism to Creativity. Executive Summary*. http://eacea.ec.europa.eu/llp/studies/documents/study_on_the_contribution_of_multilingualism_to_creativity/executive_summary_en.pdf (12.07.2010).

Eurydice 2005: *Key data on Teaching Languages at school in Europe*. 2005 Edition. Brussels. http://eacea.ec.europa.eu/eurydice/ressources/eurydice/pdf/0_integral/049EN.pdf (13.07.2010).

Eurydice 2008: *Key Data on Teaching Languages at School in Europe*. 2008 Edition. Brussels. http://eacea.ec.europa.eu/about/eurydice/documents/KDL2008_EN.pdf (10.08.2010).

1995: *Framework Convention for the Protection of National Minorities – Strasbourg, 1.II.1995*. Online document: http://conventions.coe.int/Treaty/en/Treaties/Html/157.htm (27.07.2010).

Grin, F. and Moring, T. (2002) *Support for minority languages in Europe. Final report*. Dublin/Flensburg: European Bureau für Lesser-Used Languages and European Center for Minority Issues. Online document: http://ec.europa.eu/education/languages/pdf/doc639_en.pdf (21.09.2011).

Helsinki Conclusions 1999: *Helsinki European Council 10 and 11 December 1999. Presidency Conclusions.* Online document: http://www.europarl.europa.eu/summits/hel1_en.htm (10.08.2010).

High Level Group 2007: *Final Report. High Level Group on Multilingualism.* (2007) Online document: http://ec.europa.eu/education/policies/lang/doc/multireport_en.pdf (26.07.2010).

Jessner, U. (2007) Multicompetence approaches to language proficiency development in multilingual education. Online document: http://www.uibk.ac.at/anglistik/staff/jessner/publication/downloads/11859.pdf (27.09.2010).

Kelle, U. (2001) Sociological explanations between micro and macro and the integration of qualitative and quantitative methods [43 Absätze]. *Forum Qualitative Sozialforschung/ Forum: Qualitative Social Research* 2(1), Art.5. Online document: http://www.qualitative-research.net/index.php/fqs/article/view/966/2109 (30.11.2010).

Languages Mean Business 2008: *Languages mean Business. Companies work better with languages. Recommendations from the Business Forum for Multilingualism established by the European Commission* (2008). Online document: http://ec.europa.eu/dgs/education_culture/publ/pdf/language/davignon_en.pdf (12.07.2010).

Lisbon Conclusions 2000: *Lisbon European Council 23 and 24 March 2000. Presidency conclusions* (2000). Online document: *http://www.europarl.europa.eu/summits/lis1_en.htm* (12.07.2010).

Maalouf 2008: *A rewarding challenge. How the multiplicity of languages could strengthen Europe. Proposals from the Group of Intellectuals for Intercultural Dialogue set up at the initiative of the European Commission* (2008). Online document: http://ec.europa.eu/education/languages/pdf/doc1646_en.pdf (02.08.2010).

OJ 1958 L 17: Regulation No 1 determining the languages to be used by the European Economic Community. In OJ L 17, 6. 10. 1958, 385–386. Online document: http://eur-lex.europa.eu/LexUriServ/LexUriServ.do?uri=CELEX:31958R0001:EN:HTML (14.07.2010).

OJ 1974 C 98: Resolution of the Ministers of Education, meeting within the Council, of 6 June 1974 on cooperation in the field of education. In OJ C 98, 20.08.1974, 2. Online document: http://eur-lex.europa.eu/LexUriServ/LexUriServ.do?uri=CELEX:41974X0820:EN:HTML (13.07.2010).

OJ 1976 C: Resolution of the Council and of the Ministers of Education, meeting within the Council, of 9 February 1976 comprising an action programme in the field of education. In OJ C 38, 19.02.1976, 1–5. – Online Document: http://eur-lex.europa.eu/LexUriServ/LexUriServ.do?uri=CELEX:41976X0219:EN:HTML (12.07.2010).

OJ 1977 L 199: Council Directive 77/486/EEC of 25 July 1977 on the education of the children of migrant workers. In *OJ L 199*, 06.08. 1977, 32–33. Online Document: http://eur-lex.europa.eu/LexUriServ/LexUriServ.do?uri=CELEX:31977L0486:EN:HTML (14.07.2010).

OJ 1981 C 287: Resolution on a Community charter of regional languages and cultures and on a charter of rights of ethnic minorities. Resolution prepared by Mr Gaetano Arfé and adopted by the European Parliament on 16 October 1981. In *OJ C 287*, 09.11.1981, 106. Online document: http://www.ciemen.org/mercator/UE18-GB.HTM (13.07.2010).

OJ 1983 C 68: Resolution on measures in favour of minority languages and cultures. Resolution prepared by Mr. Gaetano Arfé and adopted by the European Parliament on 11 February 1983. In *OJ C 68*, 14.03.1983, 103. Online document: http://www.ciemen.org/mercator/UE20-GB.HTM (27.07.2010).

OJ 1987 C 318: European Parliament resolution on the languages and cultures of regional and ethnic minorities in the European Community (Resolution prepared by Willy Kuijpers, and adopted by the European Parliament on 30 October 1987). In *OJ C 318*, 30.11.1987, 160. Online document: http://com482.altervista.org/documents/ legjislazion/kuijpers_en.pdf (13.07.2010).

OJ 1989 L 239: Council decision of 28 July 1989 establishing an action programme to promote foreign language competence in the European Community (Lingua) (89/489/ EEC) In *OJ L 239, 16.8.1989, 24–32*. Online document: http://eur-lex.europa.eu/Notice. do?val=149489:cs&lang=en&list=149490:cs,149489:cs,149488:cs,149487:cs,14888 2:cs,148881:cs,149441:cs,159174:cs,148880:cs,148879:cs,&pos=2&page=1&nbl=12 &pgs=10&hwords=&checktexte=checkbox&visu=#texte (13.07.2010).

OJ 1992 C 191: Treaty on European Union. In *OJ C 191*, 29.07.1992, 1–115. Online document: http://eur-lex.europa.eu/en/treaties/dat/11992M/tif/JOC_1992_191__1_ EN_0001.pdf (12.07.2010).

OJ 1994 L 11: Council Regulation (EC) No 40/94 of 20 December 1993 on the Community trade mark. In *OJ L 11*, 14.01.1994, 1–36. Online document: http://eur-lex.europa.eu/ LexUriServ/LexUriServ.do?uri=CELEX:31994R0040:EN:HTML (27.04.2011).

OJ 1994 C 61: Resolution on linguistic and cultural minorities in the European Community. In *OJ C 61*, 28.02.1994, 110. Online document: http://www.minelres.lv/eu/epres/ re940209.htm (09.08.2010).

OJ 1995 L 87: Decision No 819/95/EC of the European Parliament and of the Council of 14 March 1995 establishing the Community action programme 'Socrates'. In *OJ L 87*, 20.4.1995, 10–24. Online document: http://eur-lex.europa.eu/LexUriServ/ LexUriServ.do?uri=CELEX:31995D0819:EN:HTML (13.07.2010).

OJ 1996 L 306: Council Decision of 21 November 1996 on the adoption of a multiannual programme to promote the linguistic diversity of the Community in the information society. In *OJ L 306*, 28.11.1996, 40–48. Online document: http://eur-lex.europa. eu/LexUriServ/LexUriServ.do?uri=CELEX:31996D0664:EN:HTML (12.07.2010).

OJ 1997 C 340: Treaty on European Union (consolidated version): EU Treaty (Maastricht 1992). In *OJ C 340*, 10.11.1997, 145-172. - Online document: http://eur-lex.europa.eu/LexUriServ/LexUriServ.do?uri=CELEX:11997M/ TXT:EN:HTML (1.12.2010).

OJ 1998 C 1: Council Resolution of 16 December 1997 on the early teaching of European Union languages. In *OJ C 1*, 03.01.1998, 2-3. Online document: http://eur-lex.europa. eu/LexUriServ/LexUriServ.do?uri=OJ:C:1998:001:0002:0003:EN:PDF (13.07.2010).

OJ 1999 L 146: Council Decision of 26 April 1999 establishing the second phase of the Community vocational training action programme 'Leonardo da Vinci' (1999/382/ EC). In *OJ 1999 L 146*, 11.06.1999, 33-47. Online document: Error! Hyperlink reference not valid. (10.08.2010).

OJ 2000 C 364: Charter of Fundamental Rights of the European Union. In *OJ C 364*, 18.12.2000, 1–22. Online document: http://www.europarl.europa.eu/charter/pdf/ text_en.pdf (12.07.2010).

OJ 2000 L 232: Decision No 1934/2000 EC of the European Parliament and of the Council of 17 July 2000 on the European Year of Languages 2001. In *OJ L 232*, 14.9.2000, 1–5. Online document: http://eur-lex.europa.eu/LexUriServ/LexUriServ.do?uri=OJ:L:20 00:232:0001:0005:EN:PDF (12.07.2010).

OJ 2000 L 28: Decision No 253/2000/EC of the European Parliament and of the Council of 24 January 2000 establishing the second phase of the Community action programme in the field of education 'Socrates'. In *OJ L 28*, 3.2.2000, 1–15. Online document:

http://eur-lex.europa.eu/LexUriServ/LexUriServ.do?uri=OJ:L:2000:028:0001:0015:E N:PDF (13.07.2010).
OJ 2002 C 142: Detailed work programme on the follow-up of the objectives of Education and training systems in Europe. In: *OJ C 142*, 14.06.2002, 1–22. Online document: http://eur-lex.europa.eu/LexUriServ/LexUriServ.do?uri=OJ:C:2002:142:0001:0022: EN:PDF (13.07.2010).
OJ 2002 C 50: Council Resolution of 14 February 2002 on the promotion of linguistic diversity and language learning in the framework of the implementation of the objectives of the European Year of Languages 2001. In *OJ C 50*, 23.2.2002, 1–2. Online document: http://eur-lex.europa.eu/LexUriServ/LexUriServ.do?uri=OJ:C:2002:050: 0001:0002:EN:PDF (12.07.2010).
OJ 2004 C 310: Treaty establishing a Constitution for Europe. In *OJ C 310*, 16.12.2004, 1–474. Online document: http://eur-lex.europa.eu/JOHtml.do?uri=OJ:C:2004:310: SOM:EN:HTML (11.08.2010).
OJ 2004 L 169: Council Regulation (EC) No 930/2004 of 1 May 2004 on temporary derogation measures relating to the drafting in Maltese of the acts of the institutions of the European Union. In *OJ L 169*, 01.05.2004, 1–2. Online document: http://eur-lex.europa.eu/LexUriServ/LexUriServ.do?uri=OJ:L:2004:169:0001:0002:EN:PDF (14.07.2010).
OJ 2005 C 256 E: European Parliament resolution on measures to promote multilingualism and language learning in the European Union: European Indicator of Language Competence (2005/2213(INI)). In *OJ C 296 E*, 06.12.2006, 271–273. Online document: http://eur-lex.europa.eu/LexUriServ/LexUriServ.do?uri=OJ:C:2006:29 6E:0271:0273:EN: PDF (13.07.2010).
OJ 2005 L 156: Council Regulation (EC) No 920/2005 of 13 June 2005 amending Regulation No 1 of 15 April 1958 determining the language to be used by the European Economic Community and Regulation No 1 of 15 April 1958 determining the language to be used by the European Atomic Energy Community and introducing temporary derogation measures from those Regulations. In *OJ L 156*, 18.06.2005, 3–4. Online document: http://eur-lex.europa.eu/LexUriServ/LexUriServ.do?uri=OJ:L:2005:156: 0003:0004:EN:PDF (14.07.2010).
OJ 2006 C 251 E: Common Position No 15/2006 adopted by the Council on 24 July 2006 with a view to adopting a Decision No …/2006/EC of the European Parliament and of the Council of … establishing an action programme in the field of lifelong learning. In *OJ C 251 E*, 17.10.2006, 37–61. Online document: http:// eur-lex.europa.eu/LexUriServ/LexUriServ.do?uri=OJ:C:2006:251E:0037:0061:en:P DF (13.07.2010).
OJ 2006 L 412: Decision No 1983/2006/EC of the European Parliament and of the Council of 18 December 2006 concerning the European Year of Intercultural Dialogue (2008). In *OJ L 412*, 30.12.2006, 44–50. Online document: http://eur-lex.europa.eu/LexUriServ/site/en/oj/2006/l_412/l_41220061230en00440050.pdf (12.07.2010).
OJ 2007 C 306: Treaty of Lisbon amending the Treaty on European Union and the Treaty establishing the European Community, signed at Lisbon, 13 December 2007. In *OJ C 306*, 17.12.2007, 1–271. Online document: http://eur-lex.europa.eu/JOHtml.do?uri= OJ:C:2007:306:SOM:EN:HTML (10.08.2010).
OJ 2008 C 115: Consolidated versions of the Treaty on European Union and the Treaty on the Functioning of the European Union. In *OJ C 115*, 09.05.2008,

13–45. Online document: http://eur-lex.europa.eu/LexUriServ/LexUriServ.do?uri=CELEX:12008M/TXT:EN:HTML (01.12.2010).

OJ 2008 C 140: Council conclusions of 22 May 2008 on multilingualism. In *OJ C 140*, 06.06.2008, 14–15. Online document: http://eur-lex.europa.eu/LexUriServ/LexUriServ.do?uri=OJ:C:2008:140:0014:0015:EN:PDF (12.07.2010).

OJ 2008 C 257: Opinion of the Committee of the Regions on 'Multilingualism'. In *OJ C 257*, 09.10.2008, 30–35. Online document: http://eur-lex.europa.eu/LexUriServ/LexUriServ.do?uri=OJ:C:2008:257:0030:0035:EN:PDF (11.08.2010).

OJ 2008 C 320: Council Resolution of 21 November 2008 on a European strategy for multilingualism. In *OJ C 320*, 16.12.2008, 1–3. Online document: http://eur-lex.europa.eu/LexUriServ/LexUriServ.do?uri=OJ:C:2008:320:0001:0003:EN:PDF (27.07.2010).

OJ 2009 C 77: Opinion of the European Economic and Social Committee on Multilingualism. In *OJ C 77*, 31.03.2009, 109–114. Online document: http://eur-lex.europa.eu/LexUriServ/LexUriServ.do?uri=OJ:C:2009:077:0109:0114:EN:PDF (13.07.2010).

OJ 2010 C 83 Charter: Charter of Fundamental Rights of the European Union. In *OJ C 83*, 30.03.2010, 389–403. Online Version: http://eur-lex.europa.eu/LexUriServ/LexUriServ.do?uri=OJ:C:2010:083:0389:0403:EN:PDF (14.07.2010).

OJ 2010 C 83 Treaty: Consolidated versions of the Treaty on European Union and the Treaty on the Functioning of the European Union. In *OJ C 83, 30.03.2010, 1–388*. *Online document:* http://eur-lex.europa.eu/LexUriServ/LexUriServ.do?uri=OJ:C:2010:083:FULL:EN:PDF (14.07.2010).

Promotion of Multilingualism 2008: *Promotion of Multilingualism in the 31 countries of the lifelong-learning programme. Final Report March 2008.* Online document: http://ec.europa.eu/education/languages/pdf/doc1631_en.pdf (28.07.2010).

Rapport DGLFLF 2010: *Délégation générale à la langue française et aux langues de France: Rapport au Parlement sur l'emploi de la langue française.* (2009) Online document: http://www.dglf.culture.gouv.fr/rapport/2010/Rapport_Parlemen_10.pdf 05.05.2011).

SEC(2002)1234: *Commission staff working paper. Promoting Language Learning and Linguistic Diversity – Consultation.* (2002) Online document: http://ec.europa.eu/education/languages/pdf/doc308_en.pdf (13.07.2010).

Seidlhofer, B. (2003) *A concept of 'international English' and related issues: From 'real English' to 'realistic English'.* Strasbourg: Council of Europe. http://www.coe.int/t/dg4/linguistic/source/seidlhoferen.pdf (27.04.2011).

Special Eurobarometer 243: *Special Eurobarometer 243. Europeans and their Languages.* (2006) Online document: http://ec.europa.eu/public_opinion/archives/ebs/ebs_243_en.pdf (24.08.2010).

Standing Conference 10/1977: *Standing Conference of European Ministers of Education. 10th Session (Strasbourg, France, 28–30 June 1977).* Online document: http://www.coe.int/t/e/cultural_co-operation/education/standing_conferences/p.10thsession_strasbourg1977.asp#TopOfPage (01.12.2010).

Standing Conference 9/1975: *Standing Conference of European Ministers of Education. 9th Session (Stockholm, Sweden, 9–12 June 1975).* Online document: *http://www.coe.int/t/e/cultural_co-operation/education/standing_conferences/q.9thsession_stockholm1975.asp#TopOfPage* (01.12.2010).

Strubell, M., Vilaró, S., Williams, G. and Williams, G.O. (2007) *The diversity of language teaching in the European Union. Final report to the European Commission, Directorate General for Education*

and culture. Brussels: European Communities. Online document: http://ec.europa.eu/ education/languages/eu-language-policy/docs/diversity_en.pdf (26.09.2011).
The Hague Communiqué 1969: *Communiqué of the meeting of Heads of State or Government of the Member States at The Hague (1 and 2 December 1969)*. Online document: http://www.ena.lu/final_communique_hague_summit_december_1969-2-1565 (13.07.2010).
UNESCO 1996: *Universal Declaration on Linguistic Rights*. Online document: http://www.unesco.org/most/lnngo11.htm (27.09.2011).
UNESCO 2001: *UNESCO Universal Declaration on Cultural Diversity*. Online document: http://portal.unesco.org/en/ev.php-URL_ID=13179&URL_DO=DO_TOPIC&URL_SECTION=201.html (27.09.2011).
VALEUR-Report 2007: McPake, J., Tinsley, T., Broeder, P., Mijares, L., Latomaa, S. and Martyniuk, W. (2007) *VALEUR. Valuing All Languages in Europe*. Council of Europe Publishing (= ECML Research and Development Research Report Series). Online document: http://www.ecml.at/mtp2/VALEUR/html/A1_Valeur_reportE.pdf (01.12.2010).
VOICE: Vienna-Oxford International Corpus of English: http://www.univie.ac.at/voice (26.04.2011).
Wodak, R. (2011) Language, power and identity. In *Language Teaching. Plenary Speeches*. 1–19. http://journals.cambridge.org/download.php?file=%2FLTA%2FS0261444811-000048a.pdf&code=c83d890583f0a333ff41ae708a1ef5e1 (23.04.2011).

Online Documents – LINEE:

Area Report A 2008: *Research Area Report (D7). Thematic Area A: Language, Culture and Identity*. 08.11.2008. Online document: http://linee.info/index.php?eID=tx_nawsecuredl&u=0&file=fileadmin/user_upload/pdf/AreaReport_A_D7_080808.pdf&t=1290003780&hash=31e0510fdde7d69ad566185658e8183b (16.08.2010).
Area Report A 2009: *Research Area Report (D25). Thematic Area A: Language, Culture and Identity*. 09.11.2009. Online document: http://linee.info/index.php?eID=tx_nawsecuredl&u=0&file=fileadmin/user_upload/pdf/D25_AreaA_151209.pdf&t=1290003903&hash=630c80080ad9dc554c782b8defbc9753 (16.08.2010).
Area Report B 2008: *Research Area Report (D8). Thematic Area B: Language Policy and Planning*. 13.08.2008. Online document: http://linee.info/index.php?eID=tx_nawsecuredl&u=0&file=fileadmin/user_upload/pdf/AreaReport_B_D8_080808.pdf&t=1290003903&hash=65bb1d775e96ed0217fc304bfd4e9608a (17.08.2010).
Area Report B 2009: *Research Area Report (D26). Thematic Area B: Language Policy and Language Planning*. 07.11.2009. Online document: http://linee.info/index.php?eID=tx_nawsecuredl&u=0&file=fileadmin/user_upload/pdf/D26_AreaB_151209.pdf&t=1290003903&hash=d94ab0d0ac6132285843af64ec4bc4b3 (16.08.2010).
Area Report C 2008: *Research Area Report (D9). Thematic Area C: Multilingualism and Education*. 11.08.2008. Online document: http://linee.info/index.php?eID=tx_nawsecuredl&u=0&file=fileadmin/user_upload/pdf/AreaReport_C_D9_080808.pdf&t=1290003903&hash=05838c0e7ddca4241eaab35f0be37a78 (17.08.2010).
Area Report C 2009: *Research Area Report (D27). Thematic Area C: Multilingualism and Education*. 30.11.2009. Online document: http://linee.info/index.php?eID=tx_nawsecuredl&u=0&file=fileadmin/user_upload/pdf/D27_AreaC_151209.pdf&t=1290003903&hash=6ac72257e9e6b13cde81b1f03ff98ad1 (24.08.2010).

Area Report D 2008: *Research Area Report (D10)*. *Thematic Area D: Language and Economy*. 16.10.2008. Online document: http://linee.info/index.php?eID=tx_nawsecuredl&u=0&file=fileadmin/user_upload/pdf/AreaReport_D_D10_080912.pdf&t=1290003903&hash=74ef1a0d717bcc313ef3d8f04402bc8e (17.08.2010).
Area Report D 2009: *Research Area Report (D28)*. *Thematic Area D: Language and Economy*. 10.12.2009. Online document: http://linee.info/index.php?eID=tx_nawsecuredl&u=0&file=fileadmin/user_upload/pdf/D28_AreaD_151209.pdf&t=1290003903&hash=9f0d6449a4bf41040eb3587039f3b964 (17.08.2010).
LINEE Annex I 2006: For the Annex to the Contract of the *LINEE*-Project, which is not accessible for non-LINEE members, cf. Appendix.
LINEE Online: Homepage of the *LINEE*-Project – www.linee.info (04.10.2011).
PoPa EL 2008: Studer, P., Božić, S., Dovalil, V. and Peckham D.W.: *Position Paper on European Level (D12)*. *Discourses on European Linguistic and Cultural Diversity*. 09.12.2008. Online document: http://linee.info/index.php?eID=tx_nawsecuredl&u=0&file=fileadmin/user_upload/pdf/Recommendations_European_level.pdf&t=1290003903&hash=44dec82daa97a6e1dac86eb9ccd34093 (25.08.2010).
PoPa EL 2009: Sherman, T., Bozić, S., Studer, P. and Jenkins, J.: *Position Paper on European Level (D30)*. 01.12.2009. Online document: http://linee.info/index.php?eID=tx_nawsecuredl&u=0&file=fileadmin/user_upload/pdf/D30_PoPa_Europ_151209.pdf&t=1290003903&hash=ff2d0d531722d4f7f7e442ee31f71078 (24.08.2010).
PoPa NL 2008: Vigers, D., Bertosa, M., Ioannidou, E., Dal Negro, S., Vasiljev, I. and Ludwar-Ene, G.: *Position Paper on National Level (D13)*. 09.12.2009. Online document: http://linee.info/index.php?eID=tx_nawsecuredl&u=0&file=fileadmin/user_upload/pdf/Recommendations_national_level.pdf&t=1285832791&hash=df500ee4bd8ca8f97e1818b985f4f76d (29.09.2010).
PoPa NL 2009: Muhvić-Dimanovski, V., De Angelis, G., Mar-Molinero, C. and Vasiljev, I.: *Position Paper on National Level (D31)*. 30.11.2009. Online document: http://linee.info/index.php?eID=tx_nawsecuredl&u=0&file=fileadmin/user_upload/pdf/D31_PoPa_nat_151209.pdf&t=1290003903&hash=b51887a6f63a64cdc6f007184b6c774f (28.09.2009).
PoPa RLL 2008: Fenyvesi, A., Muhvić-Dimanovski, V. and Sherman, T.: *Position Paper on Regional and Local Level (D14)*. 09.12.2008. Online document: http://linee.info/index.php?eID=tx_nawsecuredl&u=0&file=fileadmin/user_upload/pdf/Recommendations_regional_level.pdf&t=1317898372&hash=22e63fe7f6ab160ebfab23d8131dcc51 (05.10.2011).
PoPa RLL 2009: Sloboda, M., Barát, E. and Fenyvesi, A.: *Position Paper on Regional and Local Level (D32)*. 09.12.2009. Online document: http://linee.info/index.php?eID=tx_nawsecuredl&u=0&file=fileadmin/user_upload/pdf/D32_PoPa_Reg_151209.pdf&t=1290003903&hash=f1dcad013c1e62c23cce788bf6362096 (24.08.2010).
RePa WP: For LINEE research papers (Siglum starting with 'RePa WP …'), which are not accessible for non-LINEE members cf. Appendix.

Appendix

LINEE Annex I 2006: Annex I (final version - 7 July 2006) to: Commission of the European Communities, Research Directorate-General: *Contract on the Network of Excellence LINEE (Languages in a Network of European Excellence)*. Contract Number 028388.

Research structure
cf. http://linee.info/work-packages/overview.html (05.10.2010)

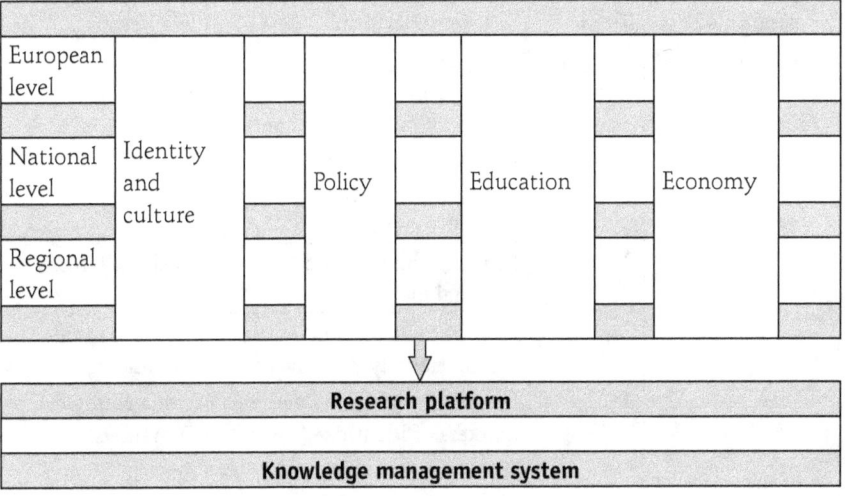

Research within LINEE is organised in four Thematic Areas:

- **Language, Identity and Culture:** Examines how language, identity and culture relate to each other and by what other factors they might be influenced in which way.
- **Language Policy and Planning:** Examines the adequacy of the existing language policy and language planning efforts in the EU countries.
- **Multilingualism and Education:** Examines how young people develop an embracing capacity to behave in a flexible and adequate manner in concrete multilingual contexts.

- **Language and Economy:** Examines the interplay between language and economy and aims to provide results that can impact on the building of a knowledge-based society.

Each thematic area is divided into three levels: European, national and regional. This structure (4 thematic areas, 3 levels of analysis) results in 12 Work Packages (WPs). In each of the two LINEE phases, the research of these two groups of Work Packages (WP1–12 and WP1a–12a) is then integrated into an overarching project called 'Research Platform'.

Thematic area and supervisors	WP number	Title	WP leader
(Rosita Rindler Schjerve)	0	Research Platform	Eva Vetter
A (Anita Sujoldžić)	1	Carriers and symbols of European culture and identity	Senka Božić
	1a	Europeanisation and the reshaping of cultural tourism and cultural industry	
	2	Language and concepts of national identity	Mislava Bertoša
	2a	Promoting national identity internationally	Vesna Muhvić-Dimanovski
	3	Local and regional varieties as markers of identity	Vesna Muhvić-Dimanovski
	3a	Politics and strategies of identity in multicultural European cities	Erzsébet Barát
B (Patrick Stevenson)	4	European discourses on multilingualism: language policy planning at the supranational level	Patrick Studer
	5	Language spread policies, migration and citizenship	Clare Mar-Molinero
	5a	The impact of 'new' migration and contested linguistic spaces	

	6	Regional and minority languages in the process of EU enlargement: challenge or burden?	Jeroen Darquennes Marianne Broermann Jenny Carl
	6a	Language management in the linguistic landscapes of multilingual cities	Marián Sloboda
C (Rita Franceschini)	7	English and multilingualism or English only in a multilingual Europe?	Donald W. Peckham
	7a	Learning, use and perceptions of English as a lingua franca communication in European contexts	Jennifer Jenkins
	8	Traditional pedagogic cultures in foreign language education and the need for multi-competence	Ros Mitchell
	8a	In search of multi-competence: exploring language use and language values among multilingual immigrant students in England, Italy and Austria	Gessica De Angelis Elena Ioannidou
	9	Regional case studies of multilingual education in (inter)regional settings	Paul Videsott
	9a	In search of multi-competence: exploring language use and language values among multilingual immigrant students in England, Italy and Austria	Anna Fenyvesi
D (Jiří Nekvapil)	10	Labour markets, the Knowledge Economy, language and mobility in Europe	Vít Dovalil

	10a	Large multinational companies: linguistic diversity and communication in parent and daughter companies	Tamah Sherman
	11	Multilingualism amongst minority population: a case of trans-cultural capital or social exclusion?	Ulrike Hanna Meinhof
	11a	Multilingualism, trans-cultural capital and social exclusion amongst migrant minority populations	Ivo Vasiljev
	12	Linguistic diversity in large multinational companies and their regional allocation	Tamah Sherman
	12a	Economic participation, language practices and collective identities in the multilingual city	Jaine Beswick

The Work Packages 13–18 fulfil supportive and managerial functions within the LINEE network. These Work packages are as follows:

WP number	Title	WP leader
13	Communication and dissemination	Thomas Gantenbein
14	Review and assessment	Iwar Werlen
15	Management and coordination	Maddalena Tognola
16	Media and infrastructure	Peter Weber
17	Gender issues	Erzsébet Barát
18	Training and mobility	Mislava Bertosa

Appendix 217

Research Papers (RePa):
Phase I:

Siglum	Themat. Area	WP	Title of Research Paper	Contributors
RePa WP1 2008	A	WP1	*Carriers and symbols of European culture and identity*	Senka Bozic Olja Orlic Mario Vrbancic
RePa WP2 2008		WP2	*Language and concepts of national identity*	Mislava Bertoša
RePa WP3 2008		WP3	*Local and regional varieties as markers of identity*	Sandra Antulov Vesna Muhvić-Dimanovski Marian Sloboda Dace Strelēvica-Ošiņa Anita Sujoldžić
RePa WP4 2008	B	WP4	*(Contradictory¿) European discourse(s) on multilingualism and multiculturalism*	Patrick Studer
RePa WP5 2008	B	WP5	*Language policies, citizenship and migration*	Clare Mar-Molinero Dick Vigers
RePa WP6 2008		WP6	*Regional and minority languages in the process of EU enlargement: challenge or burden¿*	Marianne Broermann Jenny Carl Daniela Dorner
RePa WP7 2008	C	WP7	*English and multilingualism, or English only in a multilingual Europe¿*	Karolina Kalocsai Emőke Kovács Donald W. Peckham Tamah Sherman

RePa WP8 2008		WP8	Traditional pedagogic cultures in foreign language education and the need for multi-competence	Silvia Dal Negro Gessica De Angelis Elena Ioannidou Ros Mitchell Katalin Petneki Gerda Videsott
RePa WP9 2008		WP9	(Inter)regional case studies of multilingual education	Zsuzsanna Dégi Anna Fenyvesi Zsuzsanna Éva Kiss Ágnes Ódry István Rabec Eszter Szabó-Gilinger Gerda Videsott Paul Videsott
RePa WP10 2008	D	WP10	Labour markets, the Knowledge Economy, language and mobility in Europe	Vít Dovalil
RePa WP11 2008		WP11	Multilingualism amongst minority populations: a case of trans-cultural capital or social exclusion? Francophone Sub-Saharan Africans in Germany	Gudrun Ludwar-Ene
	D	WP11		Ivo Vasiljev
			The Vietnamese business community in Czech Republic	
RePa WP12 2008		WP12	Linguistic diversity in large multinational companies and their regional allocation	Tamah Sherman

Appendix 219

Phase II:

Siglum	Themat. Area	WP	Title of Research Paper	Contributors
RePa WP1a 2009		WP1a	Europeanisation and the reshaping of cultural tourism and cultural industry	Camilla Badstübner-Kizik Agnieszka Blazek Senka Bozic Maria Drażyńska-Deja Magdalena Dudzinska Magdalena Koper Olga Orlic Waldemar Pfeiffer Mario Vrbancic
RePa WP2a 2009	A	WP2a	Promoting national identity internationally	Mislava Bertoša L. Caroll-Davies Magdalena Dudzinska A. Skelin Horvat Magdalena Koper Vesna Muhvić-Dimanovski
RePa WP3a 2009	A	WP3a WP3a	Politics and strategies of identity in multicultural European cities	Irén Annus Erzsébet Barát Jaine Beswick Ivana Burek Mirna Jernej Lucija Katulic Vanessa Mar-Molinero Éva Misits Lucija Simicic Marian Sloboda Anita Sujoldzic Malgorzata Suszczynska
RePa WP4a 2009	B	WP4a	European discourses on multilingualism: language policy-planning at the supranational level	Niku Dorostkar Vit Dovalil Mi-Cha Flubacher Felicia Kreiselmaier Patrick Studer

RePa WP5a 2009		WP5a	The impact of 'new' migration on contested linguistic spaces: implications for national language policies	Clare Mar Molinero Dick Vigers Darren Paffey Verena Tunger Cecylia Barłog
RePa WP6a 2009		WP6a	Language management in the linguistic landscapes of multilingual cities	Lucija Šimičić Marián Sloboda Eszter Szabó-Gilinger Dick Vigers
RePa WP7a 2009		WP7a	Learning, use and perceptions of English as a lingua franca communication in European contexts	Alessia Cogo Jennifer Jenkins Karolina Kolocsai Don Peckham Tamah Sherman Dagmar Sieglova
RePa WP8a 2009	C	WP8a	In search of multi-competence: exploring language use and language values among multilingual immigrant students in England, Italy and Austria	Enrica Cortinovis Silvia Dal Negro Gessica De Angelis Amanda Hilmarsson-Dunn Ros Mitchell Marie-Luise Volgger
RePa WP9a 2009	C	WP9a WP9a	Language use and language values in minority school settings	Zsuzsanna Dégi Anna Fenyvesi Veronica Irsara Zsuzsanna Kiss István Rabec Christina Reissner Paul Videsott
RePa WP10a 2009	D	WP10a	Large multinational companies: linguistic diversity and communication in parent and daughter companies	Erszebet Balogh Jenny Carl Vít Dovalil Oliver Engelhardt Mi-Cha Flubacher Jiří Nekvapil Tamah Sherman Dagmar Sieglová Agnes Tapaine-Balla

RePa WP11a 2009		WP11a	*Multilingualism, transcultural capital and social exclusion amongst migrant minority populations*	Zsuzsanna Dégi Gudrun Ludwar-Ene Ivo Vasiljev
RePa WP12a 2009		WP12a	*Economic participation, language practices and collective identities in the multilingual city*	Jaine Beswick Daniela Dorner Amanda Hilmarsson-Dunn Karl Ille Mirna Jernej Vanessa Mar-Molinero Dagmar Sieglova Marian Sloboda Ivo Vasiljev

For Product Safety Concerns and Information please contact our EU Authorised Representative:

Easy Access System Europe

Mustamäe tee 50

10621 Tallinn

Estonia

gpsr.requests@easproject.com

www.ingramcontent.com/pod-product-compliance
Lightning Source LLC
Chambersburg PA
CBHW070604300426
44113CB00010B/1397